Labour Turnover and Work-Related Training

Lorraine Dearden
Stephen Machin
Howard Reed
David Wilkinson

The Institute for Fiscal Studies
7 Ridgmount Street
London WC1E 7AE

Published by
The Institute for Fiscal Studies
7 Ridgmount Street
London WC1E 7AE
tel. (44) 171 636 3784
fax (44) 171 323 4780
email: mailbox@ifs.org.uk
internet: http//www.ifs.org.uk

Printed by
KKS Printing
The Printworks
12-20 Rosina Street
London E9 6JE

Preface

The authors are grateful to the ESRC Data Archive and Peter Shepherd and Kate Smith at City University for providing them with the data used in this analysis. This research has benefited considerably from the time, criticism and direction given by Francis Green and Christine Greenhalgh, advisers to the project. The authors would also like to thank Richard Blundell, Francesca Osowska and Dominic Rice who provided constructive comments and suggestions at every stage of the project. John Temple and Bill Wells also provided useful comments and suggestions on the final draft report, for which the authors are grateful. They would also like to thank seminar participants at University College London and the Institute for Fiscal Studies. Funding from the Department for Education and Employment is gratefully acknowledged, as is support from the ESRC Centre for the Microeconomic Analysis of Fiscal Policy at the Institute for Fiscal Studies. The authors would like to thank Judith Payne for preparing this report for publication.

The views expressed in this report are those of the authors alone, and not those of the Department for Education and Employment; nor of the Institute for Fiscal Studies or the Centre for Economic Performance at the London School of Economics, which have no corporate views.

Lorraine Dearden is a Programme Co-ordinator at the Institute for Fiscal Studies.

Stephen Machin is Professor of Economics at University College London; Executive Programme Director of the Industrial Relations Programme at the Centre for Economic Performance, London School of Economics; and a Research Associate of the Institute for Fiscal Studies.

Howard Reed is a Research Economist at the Institute for Fiscal Studies.

David Wilkinson is a Research Assistant at the Centre for Economic Performance, London School of Economics.

Contents

Summary

This report examines the link between training and job mobility in Britain, drawing on two large-scale microeconomic data sources — the National Child Development Survey (NCDS) and the Quarterly Labour Force Survey (QLFS). The analysis of both data sources uncovers a similar story for each. Mobility, measured in terms of job-to-job moves, is, if anything, lower for individuals who received training in previous periods. This is particularly true if the training was employer-funded and generally regardless of whether this employer-funded training involved a qualification being obtained. This suggests that employers who provide training, including qualification training, in general face a lower-than-average probability of losing those workers in the next year than employers who do not provide such training. All this supports the notion that employers train workers they wish to retain so that they can benefit from any skill upgrading that results from training.

Looking at the relationship between training and previous mobility, we find that, for men, there is no clear evidence that training receipt is lower or higher for recent job movers. For women, there is some evidence of a positive link with recent job moves and a negative link with the total number of jobs held, but the results are not strong. For both men and women, a job move in the current quarter is associated with an increase in the probability of being trained in that quarter, and this relationship is probably driven by induction training when a person first moves into a new job. Overall, a skill accumulation interpretation of the mobility–training relationship seems consistent with the data.

However, certain ambiguities in the results do remain, particularly if one wishes to place the empirical results in an appropriate theoretical context. Some of these could be resolved by obtaining more precise data on training structures. The fact that different effects emerge for different forms of training makes it especially important that data collection agencies are careful to distinguish what is meant by questions that try to elicit information on forms of training. For example, our results seem to suggest that the distinction between employer-funded and non-employer-funded training is important. This suggests that understanding how individuals respond to questions asking them who financed training appears to be important and it would be useful to probe this further in future surveys. This would involve asking questions about whether wage levels were adjusted during training periods.

Furthermore, the results we present, when taken in conjunction with the theoretical work discussed in the report, make it clear that the link between training and job mobility is a complex one. This implies that one should exercise some caution in moving from the basic empirical relationships to policy analysis. The latter would require more knowledge on who finances different training spells, the size of hiring markets for workers with different skill attributes, the extent of information asymmetries, the distribution of returns between workers and employers, and information on the social scarcity of alternative skills. At present, we know very little about most of these. Some could be learnt were there good-quality data on training strategies of employers and their workers but, as of now, there is no data source that contains such high-quality data on workers and their employers. A better understanding of the links between mobility and training could be developed if such data were collected.

CHAPTER 1
Introduction

put here

Training is seen by many commentators as vital to the future performance of the economy.[1] According to this view, the role that training may play in developing and sustaining the skills base of the work-force is crucial for economic performance, both for individual companies and their employees and for maintaining international competitiveness. In the light of these views, it is important to examine the links between training and the development of the UK skills base. An important aspect of this is the relationship between training incidence and the labour force mobility of workers, which is the subject of this report.

Standard human capital theory argues that firms will only bear the costs of firm-specific training and not of general training, since general training is also productivity-enhancing in other firms and therefore there is a distinct potential for 'generally' trained workers to be subject to poaching. The notion of poaching has been widely quoted as leading to under-provision of general

---

[1] Some clear examples from the two main political parties are:

'To compete internationally the UK [needs] employers who see the importance of developing the skills of their workforce' (*Forging Ahead*, Competitiveness White Paper, 1995, p. 78).

'Our aim is to make this country the unrivalled Enterprise Centre of Europe ... one which provides the education and training we need for the world of today and tomorrow' (*Creating the Enterprise Centre of Europe*, Competitiveness White Paper, 1996, Foreword).

'Labour is determined to reverse the falling level of skills within our workforce ... by widening access to retraining for those in work' (*Winning for Britain*, Labour Party, 1994, p. 19).

training and as contributing to many of the skills problems that, so it is argued, characterise the British workforce.

The human capital approach goes on to argue that,
since workers receive all of the return to general training, such general training must be financed by the individual. It is clear in practice, however, that most
employer-funded training will not be entirely firm-
specific and, in any case, that some firms do bear some
of the costs of more general training.[2]

It is also argued that human capital accumulation,
including that generated by work-related training, is an
important determinant of labour market success. An integral part of the latter is the ability of individuals to
move jobs, either within firms or by changing employer.
Hence, while labour turnover may affect the probability
of receiving work-related training, it is also possible that
training will affect labour turnover. This possible simultaneity needs to be considered if one wishes to gauge the
relationship between labour turnover and employer-
funded training accurately.

The research in this report explores the relationship
between labour turnover and work-related training in
several (related) dimensions. The questions the research
sets out to answer are:

---

[2]The UK Labour Force Survey shows that, in 1985, employers paid the
fees of about 64 per cent of job-related training for employees. Self-finance
(from self, family or relatives) accounted for about 18 per cent, about 8 per
cent was financed by government or local authority, 7 per cent of training
had no fee, and the source of fees for the residual 3 per cent was not
known. Trends over time suggest an increased importance of employer-
paid fees as, by 1994, employers paid the fees of 68 per cent of training
while 17 per cent of training was self-financed and 5 per cent had no fee
(see Government Statistical Service (1994, Table D1)). Of course, this
abstracts from the notion that employers may finance training by paying
workers a wage beneath their marginal product during their training period.
We discuss this below.

- What sort of individuals are more likely to receive different types of work-related training and how important is an individual's current stock of human capital in determining the probability of receiving training? What sorts of firms undertake training and to whom do they give it? To what extent is training just given to people as they enter new jobs? Or is it a more integral part of developing an individual's skills whilst in employment?

- What impact does work-related training have on the probability of staying in a job? Does receiving different types of training increase or decrease job mobility? What are the other determinants of labour turnover and job mobility?

- Does labour turnover (variously defined) increase or decrease the probability of receiving different types of work-related training?

The research uses two microeconomic datasets — the UK Labour Force Survey (LFS) and British National Child Development Survey (NCDS) — in an attempt to answer these important questions. Both of these data sources allow us to track individuals' labour market statuses over time and therefore to look directly at labour turnover. Both have advantages and disadvantages, but for the most part we feel the data sources are complementary, hence our focus on both. The data sources allow us to measure directly the effects of training in one period on labour market status in future periods, as well as the relationship between labour market transitions and the subsequent probability of receiving different types of work-related training.

Understanding the relationship between training and labour turnover is a crucial ingredient in developing appropriate policies aimed at increasing the skills base of the economy. In Chapter 2, we review previous theoretical and empirical work on the relationship between em-

5

ployer-funded training and job turnover. In Chapter 3, we discuss in more detail the data we use in this report, and Chapter 4 sets out the methodology used in this report to look at the relationship between work-related training and job turnover. The results of our study are presented in Chapter 5, and Chapter 6 summarises the findings of the report.

CHAPTER 2
Work-Related Training and Job Turnover:
Theory and Evidence

2.1 Theoretical Models of Training and Job Turnover

The standard human capital approach, as formulated by Becker (1964), recognised that an individual's human capital is affected by more than the level of education they have invested in. Ability and work-related (what he terms 'on-the-job') training will also play a part. Becker distinguishes between *general* on-the-job training, which increases an individual's productivity to different employers, and *specific* on-the-job training, which increases an individual's productivity only at the firm in which the individual is employed.

He argues that the cost of *specific training* is shared by the worker and the firm. The employee might be paid a wage greater than marginal product during the training period, but after the training the employee's wage is below marginal product, although above what the employee could get elsewhere since the training only increases productivity in the current job. For *general training*, where the employees acquire skills that are productivity-enhancing elsewhere, they alone pay for the training costs in terms of lower wages while they receive training. Their wage during training is equal to their marginal product at this time, which will be lower than their marginal product if they were not undertaking training because of the costs associated with the time spent off work and/or the need for supervision. They accept this lower wage because they expect that, as a result of this training, the present value of the stream of lifetime benefits net of this cost will be higher than if they had not undertaken the training. In this model, firms will not bear any of the costs of general training because general training is also productivity-enhancing in other firms and therefore there is a distinct potential for 'generally' trained workers to be subject to poaching. There is no poaching externality problem in the human capital model. If firms were to share some of the costs of general training, then there is likely to be a poaching externality leading to under-provision of general training.

Human capital models, such as the Ben-Porath (1967) model, also predict that investment in general training declines with age, because of the shorter investment horizon. Older individuals have less time left in the labour market to reap the benefits of such investments. With entirely firm-specific training, the investment horizon is not the expected remaining time in work but the expected remaining time in the current job, since the returns to such investments can only be realised by both the individual and their employer while they stay in their current employment. Human capital theory therefore predicts that individuals and/or firms are, *ceteris paribus*, more likely to invest in firm-specific training, the longer the expected job duration of the individual. This suggests that there should be a negative relationship between receipt of firm-specific training and the probability of moving jobs in the future. If firms view an individual's past mobility as a predictor of their future mobility, then this may also suggest a negative relationship between past mobility and the probability of receiving firm-specific training.

The human capital model assumes that the labour market is perfectly competitive. Stevens (1994) has developed a theoretical model which shows that if a firm operates in a market with imperfect competition, then

firms may obtain some return to an investment in general training. Because other firms may also benefit from this general training, there is an externality which may lead to under-investment in general training and over-investment in more firm-specific training. One implication of her model is that future labour turnover will be lowest for workers who receive relatively firm-specific training. This is also a prediction of the human capital model. In the Stevens model, however, there is a poaching externality leading to under-investment in general training, whereas in the human capital model there is no such poaching externality.

Furthermore, the work by Stevens makes it clear that the Beckerian concepts of general and specific training are special cases and she points out that they are extreme cases of what she terms 'transferable training'. When one adopts this richer definition, many aspects of which cannot be characterised as a linear combination of general and specific training, it becomes clear that obtaining policy predictions about the likely economic effects of different kinds of training is, in fact, a complex area of study. Stevens also makes it clear that any value of training not captured by the training employer does not automatically go to a new employer if the worker moves jobs. This is because any externality would have to be shared by the worker who moves and the new employer, and the worker will try to extract the highest wage possible from his or her new employer. A third important point made by Stevens is that employers may well customise their training, so that it becomes more firm-specific and therefore reduces inter-firm mobility. This may not reflect an optimal outcome if it results in a deficit of transferable skills in the economy. Furthermore, if receipt of training is associated with reduced job mobility, this may well reflect a bias of employer-funded training towards firm-specific skill accumulation.

Katz and Ziderman (1990) develop a model which shows that firms will share the costs of general training because of informational asymmetries. They assume that potential recruiters of trained workers do not possess much information on the extent and type of workers' on-the-job training, which imposes substantial information-based costs on firms that recruit rather than train. This means that 'poaching' firms will place a lower value on workers with general training than the firms that trained them. One implication of their model is that firms may find it feasible to finance part, or all, of a worker's general training. They argue that firms are less likely to do this if formal certification is involved as this increases the information available to potential 'poachers'. They recognise that the case of West Germany is an anomaly in terms of this prediction.

Related to this is the fact that there is increasing empirical evidence that training policies are part of more widely defined 'bundles' of human resource policies. It is clear that other components of these bundles have direct impacts on mobility by raising the commitments of workers to their firms. From a theoretical perspective, it makes sense that a profit-maximising employer may well wish to link together such human resource policies (i.e. to protect their training investment) and that a prediction of reduced job mobility from training will emerge without one needing to develop a model based on information asymmetries. There may also be less direct reasons for a link between training and other company human resource policies: for example, Brown, Reich and Stern (1993) argue that job security, employee involvement and training are self-reinforcing strategies, in the sense that it may be difficult for an employer to introduce one element without the others. If this is true, then we would expect employer-funded training, whether general or specific, to reduce future job mobility.

Finally, Acemoglu and Pischke (1995) have developed a model which shows that workers may not pay for the general training they receive. Their model once again relies on informational asymmetries, but is empirically applied to explain the relationship between training and mobility in West Germany. In their model, the crucial assumption is that an individual's current employer has better information about the worker's ability than other firms. This informational advantage gives the firm some *ex-post monopsony power* over the worker which encourages the firm to provide general training. The model can lead to multiple equilibria. In one equilibrium, quits (which are assumed to be endogenous) are high and this means that employers have limited monopsony power and therefore are more reluctant to bear the costs of any general training. In the other equilibrium, there are low quits and high training. One interesting feature of this model is that the equilibrium with high quits, which involves a better match of individuals to jobs, may be less efficient because the level of training is too low. The authors also show that the effect of active poaching by other employers depends crucially on the institutional settings in the labour market. In a market where the institutional structure makes poaching more difficult (for example, the existence in Germany of work councils which can enforce consistent rules in hiring and firing), training levels will be higher than for a labour market where poaching raids are not restricted.

Acemoglu and Pischke then look at the implications of their model for individuals undertaking apprenticeship training in Germany. They argue that there are three main reasons why apprentices leave their jobs in Germany. These are (i) that they are not offered a permanent contract by their employer, (ii) that they quit voluntarily and (iii) that they are drafted to do military service. Their model predicts that stayers will earn more than laid-off workers and voluntary quitters. It predicts that military quitters leaving for exogenous reasons earn more than other quitters, and may earn more or less than stayers. They then use two cross-sections of the German 'Qualification and Career Survey' conducted in 1979 and 1985–86 to test the empirical predictions from their model. Their empirical results are consistent with the model's predictions and inconsistent with a pure specific human capital explanation.

2.2 Empirical Studies of Training and Job Mobility

There have been relatively few empirical studies looking at the relationship between training and job mobility. The studies that have examined this issue have looked at either the effect of training on mobility or the effect of mobility on training.

Wadsworth (1989) uses data from the Labour Force Survey in 1983 and 1984 to study inter-firm mobility, focusing specifically on job-to-job moves. He finds that around 6.5 per cent of employees moved jobs between 1983 and 1984, and includes a training receipt dummy variable in an econometric model of job mobility. The estimated coefficient on the training variable is negative, but statistically insignificant at conventional levels of significance.

Elias (1994) uses panel data from the 1986–90 ESRC Social Change and Economic Life Initiative (SCELI) and focuses on a subsample of adults living in Rochdale, England. He uses these data to look at whether or not job-related training influences the probability of leaving a job, controlling for other factors such as job tenure, trade union membership, and other individual and job-related characteristics. He only considers job-related training received in the job held in the preceding month of employment. He finds that such job-related training reduced the probability of turnover for women but was not an important determinant of men's job mobility. He uses a logit model and a model that allows for unobserved individual heterogeneity.[3]

Greenhalgh and Mavrotas (1996) use data from the 1984 and 1989 British Labour Force Surveys to look at the determinants of job mobility and training. They use a recursive model which looks at the determinants of mobility during the past year and then the impact this has on the probability of receiving training in the last four weeks. Their data do not allow them to look at the effect of training on subsequent mobility. They also assume that the unobserved determinants of mobility and training are uncorrelated. They find that job mobility is highest for the young and for those individuals with higher educational qualifications. These factors are also important determinants of training incidence. They find that mobility has no significant effect on training incidence for men. For women, recent job movers are more likely to be trained than those who have been in their jobs for more than 12 months. This could reflect induction training received by women when they start a new job. They also find that public sector workers have high training rates and low mobility. Sectoral R. & D. activity is associated with more training and less mobility for men in their sample. Women are more likely to train and less mobile if the rate of adoption of innovation is rapid.

Another British study is that of Booth and Satchell (1994), who use data from the fourth wave of the National Child Development Survey (which took place in 1981) to look at the impact of apprenticeships on job tenure. They found that men who completed apprenticeships had a lower exit rate from jobs than men who un-

---

[3]He assumes that these unobserved individual effects are uncorrelated with the other explanatory variables in his model, and are normally distributed with end points on the distribution (one of which represents individuals who never change their employer and one of which represents persistent changes).

dertook no training, whereas men who terminated their apprenticeship before completion had a higher exit rate.

Winkelmann (1994) looks at the effect of education and training in West Germany on labour mobility (measured as the number of job changes over a given period of time) and industry/occupational mobility (measured as a year-to-year change of industry and/or broad occupation). He uses data from the German Socio-Economic Panel (GSEOP) over the period 1974 to 1990. In looking at the determinants of labour mobility, he uses a Poisson regression model, and for occupational mobility he uses a probit model. He finds that apprenticeships and all other types of vocational training reduce labour mobility. An apprenticeship, for example, reduces the number of job changes from 0.73 to 0.50, or by 32 per cent. The mobility-reducing effects of other types of vocational training are found to be even larger. General schooling, on the other hand, has no effect on labour mobility. His results for occupational mobility are less clear, but suggest that these training effects are not occupation-specific. He argues that this supports the idea that the negative effect of training on mobility is mainly due to firm-specificness.

Campbell III (1993) also finds reduced mobility from training in his firm-level test of the efficiency wage hypothesis. He estimates quit equations to test the efficiency wage hypothesis, and includes a training variable in his set of explanatory variables. In all his specifications, training has a negative impact on the probability of quitting a job.

Royalty (1996) looks at the effect of predicted probability of job-to-job turnover and job-to-nonemployment turnover on the probability of undertaking general and firm-specific training. She argues that these predicted probabilities are proxies for the worker's total expected employment over the life cycle and the worker's expected job duration with the current employer. She uses data from the 1980–86 US National Longitudinal Survey of Youth (NLSY) and looks at the determinants of company training (which she takes to be firm-specific training) and off-the-job training (which she takes to be general training) for both men and women. Her instruments for turnover are health status and real wages in the current job. She finds that a higher estimated probability of job-to-nonemployment turnover reduces the probability of receiving company training for men and women and off-the-job training for men. A higher estimated probability of job-to-job turnover has no effect on company training and increases the likelihood of undertaking off-the-job training, though only significantly for women. She finds a significant gender difference in the probability of undertaking both types of training, but finds that it is reduced by around 25 per cent once controls for the predicted probability of job turnover are included. She also argues that the finding in previous studies of strong complementarities between education and training is due to differences in turnover for different education groups rather than being a direct effect of education on training. The finding of a positive relationship between expected turnover and general training suggests that general training may be obtained by workers in order to move to a new job rather than as training for the present job. She argues that simultaneous estimation of the relationship between turnover and training is an important extension of her work.

2.3 Summary of Existing Theory and Evidence

The theoretical discussion makes it clear that the link between job mobility and training has a number of important features and that different theoretical approaches may well generate different predictions. For example, the life-cycle human capital model generates the prediction that firm-specific training should reduce the probability of an individual leaving his or her current job. When one moves away from the perfect competition notion inherent in the Beckerian and human capital life-cycle model, predictions become more difficult. Most of the alternative models we have looked at also predict that firm-specific training should reduce future mobility, but these models also argue that there may be a poaching externality leading to under-investment in employer-funded general training. On the other hand, if the human capital model is true, there should be no employer-funded general training.

Furthermore, if one prefers to think of training in terms of a joint venture between workers and employers, in which training raises the levels of skill accumulation by fostering longer-term matches (perhaps in conjunction with other human resources policies), then all employer-funded training should have a negative impact on the probability of an individual leaving their current job. In the same vein, there is likely to be a zero or positive link between training receipt and previous (recent) job mobility as employers who wish to develop their skills base will want to provide training for newer recruits (even if this is just induction training programmes). On the other hand, if one views recent and/or frequent job mobility as a signal of problems with previous job matches, this may result in a negative association between employer-funded training receipt and previous job mobility.

The existing empirical work on the relationship between turnover and training has focused on either the effect of training on future turnover or the effect of past turnover on training (most has looked at the former). The studies have found

- negative, but often small and sometimes insignificant, effects of previous training on mobility (for men and women);

- insignificant effects of mobility on training for men, with some evidence of positive, but statistically weak, effects for women.

CHAPTER 3
Data Description

3.1 Introduction

This research uses data from the British National Child Development Survey (NCDS) and the UK Labour Force Survey (LFS) panel. Both of these datasets are longitudinal data sources which allow us to follow the same individuals over time. For the NCDS data, we have information (for various years) after the individual was born (in 1958). For the purposes of this research, we are able to look at the impact of training at different points in time on future job mobility as well as the effect of mobility on later training over a 10-year period between 1981 and 1991. From the LFS panel, we observe individuals for five consecutive quarters (since Spring 1992 when the LFS switched to being quarterly, as compared with earlier years when it was conducted on an annual basis and did not have a longitudinal component). This allows us to look at the impact of training received in early quarters on mobility in later quarters and vice versa. Both of these datasets, because of their panel element, have clear advantages over those that have been used in the past to look at the relationship between mobility and training.

3.2 Setting Up the Data

The LFS and NCDS data need to be set up in a special way to estimate these models. We now explain in some detail how this is done for each dataset and the variables we use, and then discuss the relative advantages and disadvantages of each.

3.2.1 *The National Child Development Survey (NCDS) data*

The NCDS is a continuing panel survey of all individuals born in Britain between 3 and 9 March 1958. There have been five waves of the NCDS, with the most recent survey being conducted in 1991. The project predominantly uses information from NCDS4 (when the individuals were aged 23 years, in 1981) and NCDS5 (when aged 33, in 1991).

NCDS5 first asks for information on the two highest qualification courses the person has undertaken between 1981 and 1991. It then goes on to ask about the number of other training courses lasting three days or more received by the individual between 1981 and 1991 'designed to help you develop skills that you might use in a job'. For the three most recent of these courses as well as the two highest qualification courses, it has detailed information on items such as when the training took place, whether it was provided by an employer at the time, where it took place, whether the employer paid for all or part of the course, whether the person has started a new job since leaving the course, and whether the respondent thought that the course helped them get any job since they finished the course.

We have constructed a series of quarterly cross-sections from the NCDS from the first quarter of 1981 until the fourth quarter of 1990. The dataset incorporates panel information by using an individual's known job history (both retrospective and future) and training history (again, both retrospective and prospective). In each quarter of our dataset, for example, we know how long the person has been in their current job and how long they will spend in it.[4] In constructing the dataset, we have excluded

- individuals not employed at the end of the quarter in question;
- people who are self-employed;
- agricultural workers in 1981;[5]
- quarters before the individual's first work-related training course (for individuals who undertook more than five such courses between 1981 and 1991);
- individuals for whom we have missing values on any of the variables used in the analysis.

With these sample selections, we are left with a final dataset of around 60,000 observations on men and 50,000 on women. The sample consists of approximately 1,500 men and 1,250 women for each quarter of our dataset, on average. In each quarter, we record the person's current job tenure (in quarters), whether they changed jobs in the last quarter or last year excluding the current quarter, how long they will spend in their current job (calculated from the future job histories in the data up until 1991), whether they have undertaken or are currently undertaking training courses, and industry, region and employer characteristics in their 1981 job.

We use the additional information about each training spell in the NCDS data to break the training variable down in several ways. We first identify training that is

---

[4]If a person is employed at the time of the 1991 interview, we will only know, of course, how long they have been in that job and not how long they will stay in the job in the future. For such jobs, there is what is termed a 'right censoring' problem. This censoring restricts our estimating samples. If, for example, we want to look at the effect training in one quarter has on the probability of moving jobs in the following four quarters, our estimation period must end one year before the date of the person's interview in order for us to ascertain whether they moved jobs in the following year.

[5]Dropped because of small cell sizes.

employer-funded. We define training to be employer-funded if the employer wholly or partly paid for the training. All other training is defined to be non-employer-funded. We also distinguish between training that is completed in the quarter and training that is ongoing. Finally, we distinguish between training that leads to a qualification and training that does not. For individuals undertaking training leading to a qualification, we distinguish between lower, middle and higher vocational qualifications, degree qualifications and other qualifications. A full description of these qualification training variables is given in Table 3.1. Various interactions of these training variables are also considered.

TABLE 3.1

Description of qualification training variables: NCDS

Variable	Description
Qualification training undertaken since 1981:	
Degree	University or CNAA first degree
	CNAA Post-graduate Diploma
	University or CNAA higher degree
Higher vocational	Full professional qualification
	Part of a professional qualification
	Polytechnic Diploma or Certificate (not CNAA validated)
	University or CNAA Diploma or Certificate
	Nursing qualification including nursery qualification
	Non-graduate teaching qualification
	Higher National Certificate (HNC) or Diploma (HND)
	BEC/TEC Higher Certificate or Higher Diploma
	City and Guilds Full Technological Certificate
Middle vocational	City and Guilds Advanced or Final Certificate
	Ordinary National Certificate (ONC) or Diploma (OND)
	BEC/TEC National, General or Ordinary Certificate or Diploma
	A level qualification
Lower vocational	City and Guilds Craft or Ordinary Certificate
	Royal Society of Arts (RSA) awards, stage 1, 2 or 3
	Other commercial or clerical qualification
	O level qualification
Other	All other courses leading to some sort of qualification that are not identified above
None	No qualification training undertaken since 1981

21

TABLE 3.2

Description of highest educational qualification variables: NCDS

Variable	Description
Highest qualification at age 23, in 1981:	
Degree	University or CNAA first degree
	CNAA Post-graduate Diploma
	University or CNAA higher degree
Higher vocational	Full professional qualification
	Part of a professional qualification
	Polytechnic Diploma or Certificate (not CNAA validated)
	University or CNAA Diploma or Certificate
	Nursing qualification including nursery qualification
	Non-graduate teaching qualification
	Higher National Certificate (HNC) or Diploma (HND)
	BEC/TEC Higher Certificate or Higher Diploma
	City and Guilds Full Technological Certificate
A levels	At least one: GCE A level
	or Scottish Leaving Certificate (SLC)
	or Scottish Certificate of Education (SCE)
	or Scottish University Preliminary Examination (SUPE) at Higher Grade
	or Certificate of Sixth Year Studies
Middle vocational	City and Guilds Advanced or Final Certificate
	Ordinary National Certificate (ONC) or Diploma (OND)
	BEC/TEC National, General or Ordinary Certificate or Diploma
5+ O levels	At least five: GCE O level passes or Grades A–C
	or CSE Grade 1 or equivalent
Lower vocational	City and Guilds Craft or Ordinary Certificate
	Royal Society of Arts (RSA) awards, stage 1, 2 or 3
	Other commercial or clerical qualification
O levels	One to four: GCE O level passes or Grades A–C
	or CSE Grade 1 or equivalent
Other	All other courses leading to some sort of qualification that are not identified above, including CSE Grades 2–5 or equivalent and miscellaneous apprenticeship qualifications
None	No qualifications, including those with no formal schooling

The NCDS also gives us information on the person's highest school and post-school qualification as at 1981. We use this information to identify a person's highest educational qualification and follow as closely as possible the schema of Schmitt (1993) which has subsequently been used by the OECD. This education measure based on highest qualification is clearly ordered and a full description of these NCDS highest education variables is contained in Table 3.2.[6]

We also use some information from earlier waves of the NCDS to construct variables that identify whether the individual's mother was employed in 1974 and the number of times the person moved house up until the age of 16. The reasons for constructing these variables are discussed in more detail in Chapter 4 on methodology.

3.2.2 The Labour Force Survey (LFS) data

Since Spring 1992, the LFS panel has been conducted as a rotating panel where individuals enter in waves and then stay in the survey for five quarters. Thus we can follow different cohorts of individuals over five quarters. In this report, we use 11 quarters of the Quarterly Labour Force Survey (QLFS) from Spring 1992 to Autumn 1994 which allows us to construct seven panels following individuals for five quarters. In each of the quarters, individuals are asked the same basic questions, giving us labour force status, industry and occupation. The main training question is asked to employees only and is as follows: 'Over the 4 weeks ending Sunday ... have you taken part in any education or training connected with your job, or a job that you might be able to do in the future (including courses that you have told me about already)?'. From Summer 1994, interviewees have also been asked about training over the last 13 weeks in addition to training received in the last four weeks. In this report, we also undertake estimation for the cohort that was first interviewed in Summer 1994 to

---

[6]Unlike Schmitt, we do not separately identify teaching qualifications; these are included in the highest vocational qualifications if they did not lead to a degree. We also do not have a category of O levels plus commercial/clerical. People with commercial or clerical qualifications are included in the lower vocational category.

TABLE 3.3

Description of highest educational qualification variables: QLFS

Variable	Description
Highest qualification:	
Degree	Higher degree
	First degree
	Other degree-level qualification
	Diploma in Higher Education
Higher vocational	Higher National Certificate (HNC) or Diploma (HND)
	Higher BTEC/SCOTVEC
	Teaching qualification
	Nursing qualification
	Other higher qualification below degree level
	Royal Society of Arts (RSA) Higher Diploma
Middle vocational	A level
	BTEC/SCOTVEC
	RSA Advanced Diploma
	Ordinary National Certificate (ONC) or Diploma (OND)
	BEC/TEC National, General or Ordinary Certificate or Diploma
	City and Guilds Advanced Craft
	Scottish Certificate of Sixth Year Studies (CSYS) or equivalent
	Scottish Certificate of Education (SCE) Higher or equivalent
	CSYS or equivalent
Lower vocational	City and Guilds craft or other qualification
	O level or equivalent
	GCSE or equivalent
	CSE Grades 2–5
	Youth Training Certificate
	RSA Diploma or other qualification
	BTEC/SCOTVEC First Diploma or General Certificate
Other	All other courses leading to some sort of qualification that are not identified above
None	No qualifications, including those with no formal schooling

see if our results change when we use the 13-week rather than the four-week training question.[7]

In addition to these questions, there are supplementary questions on whether the training was on- or off-the-job; the main place the training took place; time spent training; whether the training was continuing;

---

[7]We only gained access to this additional data very late in the project and for this reason most of our analysis is based on the seven cohorts first interviewed from Spring 1992 to Autumn 1993.

whether the training led to a formal qualification (or a credit towards such a qualification); the type of qualification; and who paid for the training. We use the information on time, qualification and who paid for the training to construct training variables directly comparable to those we create from the NCDS data. The information on whether the training led to a qualification and whether it was continuing is only available for the 1992 panels.

The QLFS also gives us information on the person's highest educational qualification at the time of the survey. For data up until 1992, the highest education variables are divided into 15 different ordered classifications, whereas for 1993 onwards there are 28 ordered classifications. We use these ordered variables to create an ordered highest education variable with six different classifications.[8] A full description of this is given in Table 3.3.

3.2.3 An NCDS age cohort from annual LFS data

Despite our focus on the quarterly LFS data (since Spring 1992 when the longitudinal element of the LFS was initially introduced), the LFS was previously conducted on an annual cross-sectional basis since 1983 (and once every two years before that, starting in 1975). Training questions were first introduced in the 1984 survey. The large sample size in the LFS means we can also construct an age cohort from the annual LFS cross-sections to broadly match the NCDS age cohort. From these annual cross-sections, we have taken all individuals who were in the same school year as the NCDS 1958

---

[8]Because of the ordering imposed by the QLFS questionnaire, it is not possible to construct a more disaggregated ordered highest education variable that separately identifies school qualifications such as 5+ O levels and A levels. A levels are included in the middle vocational qualification, and O levels in the lower vocational category.

birth cohort from 1984 to 1991. This is very useful for cross-validating the quality of the NCDS data as we can compare the summary statistics for key variables from both datasets. We cannot, however, use this cohort from the LFS in our analysis as it has no panel element.

3.2.4 The advantages and disadvantages of the datasets

The datasets are largely complementary, given their different structures and time periods of coverage. We feel that it is necessary to look at both to obtain a clear picture of the links between training and job mobility. The relative advantages of the two data sources are as follows:

- *NCDS:* covers a substantial time period of training receipt and job experience for a cohort that ages between 23 and 33 over the period 1981–91; contains data on multiple training spells throughout time; has very detailed work history data; covers a variety of forms of training.
- *QLFS:* has an explicit panel data focus (as individuals are observed for five quarters); covers individuals of all ages; asks questions about a variety of forms of training (which are similar to those covered in the NCDS).

The relative disadvantages of each data source (which are usually compensated for by one of the advantages of the other) are

- *NCDS:* only covers a single birth cohort; involves left censoring of the training variables as data on up to three training spells are available; as with all longitudinal data sources, may have problems as a result of sample attrition.

- *QLFS:* has a short time dimension as it only covers five quarters; as detailed above, utilises a rather basic training definition (i.e. receipt in last four weeks).

Overall, however, the focus on both data sources does seem to get around many of the problems that a study based on a single data source would face.

3.3 An Initial Look at the Data

Figure 3.1 gives an aggregate picture of what has happened to training incidence in the UK between 1984 and 1995 (based on LFS data). The figure displays the well-known pattern of rising training incidence as the fraction of employees who received any training in the four weeks prior to being interviewed showed a steady upward rise between 1984 and 1990 (from just under 10 per cent to over 15 per cent) and then remained fairly flat in the 1990s.[9]

FIGURE 3.1

Training incidence: LFS 1984–95

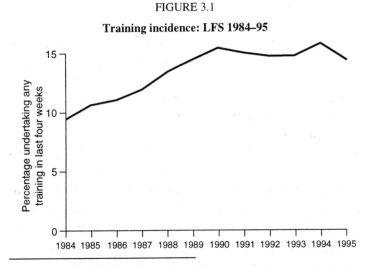

[9]See the May 1996 issue of the Department for Education and Employment's *Labour Market Quarterly Report* for more details on the trend rise in training from the LFS. Also, see Greenhalgh and Mavrotas (1994) for breakdowns of training incidence from the annual LFS for various subgroups (e.g. by gender, training type and industry).

FIGURE 3.2

Male training incidence: QLFS

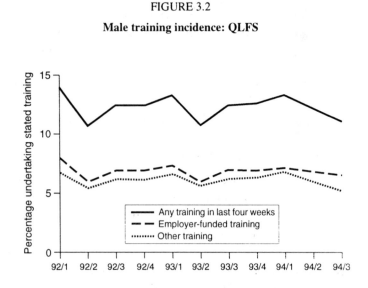

Figures 3.2–3.7 report training incidence statistics from the LFS data that we use in our empirical work. A set of analogous graphs based on NCDS data are reported in Figures 3.8–3.13. Figure 3.2 shows that, for men in the QLFS panel, there was no clear overall upward or downward trend in the incidence of training between Spring 1992 (March–May 1992 or 92/1) and Autumn 1994 (September–November 1994 or 94/3). Figures for Summer 1994 onwards are not comparable to earlier figures because of a change in the survey questionnaire.[10] Despite this, there appears to be clear seasonal variation: training was about 3 or 4 per cent less likely in the summer months. It is likely that this seasonality is driven by the fact that many further education colleges (and other training colleges) are closed

---

[10]From Summer 1994, respondents were asked a new question about training received in the 13 weeks prior to interview before they were asked the question about training received in the previous four weeks. This seems to have altered the way respondents answered the four-week question and caused a discontinuity in the data.

for much of the summer, and thus training cannot be undertaken at this time.[11] As for the breakdown into employer-funded and non-employer-funded training, these seem to be roughly equally split throughout the period. Figure 3.3 splits the training receipts for men in the QLFS into those spells that finished in a particular quarter and those that continued on past that quarter.[12] It is clear that around two-thirds of training spells in a particular quarter are continuing spells. Furthermore, in Figure 3.4 we see that only around 40 per cent of training spells in each period led to a qualification being obtained.

FIGURE 3.3

Male completed and continuing training: QLFS

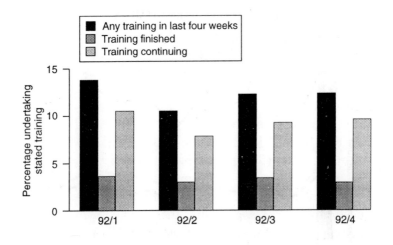

---

[11]In work arising from this report, we hope to make use of this seasonality, and the fact that vacation times differ by area, to instrument training in mobility equations (see Chapter 4).

[12]Note that information on whether training finished in a certain quarter and whether a qualification was obtained from training is only available in the QLFS for 1992. Hence we only have four quarters of statistics for Figures 3.3, 3.4, 3.6 and 3.7.

FIGURE 3.4

Male qualification and non-qualification training: QLFS

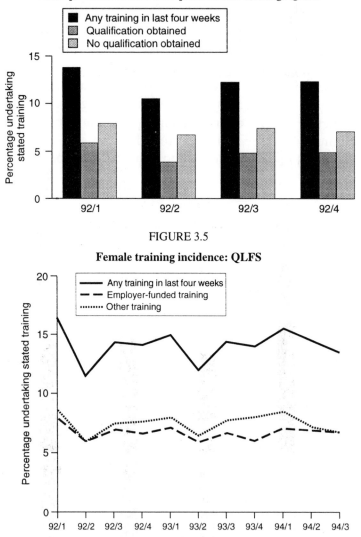

FIGURE 3.5

Female training incidence: QLFS

The comparable QLFS statistics for women are shown in Figures 3.5–3.7. The differences to note are (a) that overall training incidence is slightly higher for women than for men, (b) that women have a lower proportion of employer-funded training, and (c) that women have a slightly higher proportion of training that leads to a qualification. Once again, a seasonal dip in training receipts occurs during the summer months.

FIGURE 3.6

Female completed and continuing training: QLFS

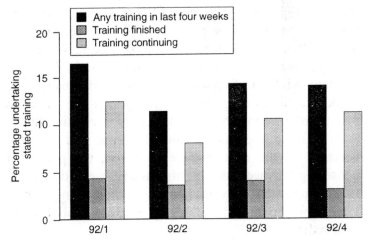

FIGURE 3.7

Female qualification and non-qualification training: QLFS

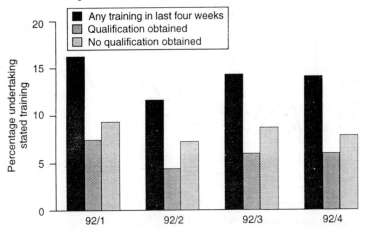

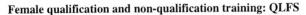

The NCDS panel data summarised in Figures 3.8–3.13 give us a longer-term picture of trends in training than does the QLFS panel. In Figure 3.8, we see that there is a clear increase in overall training receipts for men over the period Summer 1981 to Winter 1990, from about 4 per cent of the sample per quarter to about 13 per cent. This is a more dramatic increase (from a lower starting-point) than for the LFS cross-section data in Figure 3.1; this may be partially due to the censoring in the NCDS data, which means that we are less likely to observe training undertaken further back in time towards 1981 for individuals who have undertaken other work-related training courses for which we have no timing information. Nevertheless, it is interesting that it is an increase in employer-funded training that seems to account for the overall increase during the period; if censoring bias were driving the entire observed increase in training, then we would surely expect an increase in non-employer-funded training as well, but this fails to materialise.

FIGURE 3.8

Male training incidence: NCDS

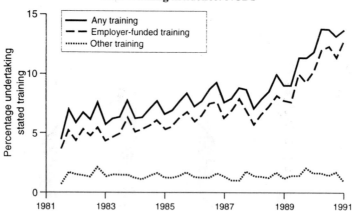

FIGURE 3.9

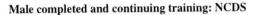

Male completed and continuing training: NCDS

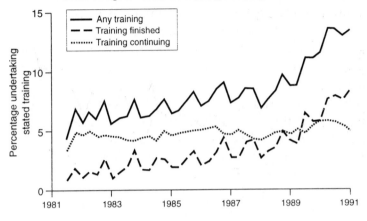

The breakdown into training spells that finished and those that were ongoing in Figure 3.9 appears to show that the proportion of completed training spells increased markedly in the late 1980s and early 1990s, whereas ongoing spells (those more likely to be the longer courses associated with qualification-related training) remained roughly constant.

FIGURE 3.10

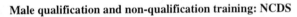

Male qualification and non-qualification training: NCDS

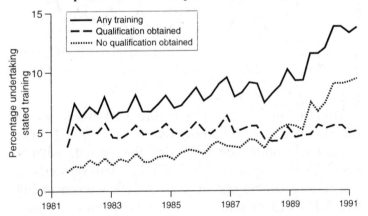

FIGURE 3.11

Female training incidence: NCDS

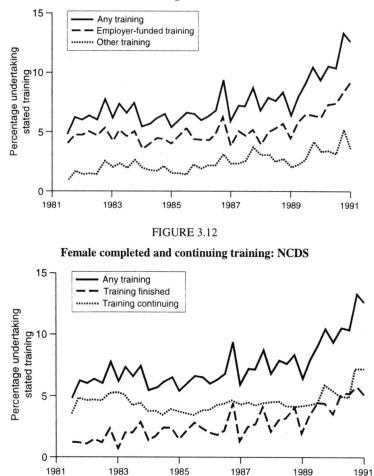

FIGURE 3.12

Female completed and continuing training: NCDS

This finding is echoed by Figure 3.10, where we see that the incidence of training that led to a qualification remained roughly constant over the period, whereas other training increased from the mid-1980s onwards.

The comparable statistics for NCDS women in Figures 3.11–3.13 present a very similar picture, although the proportion of employer-funded training (shown in

FIGURE 3.13

Female qualification and non-qualification training: NCDS

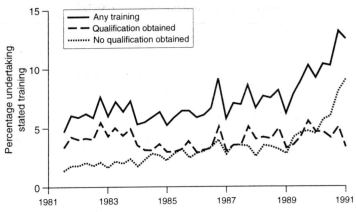

Figure 3.11) is lower than that for men. The broad results from a look at the NCDS data would therefore seem to be that the increase in training during the period (as far as we can accurately measure it) is mainly due to employer-funded training and to courses that did not lead to qualifications and were completed during the period of observation.

Turning to the data we use in our empirical work, Tables 3.4 and 3.5 present some descriptive data for men and women in the seven quarterly LFS panels, for the NCDS cohort and for the subsample of NCDS-aged individuals in the annual LFS surveys. The seven LFS panels correspond to the Spring 1992 (March–May 1992) to Autumn 1994 (September–November 1994) time periods; the NCDS quarterly panel runs from 1981 to 1990; and the LFS NCDS cohort runs from 1984 to 1991.

The mean of training receipt for men was around 15 per cent in the LFS panels, about 8 per cent in the earlier NCDS cohort and around 13 per cent in the NCDS cohort from the LFS. Comparable figures for women are

TABLE 3.4

Incidence of male training: LFS and NCDS

Men who have undertaken:	LFS panels: mean	NCDS panel: mean	NCDS cohort in LFS: mean
Any education and/or training	0.146	0.082	0.129
Employer-funded training	0.086	0.069	0.072
With qualification	0.032	0.035	—
Without qualification	0.053	0.034	—
Completed training	0.025	0.031	0.038
Continuing training	0.060	0.038	0.034
Other training	0.060	0.014	0.023
With qualification	0.020	0.010	—
Without qualification	0.037	0.004	—
Completed training	0.014	0.004	0.005
Continuing training	0.043	0.010	0.018
Training leading to no qualification	0.090	0.037	—
Training leading to qualification	0.052	0.045	—
Other qualification	0.019	0.010	—
Lower vocational	0.001	0.008	—
Middle vocational	0.013	0.004	—
Higher vocational	0.007	0.016	—
Degree	0.011	0.007	—
Sample size	26,232	59,957	7,740

Note: Training incidence in the LFS refers to any education and/or training in the last four weeks, whereas in the NCDS it refers to any training in the last quarter. Employer-funded training is defined as any training partly or wholly funded by the person's employer. The base sample for the LFS is all men in work for the five quarters of the panel. Note that, for the LFS, the subgroups beneath employer-funded and other training (i.e. with/without qualification and completed/continuing) do not add up to the total group mean as they are from different samples (the subgroup breakdowns are not available for all seven panels and are available for 15,131 observations). For the NCDS cohort in the LFS, qualification-based breakdowns are not reported as the qualifications question is only asked in 1991. For the NCDS, we include all men employed in a particular quarter over the period 1981 to 1990.

16, 7 and 13 per cent respectively. The decomposition of this aggregate measure into the more detailed training classifications displays a very consistent pattern across data sources, for both groups. Bearing in mind that the datasets have different questioning procedures, and that they cover different time periods and ages, the means in Tables 3.4 and 3.5 paint a very consistent picture of

System*Data description*

training receipt (the time series profiles are given in various graphs above).

TABLE 3.5

Incidence of female training: LFS and NCDS

Women who have undertaken:	LFS panels: mean	NCDS panel: mean	NCDS cohort in LFS: mean
Any education and/or training	0.156	0.071	0.134
Employer-funded training	0.081	0.049	0.068
With qualification	0.031	0.025	—
Without qualification	0.049	0.024	—
Completed training	0.025	0.022	0.033
Continuing training	0.056	0.027	0.034
Other training	0.075	0.022	0.033
With qualification	0.028	0.015	—
Without qualification	0.043	0.007	—
Completed training	0.015	0.005	0.005
Continuing training	0.055	0.017	0.027
Training leading to no qualification	0.092	0.031	—
Training leading to qualification	0.059	0.040	—
Other qualification	0.022	0.005	—
Lower vocational	0.005	0.009	—
Middle vocational	0.008	0.004	—
Higher vocational	0.012	0.018	—
Degree	0.010	0.003	—
Sample size	25,060	51,162	5,273

Note: Training incidence in the LFS refers to any education and/or training in the last four weeks, whereas in the NCDS it refers to any training in the last quarter. Employer-funded training is defined as any training partly or wholly funded by the person's employer. The base sample for the LFS is all women in work for the five quarters of the panel. Note that, for the LFS, the subgroups beneath employer-funded and other training (i.e. with/without qualification and completed/continuing) do not add up to the total group mean as they are from different samples (the subgroup breakdowns are not available for all seven panels and are available for 14,357 observations). For the NCDS cohort in the LFS, qualification-based breakdowns are not reported as the qualifications question is only asked in 1991. For the NCDS, we include all women employed in a particular quarter over the period 1981 to 1990.

System37

CHAPTER 4
Methodology

4.1 Introduction

How do we model the relationship between labour mobility and work-related training? Both of the datasets that we use allow us to track individuals' labour market statuses over time and therefore to look directly at labour turnover. This will allow us to measure directly the effects of different types of training in one period on labour market status in future periods, as well as the relationship between labour market transitions over a period of time and the probability of subsequently receiving different types of training.

4.2 Modelling Training and Turnover

Modelling the relationship between mobility and training is not straightforward. Using longitudinal data, as we do, gives two potential options for identifying the relationship(s) between training and mobility. The first, and much simpler, approach is to use the repeat observation nature of the panel data to identify the respective relationships between training and mobility (and vice versa) by adopting an explicit 'before-and-after' approach. This involves asking the questions 'if an individual receives training in time period t, do they move jobs in subsequent time periods (that is, $t+1$ onwards)?' and 'if an individual moves jobs in time period t, do they receive training in subsequent time periods?'. In order for this approach to be valid, we have to assume that the unobserved determinants of subsequent training are uncorrelated with mobility in the current period and that the unobserved determinants of subsequent mobility are uncorrelated with training in the current period.

If this assumption is not valid, then we need to follow a second approach which involves using instrumental variables to net out the problems of causal feedback. This requires us to find an 'instrument' for training in our mobility equation — that is, something that determines training in the current quarter but does not determine future mobility controlling for current training — as well as an 'instrument' for mobility in our training equation. The difficulty here is that theory is not very forthcoming in terms of offering suitable instruments (which probably reflects a preoccupation with abstract, and rather impractical, theory in some areas of the economics of training). Nevertheless, there are possibilities to do something about this, given the nature of our data sources.

So our empirical approach is to use both these strategies. We begin by using the 'before-and-after' approach which looks at whether an individual moves jobs or receives training after a period in which they were trained or moved job respectively. Then we attempt to adopt an instrumental variable framework which allows for the possibility that mobility and training are endogenous. Finally, we use a simultaneous model which allows current as well as lagged mobility to affect current training and vice versa. Each of these approaches is discussed in turn below. Full technical details of the models discussed below are found in Appendix A.

4.2.1 The effect of training on job turnover

Consider first the question 'if an individual receives training in time period t, do they move jobs in subsequent time periods?'. To answer this, we begin by estimating simple models for individual i in year t of the form

(4.1) $\Pr(MOBILITY_{it} = 1) = f(X_{i,t-1}, TRAIN_{i,t-1}, f_i)$

where $TRAIN_i$ and $MOBILITY_i$ are (at least to start with) 0–1 indicators of training receipt and job mobility, X_i is a vector of other relevant control variables and f_i is a vector of unobserved individual characteristics that determine the probability of moving jobs. There is an issue to do with defining the period over which mobility should be defined: in most of our work, this is taken to be the four quarters subsequent to the training time period.

To be more explicit about how the two methodologies we use are related, in our initial work we assume that the unobserved individual characteristics, f_i, that determine the probability of moving jobs are uncorrelated with training receipt (and, indeed, all our other explanatory variables), so that $E(TRAIN_{i,t-1}f_i) \neq 0$. If this condition holds, then we can consistently estimate the effect of training on mobility by estimating equation (4.1). The effect training has on the probability of moving jobs in this model is given by

(4.2) $\Pr(MOBILITY_{it} = 1 | TRAIN_{i,t-1} = 1, X_{i,t-1})$

$- \Pr(MOBILITY_{it} = 1 | TRAIN_{i,t-1} = 0, X_{i,t-1})$.

This expression is usually evaluated using mean values for the $X_{i,t-1}$.

If the unobserved individual characteristics that determine job mobility also determine training, so that $E(TRAIN_{i,t-1}f_i) \neq 0$, then we will obtain biased estimates of the effect of training on job mobility. The direction of this bias depends on whether these unobserved individual characteristics, f_i, are positively or negatively correlated with training participation and/or mobility and on the true correlation between training and mobility. This will lead us to the instrumental variable approach considered below.

4.2.2 The effect of mobility on employer-funded training

The same points apply to the impact of mobility on training. We begin by using the time dynamics to identify the relationship between training for individual i in period t and previous job mobility:

$$(4.3) \quad \Pr(TRAIN_{it} = 1) = f(X_{i,t-1}, MOBILITY_{i,t-1}, f_i).$$

The effect mobility has on the probability of undertaking training in this model is given by

$$(4.4) \quad \Pr(TRAIN_{it} = 1 \mid MOBILITY_{i,t-1} = 1, X_{i,t-1})$$
$$- \Pr(TRAIN_{it} = 1 \mid MOBILITY_{i,t-1} = 0, X_{i,t-1}).$$

It is evident that we can use the 'before-and-after' methodology when we have panel data to look at the relationship between training and previous job mobility. We adopt this approach below.

4.2.3 Instrumental variable methods

The second approach that we take is the more difficult instrumental variable (IV) approach which requires the endogenous modelling of training receipt in a job mobility equation (and vice versa). The full details of this approach are discussed in Appendix A. The idea behind the methodology can be described in the context of the following training equation:

$$(4.5) \quad \Pr(TRAIN_{it} = 1) = f(X_{i,t-1}, MOBILITY_{i,t-1}, f_i)$$

where we now allow for the possibility that $E(MOBILITY_{i,t-1}, f_i) \neq 0$ — that is, lagged mobility is endogenous.

The issue here is that, to resolve the potential endogeneity bias, we need an instrumental variable that is correlated with $MOBILITY_{i,t-1}$ but not with the error term (which contains the unobserved heterogeneity component through f_i). We discuss in Section 5.6 the specific instruments that we have developed so far.

Suppose that we have a legitimate instrument for mobility, say Z_{Mi}; then we need to estimate a second equation of the form

(4.6) $\quad \Pr(MOBILITY_{i,t-1} = 1) = f(X_{i,t-1}, Z_{Mi})$

and replace the binary indicator of mobility ($MOBILITY_{i,t-1}$) in the initial equation (4.5) with the continuous prediction index $MOBÎLITY^*_{i,t-1}$ (rather than the predicted probability) from equation (4.6). The impact of mobility on the probability of receiving training (or the marginal effect of moving) is now calculated by taking the average value of the prediction index for those who move ($\overline{M^*_1}$) and for those who do not move ($\overline{M^*_0}$), and is given by

(4.7) $\quad \Pr(TRAIN_{it} = 1 | MOBÎLITY^*_{i,t-1} = \overline{M^*_1}, X_{i,t-1})$

$\quad - \Pr(TRAIN_{it} = 1 | MOBÎLITY^*_{i,t-1} = \overline{M^*_0}, X_{i,t-1}).$

The methodology and the exact expression for this marginal effect in the probit model are discussed in Appendix A. The same IV approach can be used for modelling mobility. This again requires that we have an additional legitimate instrument for training in our mobility equation.

4.2.4 A simultaneous model of training and job mobility

In the models considered so far, we have only allowed lagged values of training and mobility to influence current mobility and training. We can extend our model to allow simultaneous determination of training and mobility, following the method of Mallar (1977). Our simultaneous model is given by

(4.8) $\Pr(MOBILITY_{it} = 1)$

$= f(X_{i,t-1}, Z_{Mi}, TRAIN_{it}, TRAIN_{i,t-1}, f_i)$

and

(4.9) $\Pr(TRAIN_{it} = 1)$

$= f(X_{i,t-1}, Z_{Ti}, MOBILITY_{it}, MOBILITY_{i,t-1}, f_i)$

where we assume that all the lagged variables in the two equations are exogenous. In order for this system of equations to be identified, we need an instrument for mobility, Z_{Mi}, which determines mobility but not training controlling for mobility, and an instrument for training, Z_{Ti}, which explains training but not mobility controlling for training. If we also want to treat lagged training and mobility as endogenous, we require at least two instruments for current and lagged training and at least two instruments for current and lagged mobility. Finding suitable instruments will be difficult in practice. In this model, we need to undertake a two-stage estimation procedure. In the first stage, we estimate reduced form probits of our endogenous binary variables and include all our exogenous variables from our two equations as explanatory variables including all the instruments. In the second stage, we include our prediction of our unobserved training and mobility variables (the prediction index from these probits) in our structural probit regressions and exclude our instruments for training from the mobility probit and our instruments for mobility from our training probit. See Appendix A for full details.

4.3 More General Models of Training and Job Mobility

In the discussion so far, we have only considered binary indicators of training and mobility and looked at how we measure the impact of training on the probability of moving jobs and the impact of moving jobs on the probability of undertaking training. The theoretical and empirical work reviewed earlier suggests that we may expect different types of training to have very different effects on the probability of moving jobs. Also, it may be the case that it is the accumulation of training rather than just a recent episode that affects an individual's decision as to whether to move jobs. This clearly needs to be explored. Also, we have only considered one measure of job turnover — the probability of leaving a job within a specified period. Another measure of job mobility that has been used in the literature (for example, the work of Winkelmann (1994) discussed in Chapter 2) is the number of jobs an individual has held at any point in time. Again, it may be the individual's whole job history that determines whether or not they receive training. Broadening the scope of our study necessarily requires us to use more complicated models, and the ideas behind these alternative models are discussed in more detail below while the more technical details are again discussed in Appendix A.

4.3.1 Models that use different types of training

We now allow for the possibility that there are two types of training — employer-funded training (*EMPTRAIN*) which we define as training for which the employer has fully or partly paid (which we may expect to be relatively firm-specific) and non-employer-funded training (*OTHTRAIN*) (which presumably involves more general training). If we have multiple measures of training, then it is easy to adapt our mobility equation to include them

FIGURE 4.1

A multinomial model of training choice

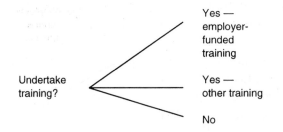

as explanatory variables. If we want to treat both these training variables as endogenous, then we need to have at least two instruments for training which explain both types of training but not mobility controlling for both types of training.

The more difficult problem is how to model the probability of receiving different types of training appropriately. In our original model, we only model the probabilities of two outcomes: the probability of undertaking training and, as a consequence, the probability of not undertaking training. If we separately identify employer-funded and non-employer-funded training, we now have three possible outcomes for which we need to model the probabilities. The way we model them depends on our assumption about how the decision process operates. One approach, which is the approach adopted by Royalty (1996), is to use a multinomial probit (or logit) model. This assumes that the decision process is not sequential and can be described diagrammatically as in Figure 4.1.

An alternative approach to modelling the probabilities of undertaking different types of training is to treat the decision process as sequential. One possibility is that an individual makes a decision regarding whether or not they should undertake training. If they decide to under-

FIGURE 4.2

A sequential model of training choice

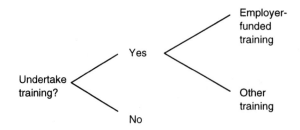

take training, they then make a decision as to what kind of training they should undertake. The decision process for this type of sequential model can be described diagrammatically as in Figure 4.2.

In this type of model, the probabilities of undertaking employer-funded and non-employer-funded training are given by

(4.10) $\Pr(EMPTRAIN_{it} = 1 \| X_{i,t-1}, MOBILITY_{i,t-1}) =$
$\Pr(EMPTRAIN_{it} = 1 \| TRAIN_{it} = 1, X_{i,t-1}, MOBILITY_{i,t-1})$
$\times \Pr(TRAIN_{it} = 1 \| X_{i,t-1}, MOBILITY_{i,t-1})$

and

(4.11) $\Pr(OTHTRAIN_{it} = 1 \| X_{i,t-1}, MOBILITY_{i,t-1}) =$
$(1 - \Pr(EMPTRAIN_{it} = 1 \| TRAIN_{it} = 1, X_{i,t-1}, MOBILITY_{i,t-1}))$
$\times \Pr(TRAIN_{it} = 1 \| X_{i,t-1}, MOBILITY_{i,t-1}).$

These probabilities can be calculated by undertaking a training probit on the whole sample and then by carrying out a further probit on all those individuals who undertake training, to obtain the conditional probability of undertaking employer-funded training, given that they have undertaken training ($\Pr(EMPTRAIN_{it} = 1 \| TRAIN_{it} = 1, X_{i,t-1}, MOBILITY_{i,t-1})$).

46

FIGURE 4.3

An alternative sequential model

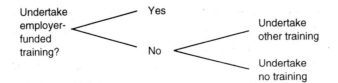

It can be argued that employers largely decide on which individuals undertake employer-funded training. If individuals do not receive employer-funded training, they may then decide whether or not to invest in other types of training. The sequential process in this type of model can be shown diagrammatically as in Figure 4.3.

In this sequential model, the probability of undertaking employer-funded training is obtained from a first-stage probit modelling the probability of undertaking employer-funded training on the whole sample. The probability of undertaking other training is calculated by undertaking a second-stage probit on all individuals who did not undertake employer-funded training and, from this, calculating the conditional probability of undertaking other training, given that they have not received employer-funded training ($\Pr(OTHTRAIN_{it} = 1 | EMPTRAIN_{it} = 0, X_{i,t-1}, MOBILITY_{i,t-1})$). In this model, the probability of undertaking employer-funded training ($\Pr(EMPTRAIN_{it} = 1 | X_{i,t-1}, MOBILITY_{i,t-1})$) is obtained directly from the first-stage regression. The probability of receiving other training in this alternative sequential model is given by

$$(4.12) \quad \Pr(OTHTRAIN_{it} = 1 | X_{i,t-1}, MOBILITY_{i,t-1}) =$$
$$\Pr(OTHTRAIN_{it} = 1 | EMPTRAIN_{it} = 0, X_{i,t-1}, MOBILITY_{i,t-1})$$
$$\times (1 - \Pr(EMPTRAIN_{it} = 1 | X_{i,t-1}, MOBILITY_{i,t-1})).$$

In this report, we estimate both of these sequential models and compare the estimates obtained from each. We can again work out the marginal effects of mobility on different types of training by evaluating the difference in the predicted probabilities when we set our mobility dummy variable to one and then zero (evaluated at sample means for all other variables). If we instrument mobility, then the marginal effect is obtained by looking at how the predicted probability of undertaking employer-funded or other training changes with respect to the continuous mobility index. Full details are given in Appendix A.

4.3.2 Models that use different measures of job mobility

In all the models discussed above, our measure of mobility has been a dummy variable that equals one if a person has moved or will move jobs within a specified period. There are clearly other measures of mobility that are of interest. In this report, we look at the impact of the number of jobs a person has held over their entire working life (excluding their current job) on the probability of receiving different types of training in their current job.

We also follow the approach of Winkelmann (1994) and use count data models to look at the effect of different types of training on the number of jobs a person has held over their working life. This involves estimating a model of the form

$$(4.13) \quad \Pr(NJOBS_{it} = j) = f(X_{i,t-1}, f_i) \quad j = 0,1,2,3,....$$

where $NJOBS_{it}$ is the number of jobs since leaving school that individual i has held at time t. The issues and econometric complications that arise in these count data models are similar to those already discussed above.

Full details of the models we use are given in Appendix A.

4.3.3 *Identifying assumptions of our models*

Training receipt displays a marked pattern over the year. Much of this variation is driven by the fact that many further education colleges (and other academic training colleges) close down or do not offer courses over the Summer, Winter and Easter holidays. As such, individuals cannot receive training of this sort during these periods. In future work, we hope to exploit this within-year variation to use holiday times as an instrument for training receipt in a job mobility equation for our LFS panel. We have conducted a survey of around 50 per cent of further education colleges in Britain and have received responses from about 170 at this stage, a response rate of around 40 per cent. We have college term dates from 1991–92 to 1995–96, from which we can construct weekly data on college opening times. We have not, as yet, been able to make use of these data as we need to gain access to disaggregated regional codes in the LFS data. A copy of the questionnaire we sent out to further education colleges is contained in Appendix C.

We have also tried a number of instruments for training using the NCDS panel, such as characteristics of the individual's first ever job. These, however, did not generally pass instrument validity tests. In terms of instruments for mobility, the NCDS contains more promising possibilities than the LFS. In this report, we have carried out both IV and simultaneous probit estimation of training equations using the number of times the cohort member moved house between 0 and 16 years of age, and a variable for whether the cohort member's mother was employed in 1974, as instruments. We argue that both these variables explain individual job moves but not training controlling for mobility. Finding suitable instruments for training and mobility is very difficult, in general, as the large majority of characteristics that determine mobility, such as employer characteristics, region and education, also determine the probability of receiving training.

CHAPTER 5
Results

5.1 Introduction

In this chapter, we report our results. We begin by reporting estimates of the reduced form determinants of training and mobility, then move on to estimate models that attempt to identify the impact of training on mobility and of mobility on training by adopting the 'before-and-after' approach discussed in the previous chapter. We then discuss the results from the more complicated sequential models of training choice and count data models looking at the impact of training on the number of jobs held by an individual. Finally, we consider instrumental variable and simultaneous models.

5.2 What Are the Determinants of Training and Job Mobility?

In this section, we look at what (exogenous) factors determine training (ignoring job mobility) and job mobility (ignoring training) in our two datasets. The specifications we use are fairly standard and for the most part reconfirm existing results in the large number of studies that have looked at the determinants of training and mobility.

Our results for the factors determining training (shown in Table B.1 in Appendix B for our NCDS panel and Tables B.2 and B.3 for our QLFS panel) show that there is a clear positive relationship between the level of qualifications attained and the likelihood of receiving training, with those with degrees and higher vocational qualifications receiving more training than individuals with lower qualifications. As for differences between industries in the LFS, for the whole sample of men, most training seems to take place in 'other services' (the base industry in the LFS regressions); construction and other manufacturing industries seem to train least. The industry effects are, by and large, significant. For women and for men under 30, the wholesale and retail trade sector is associated with less training, whilst for women the manufacturing sector as a whole (minerals, metals and other manufacturing) is associated with significantly less training. The regional dummies in the LFS training regressions provide little evidence of wide regional variations in training incidence. For men and for younger women, training incidence seems to decrease with age in the LFS, as predicted by a human capital interpretation of training expenditure (i.e. younger workers have more to gain over the life cycle from expenditure on training than older workers). For women in the LFS, there is significantly less training for part-time workers than for full-time workers. Finally, those individuals working for larger employers (with 25 or more employees) in the LFS seem to undertake more training. The probability of receiving training for men who work for large employers is, on average, 2.6 percentage points higher than it is for men who work for smaller firms. The corresponding figure for women is 2.0 percentage points.[13]

The results for the determinants of training in the NCDS panel echo the equivalent LFS results in many areas. Individuals with higher levels of educational qualifications undertake more training. The results from

---

[13]The marginal effects reported in the tables measure the average impact different types of training have on the probability of moving jobs (which will range between 0 and 1). Hence these marginal effects need to be multiplied by 100 to obtain the percentage point impact of the variable in question on the probability of moving jobs.

the NCDS in Table B.1 show that if a man's highest qualification is A levels, his probability of receiving training is 16.0 percentage points higher than that of a man with no formal educational qualifications. A similar story is found for NCDS women, with the average difference in the probability of receiving training being 14.8 percentage points between women with A levels and those with no qualifications.[14] Although the regional effects are more significant than for the LFS, it is hard to isolate any clear pattern that holds true for both men and women (the strongest findings here are that training is significantly lower in the South-West and Scotland). The industry effects from the NCDS data are a lot less significant, on the whole, than those from the LFS, perhaps because we are only able to use the 1981 industry variable from the NCDS. Individuals who were employed in larger firms in 1981 are more likely to be trained. In addition, the NCDS allows us to look at the impact of some variables that are not always available in the LFS questionnaires. For men, there is some evidence of a link between increased training and being a union member in 1981, although this is not very significant.[15] Individuals employed in the private sector in 1981 seem to train significantly less than those in the public sector. As for the changing incidence of training over the period 1981–90, the NCDS data appear to show an increase in the amount of training each year over time (especially for men), although it is not clear to what extent this is the result of a genuine increase in training over the period or of the right censoring problem discussed in Chapter 3. The results suggest that, other things being

---

[14]These figures are given by the marginal effects column in Table B.1.

[15]Including a union variable in the LFS specifications also produced a positive effect, at the cost of a reduced sample size (see Green, Machin and Wilkinson (1996b) for examples of specifications that include a union recognition variable, which is a more appropriate measure of union presence than membership).

held equal, the average training incidence has increased between 1981 and 1990 by 8.0 percentage points for men and by 6.0 percentage points for women. In summary, it is encouraging that we find no direct contradictions concerning the determinants of training in the NCDS and the LFS.

Moving on to the determinants of mobility (shown in the first column of Tables B.4 and B.8 for our NCDS sample and of Tables B.12, B.16, B.20 and B.24 for our LFS sample), in the LFS there seems to be a positive relationship between mobility and having some sort of educational qualification. Perhaps not surprisingly, finance and the wholesale and retail trade are the industries where people appear to experience the most mobility, while minerals, energy and water, and the base industry of other services are the least mobile. In general, there are few significant regional variations in mobility, the main exception being the finding that young men in the South-East and East Anglia seem to be significantly more mobile than those in most other areas. Part-time workers are much more mobile than full-timers. Men working part-time have, on average, a 7.0 percentage point higher probability of moving in the next year than men working full-time. The corresponding figure for women is 2.5 percentage points. The results also show that there is less mobility amongst non-whites and individuals working for larger employers.

The NCDS results on mobility are similar to the LFS ones with respect to education and employer size. The effects over time from 1981 to 1990 show a modest but uneven increase in mobility for men relative to 1981 (except in 1990). In this case, it is male workers in the North in 1981 who appear to be the most mobile, rather than those in the South-East. Union membership in 1981 is associated with less mobility, while individuals who worked in the private sector in 1981 are more likely to move jobs. Finally, there is a strong positive relationship between the number of times an individual in the NCDS moved house before the age of 16 and their subsequent labour market mobility. This is important, as our aim is to exploit this positive relationship by using times moved since birth as an instrument for mobility in IV regressions (see Section 5.6).

Overall, the NCDS and LFS results on the reduced form determinants of mobility seem to roughly correspond in overall pattern.

5.3 What Effect Does Training Have on Job Mobility?

We now extend our mobility equations and allow job mobility to also be dependent on previous training.

Tables 5.1 and 5.2 give some descriptive statistics for men and women. Tables 5.3 and 5.4 then report the estimated marginal effects for the training variable in job mobility probits based on NCDS data for men and women respectively (training effects significant at the 5 per cent level are denoted by ** and those significant at the 10 per cent level by *). Tables 5.5 and 5.6 then report the effects of training on mobility for all men and for men aged less than 30 respectively from the LFS panel data, while Tables 5.7 and 5.8 report the corresponding figures for women. Coefficient estimates and standard errors, as well as marginal effects for the full models, are given in Tables B.4 through B.27 in Appendix B.

Consider first the descriptive statistics in Tables 5.1 and 5.2. The tables break down job moving rates from the quarterly LFS panels and the NCDS by various characteristics of individuals and their jobs. The basic definition of job mobility is any change of jobs in the four quarters following the period in which the training incidence is defined. Whilst showing higher mobility rates for women than for men, both tables demonstrate, from both data sources, that job moves are more likely for young workers, in smaller workplaces and in industries that have lower-than-average wages (notably wholesale and retail trade).

TABLE 5.1

The characteristics of male job movers in the LFS and NCDS

Group	LFS		NCDS	
	Proportion moving job	*Number in group*	*Proportion moving job*	*Number in group*
Trained in quarter	0.057	3,829	0.151	4,785
Did not train in quarter	0.053	22,403	0.162	55,172
Age < 30	0.093	6,474	—	—
Age ≥ 30	0.041	19,758	—	—
Degree	0.055	4,070	0.221	5,827
Higher vocational	0.057	2,228	0.167	8,807
Middle vocational	0.059	5,565	0.149	15,772
Lower vocational	0.061	6,399	0.158	13,811
Other	0.053	2,522	0.163	3,368
No educational qualifications	0.037	5,448	0.147	12,372
Full-time worker	0.051	25,543	0.161	59,217
Part-time worker	0.160	689	0.150	740
White	0.054	25,375	—	—
Non-white	0.038	857	—	—
Employer size < 25	0.076	6,630	0.189	16,222
Employer size ≥ 25	0.046	19,602	0.151	43,735
Industry				
Energy and water	0.038	966	0.117	3,117
Minerals	0.029	1,357	0.146	2,534
Metals	0.051	4,593	0.161	8,779
Other manufacturing	0.043	2,877	0.147	5,269
Construction	0.060	1,845	0.194	4,517
Wholesale and retail trade	0.090	3,743	0.215	7,002
Transport and communications	0.043	2,686	0.133	4,126
Finance	0.081	2,679	0.173	3,879
Other services	0.034	5,486	0.171	7,314
All men	0.053	26,232	0.161	59,957

Note: Moving job in the LFS refers to any job move in quarters 2 to 5, whereas training refers to training in quarter 1. A job move in the NCDS refers to any job move in the current or next three quarters, whereas training refers to training in the previous quarter. The group characteristics are measured in the first quarter of the LFS panel and in 1981 (except for training variables) in the NCDS panel. Industry numbers do not sum to the total in the NCDS data because of missing values.

TABLE 5.2

The characteristics of female job movers in the LFS and NCDS

Group	LFS		NCDS	
	Proportion moving job	*Number in group*	*Proportion moving job*	*Number in group*
Trained in quarter	0.074	3,907	0.242	3,540
Did not train in quarter	0.072	21,153	0.237	47,622
Age < 30	0.123	6,548	—	—
Age ≥ 30	0.054	18,512	—	—
Degree	0.078	2,414	0.269	5,725
Higher vocational	0.059	2,970	0.239	10,711
Middle vocational	0.089	3,026	0.220	9,371
Lower vocational	0.084	8,857	0.240	13,510
Other	0.051	1,452	0.254	2,089
No educational qualifications	0.056	6,341	0.225	9,756
Full-time worker	0.067	14,444	0.237	46,190
Part-time worker	0.079	10,616	0.238	4,972
White	0.073	24,288	—	—
Non-white	0.051	772	—	—
Employer size < 25	0.088	9,069	0.257	16,764
Employer size ≥ 25	0.063	15,991	0.227	34,398
Industry				
Energy and water	0.041	242	0.159	691
Minerals	0.053	438	0.274	1,084
Metals	0.078	1,261	0.257	2,830
Other manufacturing	0.085	1,723	0.264	4,032
Construction	0.084	406	0.262	282
Wholesale and retail trade	0.106	5,295	0.271	7,018
Transport and communications	0.073	820	0.219	1,885
Finance	0.074	3,168	0.218	6,110
Other services	0.054	11,707	0.235	3,862
All women	0.072	25,060	0.237	51,162

Note: See note to Table 5.1.

Table 5.3 reports the results from our job mobility probits for our NCDS sample of men and Table 5.4 for our NCDS sample of women. In the tables, we only report the marginal effects of training — that is, the effect different types of training have (in percentage point terms) on the probability of moving jobs. We only look at the probability of moving within four quarters of receiving training; however, the results do not change dramatically if we extend this to longer periods in the NCDS. In the tables, we report results for a variety of

TABLE 5.3

The effect of training on male mobility: NCDS

Type of training	Marginal effect	Significance
1. Any training	−0.010	*
2. Employer-funded	−0.029	**
2. Other	0.025	**
3. Completed training	−0.018	**
3. Training continued	−0.004	
4. Employer-funded & completed	−0.031	**
4. Employer-funded & not completed	−0.028	**
4. Other & completed	−0.002	
4. Other & not completed	0.052	**
5. Qualification	−0.006	
5. No qualification	−0.015	*
6. Employer-funded & qualification	−0.027	**
6. Employer-funded & no qualification	−0.032	**
6. Other & qualification	0.049	**
6. Other & no qualification	0.005	
7. No qualification	−0.015	*
7. Other qualification	−0.034	**
7. Lower qualification	−0.001	
7. Middle qualification	−0.026	
7. Higher qualification	−0.020	*
7. Degree qualification	0.085	**
Sample size	59,957	

Note: * Significant at 10 per cent level.
** Significant at 5 per cent level.

specifications where the training variable is defined differently in each case. Specification 1 uses the overall training variable, 2 splits training into employer-funded and other training, 3 splits it into whether training finished in the quarter or was ongoing, 4 interacts continuing and completed training with employer-funded and other training, 5 divides training according to whether or not a qualification was obtained, 6 interacts the qualification split with whether or not the training was employer-funded, and finally 7 breaks the qualifications gained down into more disaggregated categories.

In the results reported in Tables 5.3 and 5.4, we have only included people who were employed in 1981 (so that we can have 1981 employer characteristics as explanatory variables) and we have dropped all quarters within a year of the 1991 interview, as in these periods we cannot clearly identify whether the individual moved jobs in the following four quarters.

The results in Table 5.3 suggest that, for men, receiving work-related training significantly decreases the probability of moving jobs over the following year by, on average, 1.0 percentage point. The estimated average probability of moving in the following year for non-trainees is 15.7 per cent, compared with 14.7 per cent for trainees.[16] Breaking this down, it is apparent that the negative effect is only the case for employer-funded training. If a man undertakes employer-funded training, then the probability of moving jobs in the next year is decreased by an average of 2.9 percentage points (from 15.7 per cent to 12.8 per cent). This is in line with the theoretical discussions, which state that specific training is far less likely to lead to job turnover. Training finishing in a given quarter also shows different effects from ongoing training, with the negative impact of previous training on job mobility only being significant for training that has been completed. Presumably this reflects the fact that employers wish to retain more highly trained workers who have just completed training courses. Finally, NCDS men are less likely to change jobs if their training does not lead to a formal qualifica-

---

[16]These probabilities are derived from the estimates of our probit equations where we have set all other explanatory variables equal to the mean values for the particular sample. Hence these probabilities are different from the raw mean probabilities of trainees and non-trainees reported in Table 5.1 for our male NCDS cohort.

TABLE 5.4

The effect of training on female mobility: NCDS

Type of training	Marginal effect	Significance
1. Any training	0.006	
2. Employer-funded	0.002	
2. Other	0.012	
3. Completed training	−0.007	
3. Training continued	0.014	
4. Employer-funded & completed	0.001	
4. Employer-funded & not completed	0.002	
4. Other & completed	−0.018	
4. Other & not completed	0.030	**
5. Qualification	0.034	**
5. No qualification	−0.034	**
6. Employer-funded & qualification	0.002	
6. Employer-funded & no qualification	0.000	
6. Other & qualification	0.084	**
6. Other & no qualification	−0.067	**
7. No qualification	−0.034	**
7. Other qualification	0.022	
7. Lower qualification	0.047	**
7. Middle qualification	0.031	
7. Higher qualification	0.041	**
7. Degree qualification	−0.008	
Sample size	51,162	

Note: ** Significant at 5 per cent level.

tion than if it does. However, it is clear that this varies depending on the type of qualification being undertaken, with men undertaking a degree qualification much more likely to move.

Turning to women (as reported in Table 5.4), the overall effect of training is not significantly different from zero and numerically very small. The only significant results for women relate to qualification training. Women undertaking qualification training are much more likely to move jobs, particularly those undertaking lower or higher vocational qualifications. This suggests that this type of qualification training may be obtained

TABLE 5.5

The effect of training on male mobility: QLFS

Type of training	Marginal effect	Signifi-cance	Sample size
1. Any training	–0.004		26,232
1. Any training (13-week question)	–0.006		4,520
2. Employer-funded	–0.011	**	26,232
2. Other	0.006		26,232
3. Completed training	–0.014	*	15,131
3. Training continued	–0.002		15,131
4. Employer-funded & completed	–0.021	**	15,131
4. Employer-funded & not completed	–0.008		15,131
4. Other & completed	–0.003		15,131
4. Other & not completed	0.005		15,131
5. Qualification	–0.001		15,131
5. No qualification	–0.009		15,131
6. Employer-funded & qualification	–0.019	**	15,131
6. Employer-funded & no qualification	–0.005		15,131
6. Other & qualification	0.027	**	15,131
6. Other & no qualification	–0.013		15,131
7. No qualification	–0.008		15,131
7. Other qualification	–0.005		15,131
7. Lower qualification	0.054		15,131
7. Middle qualification	–0.003		15,131
7. Higher qualification	–0.032	*	15,131
7. Degree qualification	0.030	**	15,131

Note: *   Significant at 10 per cent level.
       ** Significant at 5 per cent level.

by women in order to move jobs rather than as training for the present job.

For men, a similar story emerges from the LFS panel, as shown in Table 5.5. This is reassuring, given the clear differences in the nature of the data being used. The results presented in this table relate to the seven pooled five-quarter panels between Spring 1992 and Autumn 1993. The clear point to note is that, in line with the NCDS work above, work-related training is once again associated with reduced job mobility. Also, there is a negative effect of similar magnitude if we instead use

TABLE 5.6

The effect of training on young men's mobility: QLFS panel

Type of training	Marginal effect	Signifi- cance	Sample size
1. Any training	−0.015	*	6,474
1. Any training (13-week question)	−0.044	*	1,028
2. Employer-funded	−0.031	**	6,474
2. Other	0.005		6,474
3. Completed training	−0.016		3,776
3. Training continued	−0.019		3,776
4. Employer-funded & completed	−0.011		3,776
4. Employer-funded & not completed	−0.034	**	3,776
4. Other & completed	−0.024		3,776
4. Other & not completed	0.001		3,776
5. Qualification	−0.016		3,776
5. No qualification	−0.021		3,776
6. Employer-funded & qualification	−0.040	**	3,776
6. Employer-funded & no qualification	−0.012		3,776
6. Other & qualification	0.018		3,776
6. Other & no qualification	−0.032		3,776
7. No qualification	−0.020		3,776
7. Other qualification	−0.024		3,776
7. Lower qualification	−0.003		3,776
7. Middle qualification	−0.017		3,776
7. Higher qualification	−0.052	**	3,776
7. Degree qualification	0.024		3,776

Note: * Significant at 10 per cent level.
** Significant at 5 per cent level.

the 13-week training question rather than the four-week training question for the Summer 1994 panel, though neither of these variables is significant at conventional levels. The same pattern of results as in the NCDS regressions for men emerges, with significant negative effects being confined to employer-funded training (model 2) and to the training spell being completed (model 3). Men undertaking employer-funded training have a 3.5 per cent chance of moving in the next year compared with the estimated 4.6 per cent chance of individuals who have not undertaken employer-funded training in the previous four weeks, a difference of 1.1 percentage points. Like the NCDS results, there is no association between mobility and previous training receipt for women (see Table 5.7), but a negative effect does emerge for employer-funded training and in particular employer-funded training that does not lead to a qualification.

Focusing only on young men aged under 30 (a similar age structure to the NCDS data), Table 5.6 shows a significant negative effect for any training (in line with the NCDS results). The marginal effect of training is to reduce the probability of moving jobs in the next year by

TABLE 5.7

The effect of training on female mobility: QLFS

Type of training	Marginal effect	Signifi-cance	Sample size
1. Any training	0.000		25,060
1. Any training (13-week question)	−0.006		4,118
2. Employer-funded	−0.016	**	25,060
2. Other	0.014	**	25,060
3. Completed training	−0.012		14,357
3. Training continued	0.003		14,357
4. Employer-funded & completed	−0.012		14,357
4. Employer-funded & not completed	−0.013		14,357
4. Other & completed	−0.014		14,357
4. Other & not completed	0.018	**	14,357
5. Qualification	0.014	*	14,357
5. No qualification	−0.011		14,357
6. Employer-funded & qualification	−0.006		14,357
6. Employer-funded & no qualification	−0.017	**	14,357
6. Other & qualification	0.033	**	14,357
6. Other & no qualification	−0.004		14,357
7. No qualification	−0.011		14,357
7. Other qualification	0.011		14,357
7. Lower qualification	0.064	**	14,357
7. Middle qualification	−0.002		14,357
7. Higher qualification	0.035	**	14,357
7. Degree qualification	0.001		14,357

Note: * Significant at 10 per cent level.
  ** Significant at 5 per cent level.

1.5 percentage points from 8.6 per cent to 7.1 per cent. The effect appears even stronger when the 13-week training question is used (reducing mobility by 4.4 percentage points). A similar pattern emerges when the overall training variable is broken down: job mobility seems lower when individuals received training that was employer-funded and/or was not completed in the quarter concerned. For young men, the marginal effect for employer-funded training (at –0.031 or 3.1 percentage points) is very similar to the NCDS result (of –0.029 or 2.9 percentage points) reported above. Finally, the strongest negative effect is where the training was employer-funded and led to a qualification: workers receiving training of this sort are much less likely to move jobs in the following four quarters. This again supports the notion that employees who receive higher-quality qualification training from their employers are more likely to stay with that employer despite the fact that this training is presumably less firm-specific than employer-funded training that does not involve a qualification.

The full regression results shown in Appendix B also tell us something about other factors that affect job mobility. It is interesting to compare the marginal effects from the mobility equations that do not include training (discussed in the last section) with the marginal effects from the mobility equations with training as a regressor. The two are compared for NCDS males in Table B.4 and for NCDS women in Table B.8. Interestingly, the coefficients and marginal effects on the other regressors vary only slightly, if at all, with the inclusion of training as an extra regressor. This implies that the relationships between mobility and other variables that we identify in the previous section cannot be discounted as spurious effects operating only due to the exclusion of the training variable. Even in Table B.6, the inclusion of recent qualification variables in the mobility equation does not displace the effects of earlier qualifications up to 1981.

TABLE 5.8

The effect of training on young women's mobility: QLFS

Type of training	Marginal effect	Signifi- cance	Sample size
1. Any training	−0.014		6,548
1. Any training (13-week question)	−0.034		1,046
2. Employer-funded	−0.034	**	6,548
2. Other	0.004		6,548
3. Completed training	−0.039		3,785
3. Training continued	−0.022		3,785
4. Employer-funded & completed	−0.011		3,785
4. Employer-funded & not completed	−0.043	**	3,785
4. Other & completed	−0.086	**	3,785
4. Other & not completed	−0.004		3,785
5. Qualification	−0.021		3,785
5. No qualification	−0.030	*	3,785
6. Employer-funded & qualification	−0.036		3,785
6. Employer-funded & no qualification	−0.033		3,785
6. Other & qualification	−0.006		3,785
6. Other & no qualification	−0.027		3,785
7. No qualification	−0.030	*	3,785
7. Other qualification	−0.003		3,785
7. Lower qualification	0.001		3,785
7. Middle qualification	−0.055	**	3,785
7. Higher qualification	0.005		3,785
7. Degree qualification	−0.042		3,785

Note: * Significant at 10 per cent level.
** Significant at 5 per cent level.

It can be implied from this that school qualifications and later qualifications obtained whilst at work have separate and distinct effects on mobility. The results for NCDS females and for the LFS seem to support these findings.

One interesting extension of these findings is to consider the effect on mobility of not just the most recent training scheme(s), but the individual's entire training history. This can be done using the training history data back to 1981 that we constructed from the NCDS retrospective questionnaire. In addition, we use information from the 1981 NCDS which identifies individuals who received employer-funded training in their 1981 job. Mobility equations were estimated using the overall training variable, and then breaking the training variable down into different types of training as discussed earlier, but this time including the training count variable and the 1981 employer-funded training variable as additional regressors. These results, presented in Tables 5.9 and 5.10, show that, for men, the 1981 training variable has a significant negative marginal effect on mobility which is not diminished by the inclusion of any other training regressors. The training count variable, by contrast, fails to be significant. The coefficients on the other training variables are broadly similar to the earlier cases where these extra variables were not included. What this seems to indicate for NCDS men is that training earlier on in an individual's labour market history (at the age of 23 in this case) has an important effect on mobility which is separate from the effects of training later on. Our finding for the effects of the 1981 training variable echoes the results of Booth and Satchell (1994). For the women in the NCDS, our results are similar, apart from the finding that in this case there is a small, significant, negative effect for the training count variable as well as for the 1981 variable.

Overall, despite some evidence of a negative training effect, the results from both data sources suggest only a very small impact of training in the previous period on job mobility. Other factors appear to be much more important determinants of job mobility, as the full specifications make clear. In particular, size of employer, industry, age, unionisation and full- or part-time job status are much more important. However, the NCDS data offer some evidence that training earlier on in an individual's work history may have a significant negative impact on mobility later on in life.

TABLE 5.9

Alternative estimates of the effect of training on male mobility: NCDS

Type of training	Marginal effect	Significance
1. Any training in last quarter	−0.008	
1. No. of other training courses since 1981	−0.001	
1. Employer-funded training in 1981 job	−0.035	**
2. Employer-funded	−0.028	**
2. Other	0.028	**
2. No. of other training courses since 1981	−0.001	
2. Employer-funded training in 1981 job	−0.035	**
3. Completed training	−0.014	
3. Training continued	−0.003	
3. No. of other training courses since 1981	−0.001	
3. Employer-funded training in 1981 job	−0.035	**
4. Employer-funded & completed	−0.028	**
4. Employer-funded & not completed	−0.027	**
4. Other & completed	0.002	
4. Other & not completed	0.054	**
4. No. of other training courses since 1981	−0.001	
4. Employer-funded training in 1981 job	−0.035	**
5. Qualification	−0.004	
5. No qualification	−0.013	
5. No. of other training courses since 1981	−0.001	
5. Employer-funded training in 1981 job	−0.035	**
6. Employer-funded & qualification	−0.025	**
6. Employer-funded & no qualification	−0.031	**
6. Other & qualification	0.051	**
6. Other & no qualification	0.009	
6. No. of other training courses since 1981	−0.001	
6. Employer-funded training in 1981 job	−0.035	**
7. No qualification	−0.012	
7. Other qualification	−0.033	**
7. Lower qualification	0.002	
7. Middle qualification	−0.025	
7. Higher qualification	−0.017	
7. Degree qualification	0.080	**
7. No. of other training courses since 1981	−0.001	
7. Employer-funded training in 1981 job	−0.035	**
Sample size	59,957	

Note: ** Significant at 5 per cent level.

67

TABLE 5.10

**Alternative estimates of the effect of training on female mobility:
NCDS**

Type of training	Marginal effect	Significance
1. Any training in last quarter	0.007	
1. No. of other training courses since 1981	−0.004	**
1. Employer-funded training in 1981 job	−0.020	**
2. Employer-funded	0.003	
2. Other	0.128	
2. No. of other training courses since 1981	−0.004	**
2. Employer-funded training in 1981 job	−0.020	**
3. Completed training	−0.002	
3. Training continued	0.013	
3. No. of other training courses since 1981	−0.004	**
3. Employer-funded training in 1981 job	−0.020	**
4. Employer-funded & completed	0.005	
4. Employer-funded & not completed	0.002	
4. Other & completed	−0.012	
4. Other & not completed	0.027	**
4. No. of other training courses since 1981	−0.004	**
4. Employer-funded training in 1981 job	−0.020	**
5. Qualification	0.034	**
5. No qualification	−0.031	**
5. No. of other training courses since 1981	−0.004	**
5. Employer-funded training in 1981 job	−0.020	**
6. Employer-funded & qualification	0.003	
6. Employer-funded & no qualification	0.003	
6. Other & qualification	0.084	**
6. Other & no qualification	−0.065	**
6. No. of other training courses since 1981	−0.004	**
6. Employer-funded training in 1981 job	−0.020	**
7. No qualification	−0.031	**
7. Other qualification	0.022	
7. Lower qualification	0.046	**
7. Middle qualification	0.030	
7. Higher qualification	0.042	**
7. Degree qualification	−0.011	
7. No. of other training courses since 1981	−0.004	**
7. Employer-funded training in 1981 job	−0.020	**
Sample size	51,162	

Note: **   Significant at 5 per cent level.

5.4 What Effect Does Job Turnover Have on Training?

We now look at the effect of job mobility on the provision of training using the NCDS and QLFS data. In this section, we assume lagged mobility is exogenous. We implement an instrumental variable strategy for lagged mobility in our NCDS sample in Section 5.6.

The estimated marginal effects of mobility on the various types of training for the NCDS male panel are given in Table 5.11. These are based on our sequential model where we assume individuals decide first whether to undertake training and then what type of training they undertake (see Figure 4.2).

Table 5.11 shows a small negative relationship between mobility in the previous period and current training spells (the first stage of the decision tree in this sequential model). A job move in the previous year reduced the probability of receiving training from 6.9 per cent to 6.3 per cent, a difference of 0.6 percentage points. We then report the results of using different binary decompositions of types of training spell for the second stage of the tree. In the case of employer-funded versus other training, it seems that it is the employer-funded training which is more negatively related to mobility. From Table B.29 in Appendix B, we see that,

TABLE 5.11

**Estimates of the effect of mobility on training:
NCDS males (sequential model 1)**

Type of training	Probit Marginal effect	Significance
Any training	−0.006	**
Employer-funded training	−0.008	**
Other training	0.002	**
Qualification obtained	−0.005	
No qualification obtained	−0.001	
Training finished	−0.003	
Training continuing	−0.003	
No training	0.006	**

Note: ** Significant at 5 per cent level.

TABLE 5.12

**Alternative estimates of the effect of mobility on training:
NCDS males (sequential model 2)**

	Probit	
Type of training	*Marginal effect*	*Significance*
Any training	−0.006	**
Employer-funded training	−0.009	**
Other training	0.002	**
No training	0.006	**

Note: ** Significant at 5 per cent level.

amongst trainees, those who moved in the last year are much less likely to have received employer-funded training. The probability of receiving employer-funded training (rather than other training) for movers is 77.7 per cent compared with 83.1 per cent for non-movers, a difference of 5.4 percentage points (the marginal effect reported in Table B.29) or 6.9 per cent. The overall impact of moving on the probability of receiving employer-funded training is calculated by evaluating equation (4.10) (the expression for the predicted probability of undertaking employer-funded training) when the mobility dummy is set to zero (setting all other explanatory variables equal to their means). This suggests that moving jobs in the last year reduced the probability of receiving employer-funded training from 5.7 per cent (6.9 × 83.1 / 100) to 4.9 per cent (6.3 × 77.7 / 100), a difference of 0.8 percentage points.[17] It is this overall marginal effect, rather than the marginal effect conditional on receiving training (reported in Table B.29 in Appendix B), which is reported in Table 5.11.

Similarly, mobility has a more negative impact on qualification-related training than on training that did

---

[17]We saw earlier that the marginal effect of moving jobs last year on the probability of receiving training was −0.6 percentage points. Of those who did not move, 6.9 per cent received training compared with 6.3 per cent of those who did. We need to use these two figures in calculating the overall marginal effect of moving on receiving employer-funded training (see equation (4.10)).

TABLE 5.13

Estimates of the effect of mobility on training:
NCDS females (sequential model 1)

	Probit	
Type of training	*Marginal effect*	*Significance*
Any training	0.017	**
Employer-funded training	0.005	**
Other training	0.012	**
Qualification obtained	0.014	**
No qualification obtained	0.003	**
Training finished	0.003	**
Training continuing	0.015	**
No training	–0.017	**

Note: ** Significant at 5 per cent level.

not lead to a qualification. The main conclusion to draw from this model of training choice seems to be that labour turnover has a very different impact on different types of training, according to whether they lead to a qualification or not and whether they are employer-funded. Bearing this in mind, we turn to Table 5.12, which shows the corresponding results from the second sequential model (where individuals decide whether or not to fund their own training only in the event that their employer will not pay for them — see Figure 4.3).

Reassuringly, this alternative tree structure produces virtually identical coefficients to the previous structure, despite the different order of estimation. We thus take some comfort from the fact that, for NCDS males, the finding that previous labour turnover is negatively related to employer-funded training is robust over these two different specifications.

The corresponding results for women in the NCDS are given in Tables 5.13 and 5.14. Interestingly, the effect of mobility on overall training levels under the first sequential probit model for women is opposite to its effect for men. Mobility increases the probability of receiving training, particularly non-employer-funded training. In addition, it seems to matter whether the

TABLE 5.14

**Alternative estimates of the effect of mobility on training:
NCDS females (sequential model 2)**

	Probit	
Type of training	*Marginal effect*	*Significance*
Any training	0.017	**
Employer-funded training	0.005	**
Other training	0.012	**
No training	−0.017	**

Note: ** Significant at 5 per cent level.

training is a continuing course; if it is, mobility has more of a positive effect than if training is finished. The results we get for qualification-related training — that it is more positively affected by mobility — are the opposite of those for men.

The corresponding results from the second sequential model are given in Table 5.14. Once again, we get very similar coefficients for the effect of mobility on overall training and for the effects of mobility on employer-funded training to those we got before, which is a reassuring result in terms of data robustness and model specification. The overall message from women in the NCDS, then, seems to be that mobility has more of a positive relationship to training levels than it does for men, and that when we subdivide the training variable into employer-funded / non-employer-funded, finishing / continuing and qualification-related / non-qualification-related, we get rather different results from those for men.

Tables 5.15 and 5.16 present the results for the overall LFS male sample, whereas Tables 5.17 and 5.18 give results for the subsample of men under 30. Note also that for the second stage of the first model, the coefficients for employer-funded versus other training are estimated on a different subsample of the LFS data from the one used to estimate the coefficients for training finished versus training continuing and qualification-

TABLE 5.15

**Estimates of the effect of mobility on training:
LFS males (sequential model 1)**

	Probit			
	Full sample		Subsamples	
Type of training	*Marginal effect*	*Signifi-cance*	*Marginal effect*	*Signifi-cance*
Any training	−0.008		−0.002	
Any training			−0.009	
(13-week question)				
Employer-funded training	−0.007			
Other training	0.000			
Qualification obtained			−0.014	
No qualification obtained			0.011	
Training finished			0.012	
Training continuing			−0.014	
No training	0.008		0.002	

TABLE 5.16

**Alternative estimates of the effect of mobility on training:
LFS males (sequential model 2)**

	Probit	
Type of training	*Marginal effect*	*Significance*
Any training	−0.005	
Employer-funded training	−0.008	
Other training	0.003	
No training	0.005	

related versus non-qualification training; this is due to missing information about these subsidiary aspects of training in some of the LFS panels that we use because the questionnaire varied over the sample period. This also means that we only have very small sample sizes in our second-stage regressions for these splits and, as a result, our estimates are poorly determined.[18] This should be borne in mind when interpreting the results.

For the overall LFS quarterly sample, the estimated marginal effects of previous mobility on different types

---

[18]For this reason, we do not report the results of these second-stage regressions in Appendix B. The results are available from the authors.

of training are generally of similar magnitude to those found in the NCDS male sample, but none of the estimated effects is statistically significant at conventional levels.[19] The corresponding results from the second sequential model are given in Table 5.16 (this time, estimated on the full LFS sample). Again, we get results that are reasonably similar to those from the NCDS sample for the effect of mobility on overall training and employer-funded training, but, again, the effects are not significant.

The results for the LFS subsample of men under 30 in Table 5.17 under sequential model 1 attribute generally larger marginal effects (in absolute terms) to the mobility variable than was the case for the overall sample of men; also, the coefficients of mobility on overall training, and on whether training finished or continued,

TABLE 5.17

**Estimates of the effect of mobility on training:
LFS males under 30 (sequential model 1)**

| | Probit | | | |
| | Full sample | | Subsamples | |
Type of training	*Marginal effect*	*Signifi- cance*	*Marginal effect*	*Signifi- cance*
Any training	−0.036	**	−0.023	*
Any training (13-week question)			−0.044	*
Employer-funded training	−0.030			
Other training	−0.006			
Qualification obtained			−0.034	
No qualification obtained			0.012	
Training finished			0.024	*
Training continuing			−0.047	*
No training	0.036	**	0.023	*

Note: * Significant at 10 per cent level.
   ** Significant at 5 per cent level.

[19]This may be partly because the second-stage results for the LFS subsample in the second column of Table 5.15 are from a sample size of only 494 and therefore the standard errors on the coefficients are large.

are statistically significant. The signs of the coefficients are very similar to those we get for the overall sample of men. As for sequential model 2 in Table 5.18, this produces very similar marginal effects on the overall and employer-funded training variables, and although larger in magnitude, these are similar to the (negative) effects in the NCDS.

Turning to the results for women, estimating sequential model 1 on the overall sample (as shown in Table 5.19) produces results similar to the NCDS — that is, that mobility has a much more positive relationship to

TABLE 5.18

**Alternative estimates of the effect of mobility on training:
LFS males under 30 (sequential model 2)**

	Probit	
Type of training	*Marginal effect*	*Significance*
Any training	−0.038	
Employer-funded training	−0.033	**
Other training	−0.005	
No training	0.038	

Note: ** Significant at 5 per cent level.

TABLE 5.19

**Estimates of the effect of mobility on training:
LFS females (sequential model 1)**

	Probit			
	Full sample		Subsamples	
Type of training	*Marginal effect*	*Significance*	*Marginal effect*	*Significance*
Any training	0.024	**	0.023	**
Any training (13-week question)			0.037	**
Employer-funded training	0.000	**		
Other training	0.024	**		
Qualification obtained			0.016	
No qualification obtained			0.007	
Training finished			0.009	
Training continuing			0.013	
No training	−0.024	**	−0.023	**

Note: ** Significant at 5 per cent level.

TABLE 5.20

Alternative estimates of the effect of mobility on training:
LFS females (sequential model 2)

Type of training	Probit	
	Marginal effect	Significance
Any training	0.024	
Employer-funded training	−0.003	
Other training	0.027	**
No training	−0.024	

Note: ** Significant at 5 per cent level.

TABLE 5.21

Estimates of the effect of mobility on training:
LFS females under 30 (sequential model 1)

	Probit			
	Full sample		Subsamples	
Type of training	Marginal effect	Signifi-cance	Marginal effect	Signifi-cance
Any training	0.023	*	0.005	
Any training (13-week question)			0.040	
Employer-funded training	−0.008	**		
Other training	0.031	**		
Qualification obtained			0.028	
No qualification obtained			−0.024	
Training finished			0.016	
Training continuing			−0.011	
No training	−0.023	*	−0.005	

Note: * Significant at 10 per cent level.
    ** Significant at 5 per cent level.

training for women than for men, but none the less it has the same relatively negative impact on employer-funded training as for men. Meanwhile, the results for the effect of mobility on training when the training variable is split into qualification-related or not, and finishing or continuing, are the opposite of those for men but similar in magnitude to those that were obtained from the NCDS for women. Also, in contrast to the LFS men, most of the effects here are significant. Estimation via sequential model 2, in Table 5.20, once again yields very similar

TABLE 5.22

Alternative estimates of the effect of mobility on training:
LFS females under 30 (sequential model 2)

| | Probit | |
Type of training	Marginal effect	Significance
Any training	0.019	
Employer-funded training	–0.010	
Other training	0.029	**
No training	–0.019	

Note: ** Significant at 5 per cent level.

coefficients of mobility on the training variables. The results for women under 30 in the LFS, shown in Tables 5.21 and 5.22, tell us little in addition to the results we have already discussed for the whole sample, and are on the whole less significant (the reverse of what was the case for men).

Finally in this section, it is instructive to examine the overall training regressions reported in Tables B.40 and B.44 in Appendix B to see whether the inclusion of previous mobility in the regression wipes out any of the factors we had identified earlier in our analysis of the determinants of training. For the LFS, we find that the inclusion of mobility in a training equation alters the coefficients and marginal effects on the other regressors little, if at all. In particular, the effects of previous labour market qualifications are virtually unchanged by the inclusion of the training variable.

The overall conclusions from this section would seem to be that there is a negative effect of mobility on overall training for men, whereas the reverse seems to be true for women; this is broadly in line with many of the previous studies of these phenomena (although, particularly for the male LFS samples, estimates are not always significant). We are able to uncover more subtle effects by using the sequential modelling of training choice, the most consistent of these being that, for men, mobility affects employer-funded training more negatively than it does non-employer-funded training. The fact that our two alternative sequential probit models seem to produce similar coefficients on the employer-funded training variable when estimated on the same data (except when the second-stage sample size is extremely small) is reassuring and gives us some confidence in the techniques used.

5.5 Models Using Different Measures of Mobility

In the work so far, we have only measured job mobility in terms of a job move within a specified period of time. It is quite conceivable that an individual's entire labour market history of job moves is more important than a move in the previous year in determining whether an individual gets training at a particular point in time in their career. This is particularly true if a high (or low) propensity to move jobs sends out a signal about the probability of a worker moving in the future, worker quality or potential productivity. Similarly, by only focusing on the impact of recent training on the probability of moving jobs within a specified period, we may be missing an important part of how training affects the likelihood of moving jobs over an extended period of time.

In this section, we use the NCDS panel to look first at the impact of training over an extended period of time on the number of jobs a person has held over a particular time period. This involves estimating count data models, and the results of doing this are given in Tables 5.23 and 5.24. Full details of the estimated equations are given in Tables B.48 and B.49 in Appendix B. In our earlier models, receiving training in the previous quarter only had a negligible effect on the probability of moving jobs in the next year. The results in Tables 5.23 and 5.24 show that we are missing an important part of the story by only considering recent training. An individual who

TABLE 5.23

The effect of training on number of jobs: NCDS males

Type of training	Poisson model	
	Marginal effect	Significance
Any training in last quarter	0.009	
Number of training courses since 1981	0.003	
Training in 1981 job	−0.641	**

Note: ** Significant at 5 per cent level.

TABLE 5.24

The effect of training on number of jobs: NCDS females

Type of training	Poisson model	
	Marginal effect	Significance
Any training in last quarter	0.188	**
Number of training courses since 1981	0.019	**
Training in 1981 job	−0.231	**

Note: ** Significant at 5 per cent level.

received employer-funded training in their 1981 job has, on average, held significantly fewer jobs than a person who did not receive such training. This effect is much larger than the effect of more recent training spells. Men who received employer-funded training in their 1981 job have held on average 2.5 jobs, compared with the 3.1 jobs held by men who did not receive such training. For women, the comparable figures are 2.8 jobs for those who received training in their 1981 job versus an average of 3.0 for those who did not. In the case of women, undertaking training since 1981 is associated with having a higher number of jobs since leaving school, which partially offsets the effect of earlier training.

Thus from these models it would appear that receiving training early in their career results in fewer job changes for both men and women. For women, however, training between the ages of 23 and 33 is associated with more job changes.

Tables B.50 and B.51 in Appendix B show the impact of the number of jobs on the probability of receiving training in a particular quarter. For those who received training, we also undertake a second-stage regression to see if the number of jobs affects the probability of receiving employer-funded training differently from the probability of receiving other training. The results of these regressions are shown in Tables B.52 and B.53. For men, there seems to be no effect on overall training receipt from an increase in the number of jobs. However, from Table B.52 we see that amongst individuals receiving training, people who have held more jobs have a lower probability of receiving employer training (and, by implication, a higher probability of undertaking other training). These opposing effects are missed if we only consider the effect of number of jobs on overall training incidence. For every additional job held among trainees, the probability of receiving employer-funded training is reduced by 0.5 percentage points. For women, we find that an additional job since 1974 increases the probability of undertaking training in a given quarter by 0.3 percentage points. From Table B.53, it appears that the effect of an increase in the number of jobs held does not differ between employer and other training (unlike for men). These results are similar to the results obtained when using our original measures of mobility. For men, increased mobility is associated with a modest reduction in the probability of receiving employer-funded training.

5.6 Instrumental Variable Estimates of the Relationship between Training and Mobility

The results of instrumental variable (IV) estimation of the effects of previous mobility on training are given in Tables 5.25 and 5.26. This involves a re-estimation of sequential model 1, as shown in Figure 4.2, on the NCDS data but this time using the number of times

TABLE 5.25

IV estimates of the effect of mobility on training: NCDS males

Type of training	IV-probit Marginal effect	Significance
Any training	0.006	**
Employer-funded training	0.004	**
Other training	0.002	
Qualification obtained	0.005	**
No qualification obtained	0.001	
Training finished	−0.003	
Training continuing	0.009	**
No training	−0.006	**

Note: ** Significant at 5 per cent level.

moved since 1974 as an instrument for mobility.[20] A comparison of Table 5.25 with Table 5.11 shows that IV estimation produces somewhat different results. Under IV, we get a positive effect of mobility on overall training, and the effect of mobility on employer-funded training is more positive than the effect of mobility on non-employer-funded training. Both of these findings are the reverse of what we found under conventional probit. Additionally, the effects of mobility on qualification-related training are greater than the effects on training that does not lead to a qualification, and continuing training is more positively related to mobility than finished training; again, these findings are very different from the straight probit estimates.

The findings for the female NCDS sample in Table 5.26 also differ from the conventional probit results for women in Table 5.13. For women, mobility now appears a much less important determinant of training than suggested by our 'before-and-after' results in Table 5.13. Although we find a significant positive relationship between previous mobility and employer-funded train-

---

[20]Because the effects of mobility on overall training and employer-funded training were very similar under sequential models 1 and 2 in most cases, it was decided not to estimate model 2 by IV.

TABLE 5.26

IV estimates of the effect of mobility on training: NCDS females

	IV-probit	
Type of training	*Marginal effect*	*Significance*
Any training	0.004	
Employer-funded training	0.007	**
Other training	−0.003	**
Qualification obtained	0.001	
No qualification obtained	0.003	
Training finished	−0.001	
Training continuing	0.005	**
No training	−0.004	

Note: ** Significant at 5 per cent level.

ing which is similar to that found earlier, mobility is now found to have a significant negative effect on the probability of receiving other training, whereas in our earlier model it had a significant positive effect. The female IV results are similar to the IV results for men. The interpretation of a positive coefficient of previous mobility on training requires some thought, however. It may be that a lot of the training being carried out just after a job move is induction training, rather than training that is necessary to upgrade skills as part of an ongoing career process. Because we are only considering quite recent mobility, we might expect to find a positive relationship between mobility and training in this type of model. To investigate this issue further, we need to consider other models.

One approach is to estimate a simultaneous probit model to see if what we are picking up are simply the effects of induction training when a person commences a job. If this is the case, we would expect current mobility to be positively correlated to current training (as a result of the induction training effect) and, having controlled for this, we may get an unbiased estimate of the 'true' relationship between previous mobility and current training. This is done in the next section.

An alternative approach is to consider the individual's whole history of job moves in order to get around this simultaneity problem. In this vein, we also estimate IV regression equations for our specification using number of jobs held, and these are reported in the second column of Tables B.50 through B.53, again using the number of times moved up to the age of 16 and mother's employment status in 1974 as instruments for the number of jobs. The instrumented mobility variable is now significant and positive in the overall training equation and positive and insignificant in the employer-funded training equation for men. For women, we now find that the probability of receiving training decreases rather than increases with the number of jobs the woman has held, though this overall effect is not significant. From Table B.53, we see that the impact of mobility on employer-funded training is positive and significant. This suggests that the number of jobs held has a positive significant effect on employer-funded training but a negative and significant effect on other training, which results in the overall insignificant impact reported in Table B.51. These results suggest that it is important to control for the endogeneity of mobility in our training equations, especially for women.

5.7 Simultaneous Models of Training and Mobility

Table 5.27 presents the marginal effects of current and lagged mobility on current training in the first equation of a simultaneous model of training and mobility. The coefficients on current mobility appear to be similar to those we see on lagged mobility in the IV models above. Meanwhile, the marginal effects of lagged mobility appear to be small and negative for men, and positive and significant for women. Therefore, the simultaneous model seems to confirm that part of the positive effect of mobility on training we were picking up earlier may

TABLE 5.27

Simultaneous model of the determinants of training: NCDS

| | Simultaneous probit | | | |
| | Males | | Females | |
Measure of mobility	*Marginal effect*	*Significance*	*Marginal effect*	*Significance*
Moved this quarter	0.005	**	0.008	**
Moved last year	−0.007	**	0.017	**

Note: ** Significant at 5 per cent level.

be due to the fact that people who have recently moved jobs receive induction training. For men, it appears particularly important to look at contemporaneous as well as lagged job moves. Movements in the current quarter are associated with an increase in the probability of being trained, whereas movements in the previous year are associated with a decrease in the probability of training. For women, both contemporaneous job moves and a move in the previous year are associated with significant increases in the probability of undertaking training.

Taking the results as a whole, we have to conclude that the impact of job-to-job mobility on the probability of receiving training is ambiguous and depends crucially on the time frame over which we examine the relationship.

CHAPTER 6
Conclusions

The relationship between the amount of training received by workers and their mobility from job to job is an important aspect of the role that training may play in developing and sustaining the skills base of the UK labour force. This project has attempted to analyse the nature of the relationship between job mobility and training in Britain.

Standard economic theory, based on a human capital approach to the acquisition of skills by individuals, argues that firms may pay for specific training (where the skills acquired are specific to the firm in which the individual is employed), but they will not pay for general training (where the skills acquired are potentially usable by other firms) because of the danger that workers, once trained, will be poached by other firms. This conclusion, however, is challenged by more recent work which emphasises market imperfections (such as imperfect competition and asymmetric information) and questions the validity of characterising training as simply general or specific in nature. The debate in the literature means that it is hard to obtain clear-cut predictions of the directions of the effects of job mobility on training or vice versa. In this context, it is more important than ever for an empirical study to examine how and in what direction such relationships operate. Previous studies in this field have found negative, but often small and sometimes statistically insignificant, effects of previous training on job mobility, and insignificant effects of mobility on training for men, with some evidence of positive but statistically weak effects for women.

This report has looked at what sort of individuals are more likely to receive different types of employer-funded training, what sorts of firms undertake such training and to whom they give it. Both the impact of employer-funded training on the amount of job mobility in the economy and the impact of job mobility on levels of training have been considered. Two microeconomic datasets — the UK Labour Force Survey (LFS) and the National Child Development Survey (NCDS) — were used in the analysis. Both of these datasets feature panels where the same individuals are tracked over time, allowing the research to examine the pattern of job-to-job moves; and each dataset also contained detailed information on the amount and type of training received by different individuals, both before and after moving jobs. Hence, for the first time in Britain, this study was able to examine both the effects of training on job mobility and the effects of job mobility on training. The NCDS is a cohort study of all individuals in the UK born in one week in 1958. Detailed information on. training and employment history was collected in 1981 and 1991; the NCDS therefore offers a good source of information on training and employment over a long period of time for individuals of a certain age. By contrast, since 1992, the LFS has operated as a quarterly panel where individuals are observed for five consecutive quarters; it therefore offers more recent data on training and mobility for people of all ages, although over a much shorter time period. Hence, the two data sources can be seen as complementary in the research. This study utilised about 60,000 quarterly observations on men and about 50,000 on women in the NCDS. From the LFS data, just under 30,000 quarterly observations on both men and women were used in most of the empirical work.

An initial look at the incidence of training in the UK between 1984 and 1995 showed a rise in the proportion

of individuals in the annual LFS cross-section who reported receiving training in the four weeks prior to interview, from around 10 per cent of respondents in 1984
to 15 per cent in 1990 and thereafter. In the quarterly
LFS panel, training divides roughly equally into employer-funded and non-employer-funded. Around one-
third of training spells in a given quarter ended in that
quarter and about 40 per cent of training spells in each
period led to a qualification. The NCDS data since 1981
appear to show that most of the increase in training over
the period 1981–90 was due to employer-funded training and training that was not qualification-related.

The first issue that the report addressed using the data
was what factors (other than job mobility) determined
training, and vice versa. For the most part, the results
obtained for the determinants of training and mobility
reconfirmed findings in the large number of existing
studies looking at this issue. The level of training is
positively affected by the level of qualifications obtained by an individual, there are some differential effects by industry and training incidence decreases with
age in the LFS. Part-time workers train less than full-
time workers, while employees working for larger employers seem to undertake more training. As for the determinants of labour market mobility, mobility is
positively related to the level of qualification, and seems
to decrease with age. Part-time workers are more mobile
than full-timers. In short, most of these findings seem to
confirm the results of the existing literature.

Turning to models of the effects of training on mobility, the datasets used gave us scope to consider the
effects of different types of training courses separately.
In particular, the data allowed us to categorise training
according to whether it was employer-funded or not,
what kind of qualification (if any) it led to and how long
the training course lasted. Similarly, some results use
individual job-to-job moves as the measure of mobility,

whereas others concentrate on the total number of jobs held by a person over a longer period. By experimenting with different definitions of training and mobility, we were able to cross-check the robustness of the results and consider a wider range of models than would otherwise have been possible. The first strategy used in examining the effects of training on mobility was to see whether individuals getting trained in a particular quarter were more or less likely to move jobs in subsequent time periods (generally the following four quarters). Simple models of this form suggested that, for men, receiving training decreased the probability of moving jobs over the following year by, on average, 1 percentage point. This finding is broadly consistent with the empirical work reviewed in Chapter 2. If the training was employer-funded, then the negative effect was stronger. For women, the results were less clear-cut; the overall effect of training on mobility seems to be insignificantly different from zero, but training that is specifically employer-funded appears to decrease mobility, whereas most types of training course that lead to a qualification appear to increase it. Also, training courses that finished in a given quarter had a more negative impact on mobility than training courses that were ongoing past that quarter. These results seem to hold for both the NCDS and the LFS, though the NCDS results are not significant for women. When just the young people in the LFS (those aged under 30) are considered separately, the effects of training on mobility appear to be more negative than for other groups.

By using the training history data back to 1981 in the NCDS, it was possible to consider the effects on mobility not just of the most recent training scheme(s), but of the individual's entire training history. This question has not previously been looked at in empirical studies because of data restrictions. The results obtained from these models suggest for both men and women that employer-funded training undertaken in the individual's 1981 job has a strong and negative effect on mobility over and above the effects of more recent training. However, it should be noted that other factors (such as employer size, industry, age, unionisation and full- or part-time job status) seem to be much more important determinants of job mobility than does previous training. Also, the effects of these other factors on mobility are not diminished by including training in the models.

Turning to the converse question — the effect of job mobility on the provision of training — a sequential model was used, where it was assumed that individuals first decide whether or not to undertake training and then decide what training they undertake. For men in the NCDS, it was found that there was a small negative relationship between moving jobs in the current period and training in future periods: moving jobs in the current period decreased the probability of receiving training in a future period by 0.6 percentage points. Mobility had a larger impact on employer-funded training. For women, the results were somewhat different. Mobility increased the probability of receiving training, particularly qualification training and non-employer-funded training. The results from the LFS again suggest that a recent job move reduces the probability of employer-funded training for men, and this effect is particularly strong for young men. As was the case for the NCDS, mobility was associated with an increased probability of receiving training for women. An alternative sequential model of training choice was also used, where employers first select certain individuals to train, and then the remaining individuals decide whether to finance their own training or not. Encouragingly, the results for the effects of mobility on training from this model were very similar to those from the other sequential model.

In the same way that it was possible to use training information from the NCDS going back to 1981 in the model, it was also possible to measure mobility in terms of the total number of jobs held by a person thus far in his or her career. Looking at the effects of training on the total number of jobs held, it was found that men who received employer-funded training in their 1981 job have held, on average, 2.5 jobs compared with the 3.1 jobs held by men who did not receive such training. For women, the comparable figures were 2.8 jobs and 3.0 jobs respectively. Hence, for both men and women, training received early in their career seems to markedly decrease overall job turnover; however, for women, later training appears to be associated with increased mobility. In most of the research reviewed in Chapter 2, there was found to be no effect of mobility on the probability of training for men, and positive, though weak, effects on the probability of training for women.

If there are unobserved determinants of training that also determine earlier job moves (or vice versa), our estimates of the impact of mobility on training may be biased. Also, it is quite conceivable that there is some simultaneity in the relationship between training and mobility — for example, a job move in a particular quarter may be associated with an increase in the probability of receiving induction training. By not considering both current and lagged mobility in our training equations, we may be ascribing to lagged mobility something that is attributable to the fact that a person has moved jobs in the current quarter.

In order to look at these possibilities, we also estimated the effects of mobility on training using instrumental variable procedures. These produced somewhat different results from those of the earlier models, particularly for men. This time, there was a positive effect of earlier mobility on overall training for men, and earlier mobility had a more positive effect on employer-funded training than on other training. In the models where we instead used the number of jobs as our measure of mobility (instrumented), there was evidence that the number of jobs increased the probability of receiving training for men. For women, we found that the probability of receiving employer-funded training was positively related to the number of jobs held, whereas the probability of undertaking other training was negatively related to the number of jobs held. These two effects largely cancelled each other out and the overall impact of the number of jobs on the probability of receiving training was found to be insignificant for women. These results suggest that the negative relationship found in our earlier models between earlier mobility and training for men, particularly employer-funded training, may have been due to other unobserved characteristics of those men who move, rather than to mobility itself. This is an interesting finding and casts doubt on earlier studies that treated mobility as exogenous.

When we estimated a simultaneous model of training determination, we found that mobility in the current quarter was associated with an increased probability of receiving training for both men and women. One explanation for these results is that mobility necessitates increased amounts of induction training rather than training that is necessary to upgrade skills as part of an ongoing career process. Job moves in the previous year reduced the probability of receiving training for men, but increased the probability of receiving training for women. Overall, a skill accumulation interpretation of the mobility–training relationship seems consistent with the data. Again, however, other factors, such as employer characteristics and educational qualifications, are much more important determinants of the probability of receiving different types of training than mobility.

The overall conclusions of this report are that mobility, measured in terms of job-to-job moves, is, if anything, lower for individuals who received training in previous periods. This negative association is specific to employer-funded training, training courses that were completed in the quarter in question and training that led to a formal qualification. All this supports the notion that employers train workers who they wish to retain so that they can benefit from any skill upgrading that results from the training. It is interesting that those firms that provide workers with training are less likely to lose workers as a result of this training, even when qualifications are involved. While this result is interesting, it says nothing about whether there is a poaching externality leading to under-investment in training by firms. All it tells us is that firms that train are less likely to lose workers; it tells us nothing about whether firms are not training or only providing firm-specific training because of a perceived threat that their workers may be poached in the future.

In all of the models looking at the determinants of mobility, training was treated as exogenous. The validity of this assumption needs to be further tested using instrumental variable techniques. This was seen to be important when looking at the impact of mobility on training and it is therefore likely that the reverse is also true. In work arising out of this project, we hope to explore this issue more by using college term and holiday times as an instrument for training. It should also be emphasised that other factors, such as educational qualifications, are much more important in determining a person's future mobility than different types of training.

However, there remain certain ambiguities in the results, which might be resolved by more precise data on training structures. The fact that different effects emerge for different forms of training makes it important that these are distinguished carefully when future data are collected. Moreover, the fact that the results show a good deal of complexity in the link between training and job mobility means that one should exercise some caution when moving from the results to policy implications. In particular, more knowledge on who finances different training spells, the size of hiring markets for workers with different skill attributes, the extent to which information is imperfect, the distribution of returns between workers and employers, and the social scarcity of alternative skills would aid a better understanding of these issues.

APPENDIX A
Technical Details of the Econometric Models

This report looks at the effects of training on mobility and of mobility on training. The models used in it are described in detail below.

A.1 Models where Both Mobility and Training Are Binary Variables

Our initial models look at the case where both mobility and training are observed as simple binary variables. In all our models where training and mobility are binary variables, we write our structural model of the unobserved latent variables as

$$(A.1) \quad MOBILITY_{it}^* = \alpha_1 X_{1i,t-1} + \gamma_1 TRAIN_{i,t-1} + \mu_{1it}$$

and

$$(A.2) \quad TRAIN_{it}^* = \alpha_2 X_{2i,t-1} + \gamma_2 MOBILITY_{i,t-1} + \mu_{2it}$$

where $TRAIN_{it} = 1$ if $TRAIN_{it}^* > 0$, $TRAIN_{it} = 0$ if $TRAIN_{it}^* \leq 0$ and similarly $MOBILITY_{it} = 1$ if $MOBILITY_{it}^* > 0$ and $MOBILITY_{it} = 0$ if $MOBILITY_{it}^* \leq 0$. In this formulation, $TRAIN_{it}$ and $MOBILITY_{it}$ are binary indicators of training receipt and job mobility respectively for individual i at time t, $X_{1i,t-1}$ and $X_{2i,t-1}$ are vectors of other relevant control variables at time $t-1$, and μ_{1it} and μ_{2it} are error terms that are assumed to have a normal distribution with mean zero and variance one.[21]

A.1.1 Lagged training and mobility exogenous

We first assume that lagged training and mobility are exogenous; that is, $E(TRAIN_{i,t-1}, \mu_{1it}) = E(MOBILITY_{i,t-1}, \mu_{2it}) = 0$. Under these assumptions, we can estimate both our regression equations by univariate probits. In this model, the estimated probability of moving jobs is given by

$$(A.3) \quad \Pr(MOBILITY_{it} = 1 | X_{1i,t-1}, TRAIN_{i,t-1})$$
$$= \Pr(MOBILITY_{it}^* > 0 | X_{1i,t-1}, TRAIN_{i,t-1})$$
$$= \Phi(\hat{\alpha}_1 X_{1i,t-1} + \hat{\gamma}_1 TRAIN_{i,t-1})$$

where $\hat{\alpha}_1$ and $\hat{\gamma}_1$ are the estimates from our mobility probit and Φ is the standard normal cumulative density function. Similarly, the probability of undertaking training is given by

$$(A.4) \quad \Pr(TRAIN_{it} = 1 | X_{2i,t-1}, MOBILITY_{i,t-1})$$
$$= \Pr(TRAIN_{it}^* > 0 | X_{2i,t-1}, MOBILITY_{i,t-1})$$
$$= \Phi(\hat{\alpha}_2 X_{2i,t-1} + \hat{\gamma}_2 MOBILITY_{i,t-1})$$

where $\hat{\alpha}_2$ and $\hat{\gamma}_2$ are the estimates from our training probit.

Hence the estimated impact of undertaking training on the probability of moving jobs (or the *marginal effect of training*) is given by

---

[21]This is a standard normalisation in this type of model. Our observed binary indicator is zero or one depending on the sign of the unobserved latent variable, not on its scale. We also assume that $E(\mu_{1it}, \mu_{2it}) = 0$ and that both μ_{1it} and μ_{2it} are serially uncorrelated — that is, $E(\mu_{1it}, \mu_{1i,t-s}) = 0$ and $E(\mu_{2it}, \mu_{2i,t-s}) = 0 \; \forall \; s \neq 0$.

(A.5) $\Pr(MOBILITY_{it} = 1 | TRAIN_{i,t-1} = 1, X_{1i,t-1})$

$- \Pr(MOBILITY_{it} = 1 | TRAIN_{i,t-1} = 0, X_{1i,t-1})$

$= \Phi(\hat{\alpha}_1 X_{1i,t-1} + \hat{\gamma}_1) - \Phi(\hat{\alpha}_1 X_{1i,t-1}).$

This expression can be evaluated for different values of the $X_{1i,t-1}$, including mean values. Similarly, the estimated marginal effect of mobility on the probability of receiving training is given by

(A.6) $\Pr(TRAIN_{it} = 1 | MOBILITY_{i,t-1} = 1, X_{2i,t-1})$

$- \Pr(TRAIN_{it} = 1 | MOBILITY_{i,t-1} = 0, X_{2i,t-1})$

$= \Phi(\hat{\alpha}_2 X_{2i,t-1} + \hat{\gamma}_2) - \Phi(\hat{\alpha}_2 X_{2i,t-1}).$

A.1.2 Lagged training and mobility endogenous

We now allow for the possibility that $E(TRAIN_{i,t-1},\mu_{1it}) \neq 0$ and/or $E(MOBILITY_{i,t-1},\mu_{2it}) \neq 0$. If lagged training and/or mobility are endogenous, then estimation of univariate probit models will result in biased estimates of the effects of earlier mobility on training and earlier training on mobility. To obtain consistent estimates, we use a two-stage instrumental variable technique. In the first stage, we estimate the following reduced form equations by a probit maximum likelihood procedure:

(A.7) $MOBILITY^*_{i,t-1} = \Pi_1 X_{i,t-1} + \mu_{1it}$

and

(A.8) $TRAIN^*_{i,t-1} = \Pi_2 X_{i,t-1} + \mu_{2it}$

where $X_{i,t-1}$ contains all the exogenous variables in $X_{1i,t-1}$ and $X_{2i,t-1}$ and we assume that $Var(\mu_{1it}) = Var(\mu_{2it}) = 1$. We then substitute the predicted values of $MOBILITY^*_{i,t-1}$ ($M\hat{O}BILITY^*_{i,t-1}$) and of $TRAIN^*_{i,t-1}$

$(T\hat{R}AIN^*_{i,t-1})$ into our structural equations (A.1) and (A.2) and estimate the model again by a probit maximum likelihood method.

In this model, the probability of moving jobs is given by

(A.9) $\Pr(MOBILITY_{it} = 1 | X_{1i,t-1}, TRAIN_{i,t-1})$

$= \Phi(\hat{\alpha}_1 X_{1i,t-1} + \hat{\gamma}_1 T\hat{R}AIN^*_{i,t-1})$

and the probability of undertaking training is given by

(A.10) $\Pr(TRAIN_{it} = 1 | X_{2i,t-1}, MOBILITY_{i,t-1})$

$= \Phi(\hat{\alpha}_2 X_{2i,t-1} + \hat{\gamma}_2 MOB\hat{I}LITY^*_{i,t-1})$.

In this model, the estimated impact of undertaking training on the probability of moving jobs (or the *marginal effect* of training) is given by

(A.11) $\Pr(MOBILITY_{it} = 1 | T\hat{R}AIN^*_{i,t-1} = \overline{T^*_1}, X_{1i,t-1})$

$- \Pr(MOBILITY_{it} = 1 | T\hat{R}AIN^*_{i,t-1} = \overline{T^*_0}, X_{1i,t-1})$

$= \Phi(\hat{\alpha}_1 X_{1i,t-1} + \hat{\gamma}_1 \overline{T^*_1}) - \Phi(\hat{\alpha}_1 X_{1i,t-1} + \hat{\gamma}_1 \overline{T^*_0})$

where $\overline{T^*_1}$ is the average of the predicted training index (from equation (A.8)) for those who train and $\overline{T^*_0}$ is the average of the predicted training index for those who do not train.[22] This expression again can be evaluated at different values of $X_{1i,t-1}$, including mean values.

---

[22]Let $\overline{X}_{T,t-1}$ be the average characteristics of trainees and $\overline{X}_{N,t-1}$ be the average characteristics of non-trainees. Then $\overline{T^*_1} = \hat{\Pi}_2 \overline{X}_{T,t-1}$ and $\overline{T^*_0} = \hat{\Pi}_2 \overline{X}_{N,t-1}$ where $\hat{\Pi}_2$ is our estimated coefficients from our reduced form training equation (A.8).

The marginal effect of mobility on training is derived in an analogous way.

A.1.3 Simultaneous model of training and mobility

We now have a model of the form

(A.12) $MOBILITY_{it}^* = \alpha_1 X_{1i,t-1} + \gamma_1 TRAIN_{it} + \mu_{1it}$

and

(A.13) $TRAIN_{it}^* = \alpha_2 X_{2i,t-1} + \gamma_2 MOBILITY_{it} + \mu_{2it}$

where $TRAIN_{it} = 1$ if $TRAIN_{it}^* > 0$, $TRAIN_{it} = 0$ if $TRAIN_{it}^* \leq 0$ and similarly $MOBILITY_{it} = 1$ if $MOBILITY_{it}^* > 0$ and $MOBILITY_{it} = 0$ if $MOBILITY_{it}^* \leq 0$. We assume in this model that lagged training is exogenous and contained in the $X_{1i,t-1}$ and similarly that lagged mobility is exogenous and contained in the $X_{2i,t-1}$.[23] This type of model was first considered by Mallar (1977) and is discussed in detail by Maddala (1983, pp. 246–7). In order for this system of equations to be identified, we need at least one instrument for mobility, Z_{Mi}, which determines mobility but not training controlling for mobility, and at least one instrument for training, Z_{Ti}, which explains training but not mobility controlling for training. Hence, Z_{Mi} is contained in our $X_{1i,t-1}$ but not our $X_{2i,t-1}$, and Z_{Ti} is contained in our $X_{2i,t-1}$ but not our $X_{1i,t-1}$.

To obtain consistent estimates, we use a two-stage estimation procedure once again. In the first stage, we estimate the following reduced form equations by a probit maximum likelihood procedure:

---

[23]If we wish to treat these variables as endogenous, we need to implement the methodology of the previous section in parallel with our simultaneous equation approach. This requires extra identifying assumptions.

(A.14) $MOBILITY_{it}^{*} = \Pi_1 X_{i,t-1} + \mu_{1it}$

and

(A.15) $TRAIN_{it}^{*} = \Pi_2 X_{i,t-1} + \mu_{2it}$

where $X_{i,t-1}$ contains all the exogenous variables in $X_{1i,t-1}$ and $X_{2i,t-1}$ (except for within-sample lagged values of training and mobility)[24] and we assume that $\mathrm{Var}(\mu_{1it}) = \mathrm{Var}(\mu_{2it}) = 1$. We then substitute the predicted values of $MOBILITY_{i,t}^{*}$ ($MOB\hat{I}LITY_{i,t}^{*}$) and of $TRAIN_{i,t}^{*}$ ($TR\hat{A}IN_{i,t}^{*}$) into our structural equations (A.12) and (A.13) and estimate the model again by a probit maximum likelihood method.

In this model, the probability of moving jobs is given by

(A.16) $\Pr(MOBILITY_{it} = 1 | X_{1i,t-1}, TR\hat{A}IN_{it}^{*})$

$= \Pr(MOBILITY_{it}^{*} > 0 | X_{1i,t-1}, TR\hat{A}IN_{it}^{*})$

$= \Phi(\hat{\alpha}_1 X_{1i,t-1} + \hat{\gamma}_1 TR\hat{A}IN_{it}^{*})$

and the probability of undertaking training is given by

(A.17) $\Pr(TRAIN_{it} = 1 | X_{2i,t-1}, MOB\hat{I}LITY_{it}^{*})$

$= \Pr(TRAIN_{it}^{*} > 0 | X_{2i,t-1}, MOB\hat{I}LITY_{it}^{*})$

$= \Phi(\hat{\alpha}_2 X_{2i,t-1} + \hat{\gamma}_2 MOB\hat{I}LITY_{it}^{*})$.

The expression for the covariance matrix for the co-efficients for the structural parameters is given by Maddala (1983, p. 247).

---

[24]We do not include the lagged values of our training or mobility variables ($TRAIN_{i,t-1}$ or $MOBILITY_{i,t-1}$) in our reduced form equations as these are, by definition, not strictly exogenous.

A.2 Models Expanding Our Measures of Training

We now allow for the possibility that there are two types of training, *TRTYPE1* and *TRTYPE2*. In the report, we distinguish between employer-provided and non-employer-provided training, completed and continuing training, and qualification and non-qualification training, for example. If we have multiple measures of training, then it is easy to adapt our mobility equation to include them as explanatory variables. If we want to treat these more disaggregated training variables as endogenous, then, for each of our training variables, we need to have at least one instrument that explains this training but not mobility controlling for training.

The more difficult problem is how to appropriately model the probability of receiving different types of training. In our original model, we only model the probabilities of two outcomes — the probability of undertaking training and, as a consequence, the probability of not undertaking training. If we have two types of training, then we have three possible outcomes for which we need to model the probabilities. The way we model them depends on our assumption about how the decision process operates, as was explained in subsection 4.3.1 of the report. For most of the work in this report, we as-

FIGURE A.1

A sequential model of training

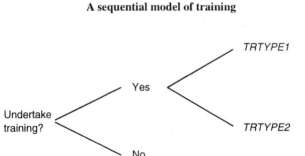

sume that the sequential training decision process operates as shown in Figure A.1.

To estimate this sequential model, we estimate by probit equation (A.2) as before on the full sample. From this model, as we saw earlier,

(A.18) $\Pr(TRAIN_{it} = 1 | X_{2i,t-1}, MOBILITY_{i,t-1})$

$= \Pr(TRAIN_{it}^* > 0 | X_{2i,t-1}, MOBILITY_{i,t-1})$

$= \Phi(\hat{\alpha}_2 X_{2i,t-1} + \hat{\gamma}_2 MOBILITY_{i,t-1})$.

We then estimate the following probit on the sub-sample of all individuals who undertake training:

(A.19) $TRTYPE1_{it}^* = \alpha_3 X_{2i,t-1} + \gamma_3 MOBILITY_{i,t-1} + \mu_{3it}$

where $TRTYPE1_{it} = 1$ and $TRTYPE2_{it} = 0$ if $TRTYPE1_{it}^* > 0$, and $TRTYPE1_{it} = 0$ and $TRTYPE2_{it} = 1$ if $TRTYPE1_{it}^* \leq 0$. From this model, we can calculate the probability of undertaking $TRTYPE1_{it}$ and $TRTYPE2_{it}$, conditional on undertaking training — that is, conditional on $TRAIN_{it} = 1$. These probabilities are given by

(A.20) $\Pr(TRTYPE1_{it} = 1 | TRAIN_{it} = 1, X_{2i,t-1}, MOBILITY_{i,t-1})$

$= \Phi(\hat{\alpha}_3 X_{2i,t-1} + \hat{\gamma}_3 MOBILITY_{i,t-1})$

and

(A.21) $\Pr(TRTYPE2_{it} = 1 | TRAIN_{it} = 1, X_{2i,t-1}, MOBILITY_{i,t-1})$

$= 1 - \Phi(\hat{\alpha}_3 X_{2i,t-1} + \hat{\gamma}_3 MOBILITY_{i,t-1})$.

From equations (A.18), (A.20) and (A.21), we can calculate the three unconditional probabilities of our three states as

(A.22) $\Pr(TRTYPE1_{it} = 1 | X_{2i,t-1}, MOBILITY_{i,t-1})$

$= \Phi(\hat{\alpha}_2 X_{2i,t-1} + \hat{\gamma}_2 MOBILITY_{i,t-1})$

$\quad \times \Phi(\hat{\alpha}_3 X_{2i,t-1} + \hat{\gamma}_3 MOBILITY_{i,t-1}),$

(A.23) $\Pr(TRTYPE2_{it} = 1 | X_{2i,t-1}, MOBILITY_{i,t-1})$

$= \Phi(\hat{\alpha}_2 X_{2i,t-1} + \hat{\gamma}_2 MOBILITY_{i,t-1})$

$\quad \times (1 - \Phi(\hat{\alpha}_3 X_{2i,t-1} + \hat{\gamma}_3 MOBILITY_{i,t-1})$

and

(A.24) $\Pr(TRAIN_{it} = 0 | X_{2i,t-1}, MOBILITY_{i,t-1})$

$= 1 - \Phi(\hat{\alpha}_2 X_{2i,t-1} + \hat{\gamma}_2 MOBILITY_{i,t-1}).$

The impact of mobility on the probability of undertaking *TRTYPE1* is given by

(A.25) $\Pr(TRTYPE1_{it} | MOBILITY_{i,t-1} = 1, X_{2i,t-1})$

$\quad - \Pr(TRTYPE1_{it} | MOBILITY_{i,t-1} = 0, X_{2i,t-1})$

$= \Phi(\hat{\alpha}_2 X_{2i,t-1} + \hat{\gamma}_2) \times \Phi(\hat{\alpha}_3 X_{2i,t-1} + \hat{\gamma}_3)$

$\quad - \Phi(\hat{\alpha}_2 X_{2i,t-1}) \times \Phi(\hat{\alpha}_3 X_{2i,t-1}),$

which we evaluate at sample mean values of the $X_{2i,t-1}$.

We can again treat mobility as endogenous by including the prediction index of mobility from our reduced

FIGURE A.2

An alternative sequential model of training

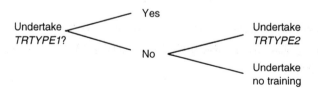

form equation (A.7) in our structural equations (A.2) and (A.19). In this case, the marginal effect of mobility on the probability of receiving *TRTYPE1* is given by

$$(A.26) \quad \Pr(TRTYPE1_{it} | MOB\hat{I}LITY_{i,t-1}^* = \overline{M_1^*}, X_{2i,t-1})$$

$$- \Pr(TRTYPE1_{it} | MOB\hat{I}LITY_{i,t-1}^* = \overline{M_0^*}, X_{2i,t-1})$$

$$= \Phi(\hat{\alpha}_2 X_{2i,t-1} + \hat{\gamma}_2 \overline{M_1^*}) \times \Phi(\hat{\alpha}_3 X_{2i,t-1} + \hat{\gamma}_3 \overline{M_1^*})$$

$$- \Phi(\hat{\alpha}_2 X_{2i,t-1} + \hat{\gamma}_2 \overline{M_0^*}) \times \Phi(\hat{\alpha}_3 X_{2i,t-1} + \hat{\gamma}_3 \overline{M_0^*})$$

where $\overline{M_1^*}$ is the average of the predicted mobility index for those who move and $\overline{M_0^*}$ is the average of the predicted mobility index for those who do not move, derived from equation (A.7).[25]

As was discussed in subsection 4.3.1 of the report, an alternative sequential model could be of the form shown in Figure A.2. In the report, when looking at the determinants of employer-provided and non-employer-provided training, we estimate both sequential models and compare the results obtained. The estimated effects of mobility on training are broadly similar for the two models.

A.3 Models that Use Different Measures of Job Mobility

In the report, we also follow Winkelmann (1994) and look at the impact of training on the number of jobs that an individual holds. This involves estimating count data

---

[25] Let $\overline{X}_{M,t-1}$ be the average characteristics of movers and $\overline{X}_{I,t-1}$ be the average characteristics of non-movers. Then $\overline{M_1^*} = \hat{\Pi}_1 \overline{X}_{M,t-1}$ and $\overline{M_0^*} = \hat{\Pi}_1 \overline{X}_{I,t-1}$ where $\hat{\Pi}_1$ is our estimated coefficients from our reduced form mobility equation (A.7).

models. With the Poisson count data model, as used in this report,

$$\text{(A.27)} \quad \Pr(NJOBS_{it} = j) = \frac{e^{-\lambda_{it}} \lambda_{it}}{j!} \quad j = 0,1,2,3,\ldots$$

where $NJOBS_{it}$ is the number of jobs since leaving school that individual i has held at time t, and

$$\text{(A.28)} \quad \ln\lambda_{it} = \alpha_1 X_{1i,t-1} + \gamma_1 TRAIN_{i,t-1} + \mu_{1it}.$$

In this model,

$$\text{(A.29)} \quad \text{E}(NJOBS_{it} \mid X_{1i,t-1}, TRAIN_{i,t-1})$$
$$= e^{\alpha_1 X_{1i,t-1} + \gamma_1 TRAIN_{i,t-1}} = \lambda_{it}.$$

In this model, the estimated impact of training on the number of jobs held by an individual is given by

$$\text{(A.30)} \quad \text{E}(NJOBS_{it} \mid X_{1i,t-1}, TRAIN_{i,t-1} = 1)$$
$$- \text{E}(NJOBS_{it} \mid X_{1i,t-1}, TRAIN_{i,t-1} = 0)$$
$$= e^{\hat{\alpha}_1 X_{1i,t-1} + \hat{\gamma}_1} - e^{\hat{\alpha}_1 X_{1i,t-1}}$$

where $\hat{\alpha}_1$ and $\hat{\gamma}_1$ are the estimated coefficients from our Poisson model.

If we treat training as endogenous, then we can once again undertake a two-stage procedure. In the first stage, we estimate the reduced form probit given by equation (A.8). We then substitute the predicted value of $TRAIN_{i,t-1}^*$ ($T\hat{R}AIN_{i,t-1}^*$) into our structural equation (A.27) and estimate the structural equation using a Poisson maximum likelihood procedure. With this two-stage estimation procedure, the estimated impact of training on the number of jobs held by an individual is given by

(A.31) $E(NJOBS_{it} \mid X_{1i,t-1}, \hat{TRAIN}^*_{i,t-1} = \overline{T^*_1})$

$- E(NJOBS_{it} \mid X_{1i,t-1}, \hat{TRAIN}^*_{i,t-1} = \overline{T^*_0})$

$= e^{\hat{\alpha}_1 X_{1i,t-1} + \hat{\gamma}_1 \overline{T^*_1}} - e^{\hat{\alpha}_1 X_{1i,t-1} + \hat{\gamma}_1 \overline{T^*_0}}$.

One limitation of the Poisson model is that the variance of the count variable is assumed to be equal to the mean. A number of other models have been developed that relax this assumption. One such model is the negative binomial model. We have also estimated our count data models using a negative binomial specification, but the results obtained from this procedure were very similar to those obtained from the Poisson and are not reported for reasons of parsimony. They are available from the authors on request.

We can also use the number of jobs (excluding the current job) as an alternative measure of mobility in equation (A.2). This will tell us whether the probability of training increases or decreases with the number of jobs a person holds. We would also include quadratics, as the relationship between number of jobs and training is unlikely to be linear. We can also use instrumental variable techniques and allow the number of jobs to be endogenous (provided we have at least one suitable instrument).

APPENDIX B
Detailed Results

TABLE B.1

Determinants of Training: NCDS

Variable	Males			Females		
	Coef.	(S.E.)	Marg. effect	Coef.	(S.E.)	Marg. effect
Constant	-2.046	(0.058)		-2.077	(0.063)	
Year dummies:						
1982	0.075	(0.041)	0.010	0.083	(0.041)	0.010
1983	0.082	(0.041)	0.011	0.094	(0.041)	0.012
1984	0.101	(0.041)	0.014	0.019	(0.043)	0.002
1985	0.143	(0.040)	0.021	0.048	(0.043)	0.006
1986	0.184	(0.040)	0.027	0.118	(0.042)	0.015
1987	0.164	(0.040)	0.024	0.150	(0.042)	0.019
1988	0.211	(0.039)	0.031	0.160	(0.042)	0.021
1989	0.332	(0.038)	0.053	0.275	(0.040)	0.038
1990	0.465	(0.038)	0.080	0.400	(0.041)	0.060
Quarter dummies:						
2nd quarter	0.035	(0.022)	0.005	-0.003	(0.025)	0.000
3rd quarter	0.085	(0.022)	0.012	0.099	(0.025)	0.012
4th quarter	0.020	(0.023)	0.003	-0.017	(0.026)	-0.002
Highest education qualification:						
Other	0.244	(0.043)	0.038	0.270	(0.056)	0.038
O levels	0.307	(0.033)	0.048	0.248	(0.037)	0.033
Lower vocational	0.255	(0.035)	0.039	0.494	(0.044)	0.080
5+ O levels	0.482	(0.036)	0.085	0.379	(0.040)	0.056
Middle vocational	0.536	(0.029)	0.090	0.539	(0.044)	0.090
A levels	0.771	(0.036)	0.160	0.781	(0.041)	0.148
Higher vocational	0.684	(0.032)	0.133	0.706	(0.038)	0.122
Degree	0.690	(0.033)	0.133	0.702	(0.039)	0.123
Industry 1981 job:						
Energy and water	-0.121	(0.040)	-0.015	0.043	(0.078)	0.005
Minerals	-0.024	(0.045)	-0.003	0.123	(0.066)	0.016
Metals	0.055	(0.027)	0.007	0.079	(0.049)	0.010
Other manufacturing	-0.042	(0.036)	-0.005	-0.146	(0.049)	-0.016
Construction	-0.170	(0.038)	-0.020	-0.228	(0.164)	-0.022
Wholesale and retail trade	-0.069	(0.033)	-0.009	0.120	(0.037)	0.015
Transport and communication	0.021	(0.034)	0.003	0.148	(0.049)	0.019
Finance	0.186	(0.033)	0.028	0.250	(0.034)	0.034
Other services	0.144	(0.027)	0.020	0.200	(0.026)	0.025
1981 region:						
South-East	0.001	(0.029)	0.000	-0.127	(0.030)	-0.014
South-West	-0.202	(0.039)	-0.023	-0.139	(0.040)	-0.015
Wales	-0.194	(0.045)	-0.022	0.090	(0.045)	0.011
West Midlands	-0.008	(0.035)	-0.001	-0.084	(0.037)	-0.009
East Midlands	-0.085	(0.037)	-0.011	-0.141	(0.041)	-0.015
East Anglia	0.041	(0.049)	0.006	-0.255	(0.053)	-0.025
Yorkshire and Humberside	0.153	(0.034)	0.022	-0.137	(0.038)	-0.015
North-West	-0.043	(0.033)	-0.006	0.006	(0.034)	0.001
North	0.223	(0.036)	0.034	-0.205	(0.050)	-0.021
Scotland	-0.179	(0.037)	-0.021	-0.124	(0.036)	-0.014
Employer size 1981 job:						
10–24	0.121	(0.033)	0.017	-0.105	(0.033)	-0.012
25–99	0.112	(0.029)	0.015	0.012	(0.029)	0.001
100–500	0.195	(0.029)	0.028	0.036	(0.030)	0.004
500+	0.133	(0.030)	0.018	0.010	(0.031)	0.001
Union member 1981	0.036	(0.019)	0.005	-0.010	(0.020)	-0.001
Private sector 1981	-0.250	(0.022)	-0.035	-0.068	(0.026)	-0.008
Part-time 1981	-0.123	(0.073)	-0.015	-0.158	(0.034)	-0.017
Number of observations		59957			51162	
Pseudo R^2		0.0703			0.0611	

TABLE B.2

Determinants of Male Training: QLFS

Variable	Males			Young Males		
	Coef.	(S.E.)	Marg. effect	Coef.	(S.E.)	Marg. effect
Constant	-0.675	(0.134)		6.671	(1.026)	
Panel dummies:						
Jun 1992	-0.145	(0.039)	-0.024	-0.375	(0.077)	-0.073
Sep 1992	-0.080	(0.038)	-0.014	-0.206	(0.072)	-0.043
Dec 1992	-0.065	(0.038)	-0.011	-0.158	(0.073)	-0.034
Mar 1993	0.008	(0.038)	0.001	-0.071	(0.073)	-0.016
Jun 1993	-0.200	(0.039)	-0.032	-0.365	(0.076)	-0.072
Sep 1993	-0.090	(0.039)	-0.015	-0.259	(0.076)	-0.053
Highest education qualification:						
Degree	0.765	(0.044)	0.182	1.176	(0.127)	0.378
Higher vocational	0.765	(0.049)	0.194	1.038	(0.130)	0.331
Middle vocational	0.665	(0.046)	0.156	0.980	(0.119)	0.287
Lower vocational	0.475	(0.042)	0.094	0.739	(0.114)	0.169
Other	0.376	(0.051)	0.080	0.523	(0.171)	0.149
Industry:						
Energy and water	-0.040	(0.056)	-0.007	-0.019	(0.137)	-0.004
Minerals	-0.173	(0.051)	-0.028	-0.135	(0.112)	-0.029
Metals	-0.294	(0.034)	-0.046	-0.141	(0.071)	-0.030
Other manufacturing	-0.416	(0.043)	-0.060	-0.449	(0.086)	-0.084
Construction	-0.376	(0.048)	-0.054	-0.294	(0.090)	-0.058
Wholesale and retail trade	-0.327	(0.037)	-0.050	-0.450	(0.071)	-0.090
Transport and communication	-0.299	(0.042)	-0.046	-0.350	(0.091)	-0.067
Finance	-0.139	(0.036)	-0.023	-0.099	(0.073)	-0.022
Region:						
South-East	0.030	(0.041)	0.005	0.021	(0.081)	0.005
South-West	0.056	(0.050)	0.010	0.113	(0.098)	0.027
Wales	0.060	(0.059)	0.011	0.115	(0.117)	0.028
West Midlands	0.056	(0.048)	0.010	0.077	(0.093)	0.018
East Midlands	0.045	(0.050)	0.008	0.044	(0.100)	0.010
East Anglia	-0.056	(0.066)	-0.010	0.152	(0.122)	0.037
Yorkshire and Humberside	0.067	(0.048)	0.012	0.114	(0.094)	0.027
North-West	-0.021	(0.046)	-0.004	-0.014	(0.089)	-0.003
North	0.021	(0.057)	0.004	-0.084	(0.113)	-0.018
Scotland	-0.048	(0.049)	-0.008	-0.059	(0.095)	-0.013
Age	-0.031	(0.006)	-0.005	-0.632	(0.087)	-0.144
Age^2/100	0.018	(0.008)	0.003	1.192	(0.183)	0.270
Part-time	0.062	(0.064)	0.011	0.056	(0.093)	0.013
Non-white	-0.069	(0.063)	-0.012	0.103	(0.118)	0.025
Employer size 25+	0.154	(0.026)	0.026	0.122	(0.048)	0.027
Number of observations	26638			5903		
Pseudo R^2	0.068			0.081		

TABLE B.3

Determinants of Female Training: QLFS

Variable	Females			Young Females		
	Coef.	(S.E.)	Marg. effect	Coef.	(S.E.)	Marg. effect
Constant	-1.165	(0.143)		4.212	(1.018)	
Panel dummies:						
Jun 1992	-0.158	(0.040)	-0.028	-0.319	(0.076)	-0.067
Sep 1992	-0.042	(0.039)	-0.008	-0.013	(0.072)	-0.003
Dec 1992	-0.057	(0.039)	-0.010	-0.123	(0.073)	-0.028
Mar 1993	0.003	(0.038)	0.001	-0.077	(0.073)	-0.018
Jun 1993	-0.214	(0.040)	-0.037	-0.279	(0.076)	-0.060
Sep 1993	-0.048	(0.039)	-0.009	-0.092	(0.073)	-0.021
Highest education qualification:						
Degree	0.921	(0.044)	0.250	1.008	(0.125)	0.325
Higher vocational	0.884	(0.043)	0.237	0.848	(0.127)	0.267
Middle vocational	0.697	(0.046)	0.177	0.684	(0.120)	0.197
Lower vocational	0.446	(0.038)	0.090	0.325	(0.114)	0.076
Other	0.341	(0.054)	0.076	0.604	(0.175)	0.184
Industry:						
Energy and Water	-0.131	(0.109)	-0.023	-0.072	(0.178)	-0.017
Minerals	-0.264	(0.086)	-0.042	-0.268	(0.155)	-0.056
Metals	-0.335	(0.056)	-0.052	-0.342	(0.101)	-0.069
Other manufacturing	-0.508	(0.054)	-0.072	-0.497	(0.089)	-0.095
Construction	-0.078	(0.085)	-0.014	-0.168	(0.165)	-0.037
Wholesale and retail trade	-0.216	(0.032)	-0.038	-0.238	(0.057)	-0.053
Transport and communication	-0.150	(0.061)	-0.026	-0.052	(0.099)	-0.012
Finance	-0.205	(0.033)	-0.035	-0.165	(0.056)	-0.037
Region:						
South-East	0.081	(0.041)	0.016	0.025	(0.076)	0.006
South-West	0.115	(0.049)	0.023	0.159	(0.093)	0.041
Wales	0.067	(0.060)	0.013	0.252	(0.109)	0.067
West Midlands	0.050	(0.049)	0.010	0.064	(0.090)	0.016
East Midlands	0.140	(0.051)	0.028	0.069	(0.098)	0.017
East Anglia	0.165	(0.063)	0.034	0.129	(0.119)	0.033
Yorkshire and Humberside	0.113	(0.048)	0.022	0.065	(0.089)	0.016
North-West	0.046	(0.046)	0.009	0.103	(0.084)	0.025
North	0.052	(0.056)	0.010	-0.017	(0.104)	-0.004
Scotland	-0.038	(0.049)	-0.007	-0.169	(0.092)	-0.038
Age	-0.010	(0.007)	-0.002	-0.428	(0.086)	-0.102
Age^2/100	0.002	(0.009)	0.000	0.816	(0.182)	0.195
Part-time	-0.233	(0.024)	-0.043	-0.153	(0.054)	-0.035
Non-white	-0.089	(0.063)	-0.016	-0.047	(0.114)	-0.011
Employer size 25+	0.110	(0.023)	0.020	0.060	(0.044)	0.014
Number of observations	25198			5995		
Pseudo R^2	0.087			0.065		

TABLE B.4

Training and the Determinants of Male Mobility I: NCDS

Variable	Coef.	(S.E.)	Marg. effect	Coef.	(S.E.)	Marg. effect
Constant	-1.345	(0.045)		-1.345	(0.045)	
Any training				-0.041	(0.024)	-0.010
Year dummies:						
1982	0.014	(0.030)	0.003	0.014	(0.030)	0.003
1983	0.056	(0.030)	0.014	0.057	(0.030)	0.014
1984	0.092	(0.030)	0.023	0.093	(0.030)	0.023
1985	0.108	(0.030)	0.027	0.108	(0.030)	0.027
1986	0.053	(0.030)	0.013	0.054	(0.030)	0.013
1987	0.062	(0.030)	0.015	0.063	(0.030)	0.016
1988	0.087	(0.030)	0.022	0.088	(0.030)	0.022
1989	0.059	(0.030)	0.014	0.061	(0.030)	0.015
1990	-0.100	(0.032)	-0.023	-0.098	(0.032)	-0.022
Quarter dummies:						
2nd quarter	-0.017	(0.018)	-0.004	-0.017	(0.018)	-0.004
3rd quarter	-0.020	(0.018)	-0.005	-0.019	(0.018)	-0.005
4th quarter	-0.027	(0.018)	-0.006	-0.026	(0.018)	-0.006
Highest education qualification:						
Other	0.094	(0.030)	0.023	0.095	(0.030)	0.024
O levels	-0.015	(0.024)	-0.003	-0.013	(0.024)	-0.003
Lower vocational	0.105	(0.024)	0.026	0.106	(0.024)	0.026
5+ O levels	-0.006	(0.028)	-0.001	-0.004	(0.028)	-0.001
Middle vocational	0.045	(0.021)	0.011	0.048	(0.021)	0.012
A levels	0.160	(0.030)	0.041	0.164	(0.030)	0.042
Higher vocational	0.078	(0.026)	0.019	0.082	(0.026)	0.020
Degree	0.350	(0.025)	0.095	0.353	(0.025)	0.096
Industry 1981 job:						
Energy and water	0.129	(0.035)	0.033	0.128	(0.035)	0.032
Minerals	0.090	(0.035)	0.023	0.090	(0.035)	0.022
Metals	0.129	(0.022)	0.032	0.129	(0.022)	0.032
Other manufacturing	0.071	(0.027)	0.018	0.071	(0.027)	0.017
Construction	0.221	(0.027)	0.058	0.220	(0.027)	0.058
Wholesale and retail trade	0.280	(0.023)	0.074	0.280	(0.023)	0.074
Transport and communication	0.101	(0.030)	0.025	0.101	(0.030)	0.025
Finance	0.091	(0.029)	0.023	0.093	(0.029)	0.023
Other services	0.268	(0.025)	0.071	0.269	(0.025)	0.071
1981 region:						
South-East	0.034	(0.024)	0.008	0.034	(0.024)	0.008
South-West	-0.061	(0.030)	-0.014	-0.062	(0.030)	-0.014
Wales	-0.074	(0.034)	-0.017	-0.074	(0.034)	-0.017
West Midlands	-0.064	(0.029)	-0.015	-0.064	(0.029)	-0.015
East Midlands	-0.051	(0.030)	-0.012	-0.051	(0.030)	-0.012
East Anglia	-0.149	(0.042)	-0.033	-0.149	(0.042)	-0.033
Yorkshire and Humberside	0.014	(0.029)	0.003	0.015	(0.029)	0.004
North-West	0.034	(0.027)	0.008	0.034	(0.027)	0.008
North	0.056	(0.031)	0.014	0.058	(0.031)	0.014
Scotland	-0.048	(0.029)	-0.011	-0.048	(0.029)	-0.011
Employer size 1981 job:						
10–24	0.006	(0.024)	0.001	0.007	(0.024)	0.002
25–99	-0.044	(0.021)	-0.010	-0.043	(0.021)	-0.010
100–500	-0.069	(0.022)	-0.016	-0.068	(0.022)	-0.016
500+	-0.117	(0.023)	-0.027	-0.116	(0.023)	-0.027
Union member 1981	-0.048	(0.015)	-0.011	-0.048	(0.015)	-0.011
Private sector 1981	0.192	(0.019)	0.044	0.191	(0.019)	0.044
Part-time 1981	-0.099	(0.058)	-0.022	-0.099	(0.058)	-0.023
Times moved 1958 to 1974	0.034	(0.003)	0.008	0.034	(0.003)	0.008
Mother employed 1974	0.007	(0.014)	0.002	0.007	(0.014)	0.002
Number of observations		59957			59957	
Pseudo R^2		0.0206			0.0206	

TABLE B.5

Training and the Determinants of Male Mobility II: NCDS

Variable	Coef.	(S.E.)	Marg. effect	Coef.	(S.E.)	Marg. effect
Constant	-1.346	(0.045)		-1.346	(0.045)	
Employer-funded training	-0.129	(0.030)	-0.029			
Other training	0.098	(0.036)	0.025			
Continuing training				-0.018	(0.030)	-0.004
Completed training				-0.077	(0.037)	-0.018
Year dummies:						
1982	0.014	(0.030)	0.003	0.014	(0.030)	0.003
1983	0.056	(0.030)	0.014	0.057	(0.030)	0.014
1984	0.092	(0.030)	0.023	0.093	(0.030)	0.023
1985	0.108	(0.030)	0.027	0.109	(0.030)	0.027
1986	0.053	(0.030)	0.013	0.054	(0.030)	0.013
1987	0.063	(0.030)	0.015	0.064	(0.030)	0.016
1988	0.086	(0.030)	0.021	0.089	(0.030)	0.022
1989	0.059	(0.030)	0.015	0.062	(0.030)	0.015
1990	-0.097	(0.032)	-0.022	-0.096	(0.032)	-0.022
Quarter dummies:						
2nd quarter	-0.017	(0.018)	-0.004	-0.017	(0.018)	-0.004
3rd quarter	-0.019	(0.018)	-0.005	-0.019	(0.018)	-0.005
4th quarter	-0.026	(0.018)	-0.006	-0.026	(0.018)	-0.006
Highest education qualification:						
Other	0.095	(0.030)	0.024	0.095	(0.030)	0.024
O levels	-0.013	(0.024)	-0.003	-0.013	(0.024)	-0.003
Lower vocational	0.107	(0.024)	0.027	0.106	(0.024)	0.026
5+ O levels	-0.005	(0.028)	-0.001	-0.004	(0.028)	-0.001
Middle vocational	0.049	(0.021)	0.012	0.047	(0.021)	0.011
A levels	0.162	(0.030)	0.041	0.164	(0.030)	0.042
Higher vocational	0.082	(0.026)	0.020	0.082	(0.026)	0.020
Degree	0.354	(0.025)	0.097	0.354	(0.025)	0.096
Industry 1981 job:						
Energy and water	0.130	(0.035)	0.033	0.128	(0.035)	0.032
Minerals	0.089	(0.035)	0.022	0.090	(0.035)	0.022
Metals	0.128	(0.022)	0.032	0.129	(0.022)	0.032
Other manufacturing	0.071	(0.027)	0.018	0.071	(0.027)	0.017
Construction	0.220	(0.027)	0.057	0.220	(0.027)	0.058
Wholesale and retail trade	0.279	(0.023)	0.074	0.280	(0.023)	0.074
Transport and communication	0.100	(0.030)	0.025	0.101	(0.030)	0.025
Finance	0.092	(0.029)	0.023	0.093	(0.029)	0.023
Other services	0.270	(0.025)	0.071	0.268	(0.025)	0.071
1981 region:						
South-East	0.035	(0.024)	0.008	0.034	(0.024)	0.008
South-West	-0.063	(0.030)	-0.015	-0.062	(0.030)	-0.014
Wales	-0.076	(0.034)	-0.017	-0.074	(0.034)	-0.017
West Midlands	-0.067	(0.029)	-0.016	-0.065	(0.029)	-0.015
East Midlands	-0.051	(0.030)	-0.012	-0.052	(0.030)	-0.012
East Anglia	-0.149	(0.042)	-0.033	-0.150	(0.042)	-0.033
Yorkshire and Humberside	0.016	(0.029)	0.004	0.015	(0.029)	0.004
North-West	0.032	(0.027)	0.008	0.034	(0.027)	0.008
North	0.059	(0.031)	0.014	0.057	(0.031)	0.014
Scotland	-0.051	(0.029)	-0.012	-0.049	(0.029)	-0.011
Employer size 1981 job:						
10–24	0.007	(0.024)	0.002	0.007	(0.024)	0.002
25–99	-0.041	(0.021)	-0.010	-0.043	(0.021)	-0.010
100–500	-0.068	(0.022)	-0.016	-0.067	(0.022)	-0.016
500+	-0.115	(0.023)	-0.027	-0.116	(0.023)	-0.027
Union member 1981	-0.048	(0.015)	-0.012	-0.048	(0.015)	-0.011
Private sector 1981	0.191	(0.019)	0.044	0.191	(0.019)	0.044
Part-time 1981	-0.098	(0.058)	-0.022	-0.099	(0.058)	-0.022
Times moved 1958 to 1974	0.035	(0.003)	0.008	0.034	(0.003)	0.008
Mother employed 1974	0.008	(0.014)	0.002	0.007	(0.014)	0.002
Number of observations		59957			59957	
Pseudo R^2		0.0211			0.0206	

TABLE B.6

Training and the Determinants of Male Mobility III: NCDS

Variable	Coef.	(S.E.)	Marg. effect	Coef.	(S.E.)	Marg. effect
Constant	-1.345	(0.045)		-1.347	(0.045)	
Non-qualification training	-0.064	(0.035)	-0.015	-0.063	(0.035)	-0.015
Qualification training	-0.024	(0.031)	-0.006			
Other				-0.155	(0.067)	-0.034
Lower vocational				-0.004	(0.069)	-0.001
Middle vocational				-0.115	(0.103)	-0.026
Higher vocational				-0.090	(0.052)	-0.020
Degree				0.309	(0.071)	0.085
Year dummies:						
1982	0.014	(0.030)	0.003	0.015	(0.030)	0.004
1983	0.057	(0.030)	0.014	0.057	(0.030)	0.014
1984	0.093	(0.030)	0.023	0.093	(0.030)	0.023
1985	0.109	(0.030)	0.027	0.109	(0.030)	0.027
1986	0.054	(0.030)	0.013	0.054	(0.030)	0.013
1987	0.064	(0.030)	0.016	0.062	(0.030)	0.015
1988	0.089	(0.030)	0.022	0.088	(0.030)	0.022
1989	0.061	(0.030)	0.015	0.061	(0.030)	0.015
1990	-0.096	(0.032)	-0.022	-0.096	(0.032)	-0.022
Quarter dummies:						
2nd quarter	-0.017	(0.018)	-0.004	-0.016	(0.018)	-0.004
3rd quarter	-0.019	(0.018)	-0.005	-0.019	(0.018)	-0.005
4th quarter	-0.026	(0.018)	-0.006	-0.026	(0.018)	-0.006
Highest education qualification:						
Other	0.095	(0.030)	0.024	0.096	(0.030)	0.024
O levels	-0.013	(0.024)	-0.003	-0.013	(0.024)	-0.003
Lower vocational	0.106	(0.024)	0.026	0.106	(0.024)	0.026
5+ O levels	-0.004	(0.028)	-0.001	-0.004	(0.028)	-0.001
Middle vocational	0.047	(0.021)	0.012	0.047	(0.021)	0.011
A levels	0.164	(0.030)	0.042	0.161	(0.030)	0.041
Higher vocational	0.081	(0.026)	0.020	0.075	(0.026)	0.018
Degree	0.353	(0.025)	0.096	0.347	(0.025)	0.094
Industry 1981 job:						
Energy and water	0.128	(0.035)	0.032	0.131	(0.035)	0.033
Minerals	0.090	(0.035)	0.022	0.090	(0.035)	0.022
Metals	0.129	(0.022)	0.032	0.128	(0.022)	0.032
Other manufacturing	0.071	(0.027)	0.018	0.069	(0.027)	0.017
Construction	0.220	(0.027)	0.057	0.222	(0.027)	0.058
Wholesale and retail trade	0.280	(0.023)	0.074	0.278	(0.023)	0.074
Transport and communication	0.101	(0.030)	0.025	0.102	(0.030)	0.025
Finance	0.093	(0.029)	0.023	0.097	(0.029)	0.024
Other services	0.269	(0.025)	0.071	0.270	(0.025)	0.071
1981 region:						
South-East	0.034	(0.024)	0.008	0.035	(0.024)	0.008
South-West	-0.063	(0.030)	-0.015	-0.060	(0.030)	-0.014
Wales	-0.075	(0.034)	-0.017	-0.076	(0.034)	-0.017
West Midlands	-0.065	(0.029)	-0.015	-0.067	(0.029)	-0.016
East Midlands	-0.052	(0.030)	-0.012	-0.052	(0.030)	-0.012
East Anglia	-0.150	(0.042)	-0.033	-0.147	(0.042)	-0.033
Yorkshire and Humberside	0.014	(0.029)	0.003	0.014	(0.029)	0.003
North-West	0.034	(0.027)	0.008	0.035	(0.027)	0.008
North	0.057	(0.031)	0.014	0.058	(0.031)	0.014
Scotland	-0.049	(0.029)	-0.011	-0.048	(0.029)	-0.011
Employer size 1981 job:						
10–24	0.007	(0.024)	0.002	0.007	(0.024)	0.002
25–99	-0.044	(0.021)	-0.010	-0.043	(0.021)	-0.010
100–500	-0.068	(0.022)	-0.016	-0.065	(0.022)	-0.015
500+	-0.117	(0.023)	-0.027	-0.115	(0.023)	-0.027
Union member 1981	-0.048	(0.015)	-0.011	-0.049	(0.015)	-0.012
Private sector 1981	0.191	(0.019)	0.044	0.194	(0.019)	0.045
Part-time 1981	-0.099	(0.058)	-0.023	-0.098	(0.058)	-0.022
Times moved 1958 to 1974	0.034	(0.003)	0.008	0.034	(0.003)	0.008
Mother employed 1974	0.007	(0.014)	0.002	0.007	(0.014)	0.002
Number of observations	59957			59957		
Pseudo R^2	0.0206			0.0211		

TABLE B.7

Training and the Determinants of Male Mobility IV: NCDS

Variable	Coef.	(S.E.)	Marg. effect	Coef.	(S.E.)	Marg. effect
Constant	-1.346	(0.045)		-1.347	(0.045)	
Employer qualification training	-0.120	(0.037)	-0.027			
Employer non-qualification training	-0.145	(0.049)	-0.032			
Other qualification training	0.188	(0.053)	0.049			
Other non-qualification training	0.022	(0.049)	0.005			
Employer continuing training				-0.123	(0.037)	-0.028
Employer completed training				-0.140	(0.050)	-0.031
Other continuing training				0.199	(0.050)	0.052
Other completed training				-0.008	(0.052)	-0.002
Year dummies:						
1982	0.014	(0.030)	0.003	0.014	(0.030)	0.003
1983	0.056	(0.030)	0.014	0.056	(0.030)	0.014
1984	0.093	(0.030)	0.023	0.092	(0.030)	0.023
1985	0.108	(0.030)	0.027	0.108	(0.030)	0.027
1986	0.054	(0.030)	0.013	0.054	(0.030)	0.013
1987	0.064	(0.030)	0.016	0.064	(0.030)	0.016
1988	0.088	(0.030)	0.022	0.087	(0.030)	0.022
1989	0.062	(0.030)	0.015	0.061	(0.030)	0.015
1990	-0.094	(0.032)	-0.022	-0.095	(0.032)	-0.022
Quarter dummies:						
2nd quarter	-0.016	(0.018)	-0.004	-0.017	(0.018)	-0.004
3rd quarter	-0.019	(0.018)	-0.005	-0.019	(0.018)	-0.005
4th quarter	-0.026	(0.018)	-0.006	-0.025	(0.018)	-0.006
Highest education qualification:						
Other	0.095	(0.030)	0.024	0.096	(0.030)	0.024
O levels	-0.013	(0.024)	-0.003	-0.013	(0.024)	-0.003
Lower vocational	0.107	(0.024)	0.027	0.107	(0.024)	0.027
5+ O levels	-0.005	(0.028)	-0.001	-0.004	(0.028)	-0.001
Middle vocational	0.049	(0.021)	0.012	0.049	(0.021)	0.012
A levels	0.160	(0.030)	0.041	0.161	(0.030)	0.041
Higher vocational	0.081	(0.026)	0.020	0.082	(0.026)	0.020
Degree	0.354	(0.025)	0.097	0.355	(0.025)	0.097
Industry 1981 job:						
Energy and water	0.131	(0.035)	0.033	0.132	(0.035)	0.033
Minerals	0.089	(0.035)	0.022	0.089	(0.035)	0.022
Metals	0.129	(0.022)	0.032	0.128	(0.022)	0.032
Other manufacturing	0.072	(0.027)	0.018	0.072	(0.027)	0.018
Construction	0.220	(0.027)	0.058	0.220	(0.027)	0.057
Wholesale and retail trade	0.279	(0.023)	0.074	0.279	(0.023)	0.074
Transport and communication	0.101	(0.030)	0.025	0.101	(0.030)	0.025
Finance	0.093	(0.029)	0.023	0.091	(0.029)	0.023
Other services	0.271	(0.025)	0.071	0.270	(0.025)	0.071
1981 region:						
South-East	0.034	(0.024)	0.008	0.034	(0.024)	0.008
South-West	-0.064	(0.030)	-0.015	-0.063	(0.030)	-0.015
Wales	-0.076	(0.034)	-0.018	-0.076	(0.034)	-0.018
West Midlands	-0.069	(0.029)	-0.016	-0.070	(0.029)	-0.016
East Midlands	-0.051	(0.030)	-0.012	-0.051	(0.030)	-0.012
East Anglia	-0.150	(0.042)	-0.033	-0.150	(0.042)	-0.033
Yorkshire and Humberside	0.014	(0.029)	0.003	0.014	(0.029)	0.003
North-West	0.031	(0.027)	0.008	0.030	(0.027)	0.007
North	0.058	(0.031)	0.014	0.057	(0.031)	0.014
Scotland	-0.052	(0.029)	-0.012	-0.052	(0.029)	-0.012
Employer size 1981 job:						
10–24	0.007	(0.024)	0.002	0.008	(0.024)	0.002
25–99	-0.041	(0.021)	-0.010	-0.040	(0.021)	-0.010
100–500	-0.069	(0.022)	-0.016	-0.068	(0.022)	-0.016
500+	-0.116	(0.023)	-0.027	-0.114	(0.023)	-0.026
Union member 1981	-0.049	(0.015)	-0.012	-0.049	(0.015)	-0.012
Private sector 1981	0.191	(0.019)	0.044	0.192	(0.019)	0.044
Part-time 1981	-0.097	(0.058)	-0.022	-0.096	(0.058)	-0.022
Times moved 1958 to 1974	0.035	(0.003)	0.008	0.035	(0.003)	0.008
Mother employed 1974	0.008	(0.014)	0.002	0.008	(0.014)	0.002
Number of observations		59957			59957	
Pseudo R^2		0.0212			0.0212	

113

TABLE B.8

Training and the Determinants of Female Mobility I: NCDS

Variable	Coef.	(S.E.)	Marg. effect	Coef.	(S.E.)	Marg. effect
Constant	-0.733	(0.043)		-0.733	(0.043)	
Any training				0.020	(0.024)	0.006
Year dummies:						
1982	0.007	(0.027)	0.002	0.006	(0.027)	0.002
1983	0.067	(0.027)	0.021	0.067	(0.027)	0.021
1984	0.013	(0.028)	0.004	0.013	(0.028)	0.004
1985	0.002	(0.028)	0.001	0.002	(0.028)	0.000
1986	-0.035	(0.028)	-0.011	-0.035	(0.028)	-0.011
1987	-0.003	(0.028)	-0.001	-0.003	(0.028)	-0.001
1988	0.011	(0.028)	0.003	0.011	(0.028)	0.003
1989	-0.007	(0.028)	-0.002	-0.007	(0.028)	-0.002
1990	-0.099	(0.030)	-0.030	-0.100	(0.030)	-0.030
Quarter dummies:						
2nd quarter	-0.015	(0.018)	-0.004	-0.015	(0.018)	-0.005
3rd quarter	-0.013	(0.018)	-0.004	-0.013	(0.018)	-0.004
4th quarter	-0.031	(0.018)	-0.009	-0.031	(0.018)	-0.010
Highest education qualification:						
Other	0.088	(0.034)	0.028	0.088	(0.034)	0.028
O levels	0.069	(0.020)	0.022	0.069	(0.020)	0.022
Lower vocational	0.119	(0.028)	0.038	0.118	(0.028)	0.038
5+ O levels	0.062	(0.024)	0.019	0.061	(0.024)	0.019
Middle vocational	-0.060	(0.030)	-0.018	-0.061	(0.030)	-0.018
A levels	0.089	(0.028)	0.028	0.087	(0.028)	0.027
Higher vocational	0.186	(0.024)	0.060	0.184	(0.024)	0.060
Degree	0.241	(0.025)	0.079	0.239	(0.025)	0.078
Industry 1981 job:						
Energy and water	-0.137	(0.060)	-0.040	-0.137	(0.060)	-0.040
Minerals	0.170	(0.044)	0.055	0.170	(0.044)	0.055
Metals	0.132	(0.031)	0.042	0.131	(0.031)	0.042
Other manufacturing	0.165	(0.027)	0.053	0.165	(0.027)	0.053
Construction	0.109	(0.083)	0.035	0.109	(0.083)	0.035
Wholesale and retail trade	0.151	(0.023)	0.048	0.151	(0.023)	0.048
Transport and communication	0.028	(0.036)	0.009	0.028	(0.036)	0.009
Finance	-0.027	(0.024)	-0.008	-0.027	(0.024)	-0.008
Other services	0.094	(0.019)	0.029	0.094	(0.019)	0.029
1981 region:						
South-East	-0.031	(0.022)	-0.009	-0.030	(0.022)	-0.009
South-West	-0.087	(0.028)	-0.026	-0.086	(0.028)	-0.026
Wales	-0.133	(0.035)	-0.039	-0.134	(0.035)	-0.039
West Midlands	-0.068	(0.027)	-0.021	-0.068	(0.027)	-0.020
East Midlands	-0.009	(0.028)	-0.003	-0.009	(0.028)	-0.003
East Anglia	-0.106	(0.035)	-0.031	-0.105	(0.035)	-0.031
Yorkshire and Humberside	-0.146	(0.028)	-0.043	-0.145	(0.028)	-0.043
North-West	-0.066	(0.025)	-0.020	-0.065	(0.025)	-0.020
North	-0.123	(0.033)	-0.036	-0.123	(0.033)	-0.036
Scotland	-0.099	(0.026)	-0.030	-0.099	(0.026)	-0.030
Employer size 1981 job:						
10–24	-0.030	(0.022)	-0.009	-0.030	(0.022)	-0.009
25–99	-0.098	(0.020)	-0.029	-0.098	(0.020)	-0.029
100–500	-0.064	(0.020)	-0.019	-0.064	(0.020)	-0.019
500+	-0.071	(0.022)	-0.022	-0.071	(0.022)	-0.022
Union member 1981	-0.110	(0.014)	-0.034	-0.110	(0.014)	-0.034
Private sector 1981	0.096	(0.018)	0.029	0.096	(0.018)	0.029
Part-time 1981	-0.047	(0.022)	-0.014	-0.046	(0.022)	-0.014
Times moved 1958 to 1974	0.007	(0.004)	0.002	0.007	(0.004)	0.002
Mother employed 1974	-0.028	(0.013)	-0.009	-0.027	(0.013)	-0.008
Number of observations		51162			51162	
Pseudo R^2		0.0107			0.0107	

TABLE B.9

Training and the Determinants of Female Mobility II: NCDS

Variable	Coef.	(S.E.)	Marg. effect	Coef.	(S.E.)	Marg. effect
Constant	-0.733	(0.043)		-0.734	(0.043)	
Employer-funded training	0.005	(0.032)	0.002			
Other training	0.038	(0.036)	0.012			
Continuing training				0.044	(0.030)	0.014
Completed training				-0.024	(0.040)	-0.007
Year dummies:						
1982	0.006	(0.027)	0.002	0.007	(0.027)	0.002
1983	0.066	(0.027)	0.021	0.067	(0.027)	0.021
1984	0.012	(0.028)	0.004	0.013	(0.028)	0.004
1985	0.001	(0.028)	0.000	0.002	(0.028)	0.001
1986	-0.036	(0.028)	-0.011	-0.034	(0.028)	-0.010
1987	-0.004	(0.028)	-0.001	-0.003	(0.028)	-0.001
1988	0.010	(0.028)	0.003	0.011	(0.028)	0.004
1989	-0.008	(0.028)	-0.002	-0.006	(0.028)	-0.002
1990	-0.101	(0.030)	-0.030	-0.099	(0.030)	-0.029
Quarter dummies:						
2nd quarter	-0.015	(0.018)	-0.005	-0.014	(0.018)	-0.004
3rd quarter	-0.013	(0.018)	-0.004	-0.012	(0.018)	-0.004
4th quarter	-0.031	(0.018)	-0.010	-0.031	(0.018)	-0.009
Highest education qualification:						
Other	0.088	(0.034)	0.028	0.088	(0.034)	0.028
O levels	0.069	(0.020)	0.022	0.069	(0.020)	0.022
Lower vocational	0.118	(0.028)	0.038	0.118	(0.028)	0.038
5+ O levels	0.061	(0.024)	0.019	0.061	(0.024)	0.019
Middle vocational	-0.061	(0.030)	-0.018	-0.061	(0.030)	-0.018
A levels	0.087	(0.028)	0.027	0.086	(0.028)	0.027
Higher vocational	0.185	(0.024)	0.060	0.184	(0.024)	0.060
Degree	0.239	(0.025)	0.078	0.240	(0.025)	0.078
Industry 1981 job:						
Energy and water	-0.138	(0.060)	-0.040	-0.137	(0.060)	-0.040
Minerals	0.170	(0.044)	0.055	0.170	(0.044)	0.055
Metals	0.131	(0.031)	0.042	0.131	(0.031)	0.042
Other manufacturing	0.165	(0.027)	0.053	0.165	(0.027)	0.053
Construction	0.110	(0.083)	0.035	0.110	(0.083)	0.035
Wholesale and retail trade	0.150	(0.023)	0.048	0.151	(0.023)	0.048
Transport and communication	0.028	(0.036)	0.009	0.028	(0.036)	0.009
Finance	-0.027	(0.024)	-0.008	-0.027	(0.024)	-0.008
Other services	0.094	(0.019)	0.029	0.094	(0.019)	0.029
1981 region:						
South-East	-0.030	(0.022)	-0.009	-0.030	(0.022)	-0.009
South-West	-0.086	(0.028)	-0.026	-0.086	(0.028)	-0.026
Wales	-0.134	(0.035)	-0.039	-0.134	(0.035)	-0.039
West Midlands	-0.068	(0.027)	-0.020	-0.068	(0.027)	-0.020
East Midlands	-0.008	(0.028)	-0.003	-0.008	(0.028)	-0.003
East Anglia	-0.105	(0.035)	-0.031	-0.105	(0.035)	-0.031
Yorkshire and Humberside	-0.145	(0.028)	-0.043	-0.146	(0.028)	-0.043
North-West	-0.065	(0.025)	-0.020	-0.066	(0.025)	-0.020
North	-0.123	(0.033)	-0.036	-0.123	(0.033)	-0.036
Scotland	-0.098	(0.026)	-0.029	-0.099	(0.026)	-0.030
Employer size 1981 job:						
10–24	-0.030	(0.022)	-0.009	-0.029	(0.022)	-0.009
25–99	-0.098	(0.020)	-0.029	-0.098	(0.020)	-0.029
100–500	-0.065	(0.020)	-0.020	-0.064	(0.020)	-0.019
500+	-0.071	(0.022)	-0.022	-0.071	(0.022)	-0.022
Union member 1981	-0.110	(0.014)	-0.034	-0.110	(0.014)	-0.034
Private sector 1981	0.096	(0.018)	0.029	0.096	(0.018)	0.029
Part-time 1981	-0.047	(0.022)	-0.014	-0.047	(0.022)	-0.014
Times moved 1958 to 1974	0.007	(0.004)	0.002	0.007	(0.004)	0.002
Mother employed 1974	-0.028	(0.013)	-0.008	-0.027	(0.013)	-0.008
Number of observations		51162			51162	
Pseudo R^2		0.0107			0.0107	

TABLE B.10

Training and the Determinants of Female Mobility III: NCDS

Variable	Coef.	(S.E.)	Marg. effect	Coef.	(S.E.)	Marg. effect
Constant	-0.736	(0.043)		-0.734	(0.043)	
Non-qualification training	-0.114	(0.038)	-0.034	-0.114	(0.038)	-0.034
Qualification training	0.108	(0.031)	0.034			
Other				0.071	(0.082)	0.022
Lower vocational				0.146	(0.062)	0.047
Middle vocational				0.097	(0.101)	0.031
Higher vocational				0.127	(0.045)	0.041
Degree				-0.026	(0.101)	-0.008
Year dummies:						
1982	0.007	(0.027)	0.002	0.007	(0.027)	0.002
1983	0.066	(0.027)	0.021	0.067	(0.027)	0.021
1984	0.014	(0.028)	0.004	0.015	(0.028)	0.005
1985	0.004	(0.028)	0.001	0.004	(0.028)	0.001
1986	-0.033	(0.028)	-0.010	-0.033	(0.028)	-0.010
1987	-0.001	(0.028)	0.000	-0.001	(0.028)	0.000
1988	0.012	(0.028)	0.004	0.012	(0.028)	0.004
1989	-0.005	(0.028)	-0.001	-0.004	(0.028)	-0.001
1990	-0.096	(0.030)	-0.029	-0.096	(0.030)	-0.029
Quarter dummies:						
2nd quarter	-0.014	(0.018)	-0.004	-0.014	(0.018)	-0.004
3rd quarter	-0.012	(0.018)	-0.004	-0.012	(0.018)	-0.004
4th quarter	-0.031	(0.018)	-0.009	-0.031	(0.018)	-0.010
Highest education qualification:						
Other	0.087	(0.034)	0.027	0.087	(0.034)	0.027
O levels	0.069	(0.020)	0.022	0.069	(0.020)	0.022
Lower vocational	0.118	(0.028)	0.037	0.117	(0.028)	0.037
5+ O levels	0.060	(0.024)	0.019	0.061	(0.024)	0.019
Middle vocational	-0.059	(0.030)	-0.018	-0.059	(0.030)	-0.018
A levels	0.086	(0.028)	0.027	0.087	(0.028)	0.027
Higher vocational	0.183	(0.024)	0.059	0.184	(0.024)	0.059
Degree	0.240	(0.025)	0.078	0.241	(0.025)	0.079
Industry 1981 job:						
Energy and water	-0.135	(0.060)	-0.039	-0.135	(0.060)	-0.039
Minerals	0.173	(0.044)	0.056	0.172	(0.044)	0.056
Metals	0.131	(0.031)	0.042	0.130	(0.031)	0.041
Other manufacturing	0.165	(0.027)	0.053	0.165	(0.027)	0.053
Construction	0.111	(0.083)	0.036	0.111	(0.083)	0.035
Wholesale and retail trade	0.151	(0.023)	0.048	0.151	(0.023)	0.048
Transport and communication	0.029	(0.036)	0.009	0.029	(0.036)	0.009
Finance	-0.025	(0.024)	-0.007	-0.025	(0.024)	-0.008
Other services	0.094	(0.019)	0.029	0.094	(0.019)	0.029
1981 region:						
South-East	-0.030	(0.022)	-0.009	-0.030	(0.022)	-0.009
South-West	-0.088	(0.028)	-0.026	-0.087	(0.028)	-0.026
Wales	-0.132	(0.035)	-0.039	-0.133	(0.035)	-0.039
West Midlands	-0.068	(0.027)	-0.021	-0.068	(0.027)	-0.020
East Midlands	-0.010	(0.028)	-0.003	-0.010	(0.029)	-0.003
East Anglia	-0.105	(0.035)	-0.031	-0.106	(0.035)	-0.031
Yorkshire and Humberside	-0.146	(0.028)	-0.043	-0.146	(0.028)	-0.043
North-West	-0.066	(0.025)	-0.020	-0.066	(0.025)	-0.020
North	-0.124	(0.033)	-0.036	-0.124	(0.033)	-0.037
Scotland	-0.101	(0.026)	-0.030	-0.101	(0.026)	-0.030
Employer size 1981 job:						
10–24	-0.027	(0.022)	-0.008	-0.028	(0.022)	-0.009
25–99	-0.097	(0.020)	-0.029	-0.098	(0.020)	-0.029
100–500	-0.064	(0.020)	-0.020	-0.065	(0.020)	-0.020
500+	-0.071	(0.022)	-0.022	-0.072	(0.022)	-0.022
Union member 1981	-0.110	(0.014)	-0.034	-0.110	(0.014)	-0.034
Private sector 1981	0.095	(0.018)	0.029	0.095	(0.018)	0.029
Part-time 1981	-0.046	(0.022)	-0.014	-0.047	(0.022)	-0.014
Times moved 1958 to 1974	0.007	(0.004)	0.002	0.007	(0.004)	0.002
Mother employed 1974	-0.027	(0.013)	-0.008	-0.027	(0.013)	-0.008
Number of observations		51162			51162	
Pseudo R^2		0.0111			0.0111	

TABLE B.11

Training and the Determinants of Female Mobility IV: NCDS

Variable	Coef.	(S.E.)	Marg. effect	Coef.	(S.E.)	Marg. effect
Constant	-0.733	(0.043)		-0.734	(0.043)	
Employer qualification training	0.007	(0.040)	0.002			
Employer non-qualification training	0.000	(0.052)	0.000			
Other qualification training	0.255	(0.047)	0.084			
Other non-qualification training	-0.241	(0.056)	-0.067			
Employer continuing training				0.005	(0.039)	0.002
Employer completed training				0.005	(0.053)	0.001
Other continuing training				0.093	(0.044)	0.030
Other completed training				-0.060	(0.059)	-0.018
Year dummies:						
1982	0.006	(0.027)	0.002	0.006	(0.027)	0.002
1983	0.066	(0.027)	0.021	0.067	(0.027)	0.021
1984	0.013	(0.028)	0.004	0.013	(0.028)	0.004
1985	0.004	(0.028)	0.001	0.002	(0.028)	0.001
1986	-0.034	(0.028)	-0.010	-0.035	(0.028)	-0.011
1987	-0.004	(0.028)	-0.001	-0.004	(0.028)	-0.001
1988	0.009	(0.028)	0.003	0.010	(0.028)	0.003
1989	-0.007	(0.028)	-0.002	-0.008	(0.028)	-0.002
1990	-0.099	(0.030)	-0.029	-0.101	(0.030)	-0.030
Quarter dummies:						
2nd quarter	-0.014	(0.018)	-0.004	-0.014	(0.018)	-0.004
3rd quarter	-0.012	(0.018)	-0.004	-0.012	(0.018)	-0.004
4th quarter	-0.032	(0.018)	-0.010	-0.031	(0.018)	-0.010
Highest education qualification:						
Other	0.085	(0.034)	0.027	0.087	(0.034)	0.027
O levels	0.069	(0.020)	0.021	0.069	(0.020)	0.022
Lower vocational	0.118	(0.028)	0.038	0.117	(0.028)	0.037
5+ O levels	0.058	(0.024)	0.018	0.061	(0.024)	0.019
Middle vocational	-0.059	(0.030)	-0.018	-0.061	(0.030)	-0.019
A levels	0.087	(0.028)	0.027	0.087	(0.028)	0.027
Higher vocational	0.187	(0.024)	0.060	0.184	(0.024)	0.059
Degree	0.240	(0.025)	0.078	0.240	(0.025)	0.078
Industry 1981 job:						
Energy and water	-0.138	(0.060)	-0.040	-0.137	(0.060)	-0.040
Minerals	0.176	(0.044)	0.057	0.169	(0.044)	0.055
Metals	0.131	(0.031)	0.042	0.131	(0.031)	0.042
Other manufacturing	0.165	(0.027)	0.053	0.165	(0.027)	0.053
Construction	0.114	(0.083)	0.036	0.110	(0.083)	0.035
Wholesale and retail trade	0.151	(0.023)	0.048	0.150	(0.023)	0.048
Transport and communication	0.030	(0.036)	0.009	0.028	(0.036)	0.009
Finance	-0.022	(0.024)	-0.007	-0.026	(0.024)	-0.008
Other services	0.094	(0.019)	0.029	0.094	(0.019)	0.029
1981 region:						
South-East	-0.030	(0.022)	-0.009	-0.030	(0.022)	-0.009
South-West	-0.088	(0.028)	-0.026	-0.086	(0.028)	-0.026
Wales	-0.132	(0.035)	-0.039	-0.134	(0.035)	-0.039
West Midlands	-0.069	(0.027)	-0.021	-0.067	(0.027)	-0.020
East Midlands	-0.007	(0.029)	-0.002	-0.007	(0.028)	-0.002
East Anglia	-0.106	(0.035)	-0.031	-0.105	(0.035)	-0.031
Yorkshire and Humberside	-0.147	(0.028)	-0.043	-0.146	(0.028)	-0.043
North-West	-0.064	(0.025)	-0.019	-0.065	(0.025)	-0.020
North	-0.123	(0.033)	-0.036	-0.122	(0.033)	-0.036
Scotland	-0.099	(0.026)	-0.029	-0.098	(0.026)	-0.029
Employer size 1981 job:						
10-24	-0.029	(0.022)	-0.009	-0.030	(0.022)	-0.009
25-99	-0.098	(0.020)	-0.030	-0.098	(0.020)	-0.029
100-500	-0.066	(0.020)	-0.020	-0.064	(0.020)	-0.020
500+	-0.073	(0.022)	-0.022	-0.071	(0.022)	-0.022
Union member 1981	-0.109	(0.014)	-0.033	-0.110	(0.014)	-0.033
Private sector 1981	0.094	(0.018)	0.029	0.096	(0.018)	0.029
Part-time 1981	-0.046	(0.022)	-0.014	-0.047	(0.022)	-0.014
Times moved 1958 to 1974	0.007	(0.004)	0.002	0.007	(0.004)	0.002
Mother employed 1974	-0.028	(0.013)	-0.009	-0.028	(0.013)	-0.009
Number of observations	51162			51162		
Pseudo R^2	0.0115			0.0108		

TABLE B.12

Training and the Determinants of Male Mobility I: QLFS

Variable	Coef.	(S.E.)	Marg. effect	Coef.	(S.E.)	Marg. effect
Constant	-1.052	(0.160)		-1.031	(0.161)	
Any training in last 4 weeks				-0.042	(0.038)	-0.004
Panel dummies:						
Jun 1992	0.094	(0.051)	0.010	0.092	(0.051)	0.009
Sep 1992	0.089	(0.050)	0.009	0.088	(0.051)	0.009
Dec 1992	0.105	(0.051)	0.011	0.104	(0.051)	0.011
Mar 1993	0.068	(0.052)	0.007	0.068	(0.052)	0.007
Jun 1993	0.089	(0.051)	0.009	0.088	(0.051)	0.009
Sep 1993	0.191	(0.050)	0.021	0.191	(0.050)	0.021
Highest education qualification:						
Degree	0.191	(0.050)	0.021	0.196	(0.050)	0.021
Higher vocational	0.152	(0.057)	0.016	0.158	(0.057)	0.017
Middle vocational	0.092	(0.045)	0.009	0.096	(0.045)	0.010
Lower vocational	0.029	(0.044)	0.003	0.032	(0.044)	0.003
Other	0.221	(0.054)	0.025	0.223	(0.054)	0.025
Industry:						
Energy and water	0.093	(0.083)	0.010	0.093	(0.083)	0.010
Minerals	-0.037	(0.079)	-0.003	-0.040	(0.079)	-0.004
Metals	0.221	(0.047)	0.024	0.217	(0.047)	0.023
Other manufacturing	0.134	(0.055)	0.014	0.129	(0.056)	0.014
Construction	0.250	(0.059)	0.029	0.246	(0.059)	0.028
Wholesale and retail trade	0.344	(0.047)	0.041	0.339	(0.048)	0.040
Transport and communication	0.129	(0.057)	0.014	0.126	(0.057)	0.013
Finance	0.378	(0.049)	0.047	0.377	(0.049)	0.047
Region:						
South-East	0.062	(0.053)	0.006	0.063	(0.053)	0.006
South-West	-0.039	(0.066)	-0.004	-0.039	(0.066)	-0.004
Wales	-0.051	(0.081)	-0.005	-0.051	(0.081)	-0.005
West Midlands	0.014	(0.063)	0.001	0.014	(0.063)	0.001
East Midlands	0.067	(0.065)	0.007	0.067	(0.065)	0.007
East Anglia	0.137	(0.078)	0.015	0.136	(0.078)	0.015
Yorkshire and Humberside	0.092	(0.062)	0.009	0.093	(0.062)	0.010
North-West	0.087	(0.059)	0.009	0.087	(0.059)	0.009
North	0.104	(0.072)	0.011	0.105	(0.072)	0.011
Scotland	0.060	(0.062)	0.006	0.060	(0.062)	0.006
Age	-0.032	(0.008)	-0.003	-0.032	(0.008)	-0.003
$Age^2/100$	0.019	(0.010)	0.002	0.019	(0.010)	0.002
Part-time	0.497	(0.065)	0.070	0.498	(0.065)	0.070
Non-white	-0.209	(0.085)	-0.017	-0.208	(0.085)	-0.017
Employer size 25+	-0.159	(0.030)	-0.016	-0.157	(0.030)	-0.016
Number of observations		26232			26232	
Pseudo R^2		0.055			0.055	

TABLE B.13

Training and the Determinants of Male Mobility II: QLFS

Variable	Coef.	(S.E.)	Marg. effect	Coef.	(S.E.)	Marg. effect
Constant	-1.034	(0.161)		-0.912	(0.212)	
Employer-funded training	-0.129	(0.051)	-0.011			
Other training	0.061	(0.052)	0.006			
Completed training				-0.176	(0.104)	-0.014
Continuing training				-0.024	(0.058)	-0.002
Panel dummies:						
Jun 1992	0.093	(0.051)	0.009	0.095	(0.051)	0.009
Sep 1992	0.089	(0.051)	0.009	0.089	(0.051)	0.009
Dec 1992	0.106	(0.051)	0.011	0.105	(0.051)	0.010
Mar 1993	0.069	(0.052)	0.007			
Jun 1993	0.088	(0.051)	0.009			
Sep 1993	0.192	(0.050)	0.021			
Highest education qualification:						
Degree	0.200	(0.050)	0.022	0.199	(0.066)	0.021
Higher vocational	0.162	(0.057)	0.017	0.160	(0.074)	0.017
Middle vocational	0.096	(0.045)	0.010	0.098	(0.055)	0.010
Lower vocational	0.031	(0.044)	0.003	-0.011	(0.060)	-0.001
Other	0.221	(0.054)	0.025	0.212	(0.074)	0.023
Industry:						
Energy and water	0.098	(0.083)	0.010	0.145	(0.104)	0.015
Minerals	-0.037	(0.079)	-0.003	-0.025	(0.104)	-0.002
Metals	0.218	(0.047)	0.024	0.236	(0.062)	0.025
Other manufacturing	0.129	(0.056)	0.013	0.044	(0.077)	0.004
Construction	0.246	(0.059)	0.028	0.166	(0.082)	0.017
Wholesale and retail trade	0.338	(0.048)	0.040	0.367	(0.064)	0.043
Transport and communication	0.127	(0.057)	0.013	0.127	(0.076)	0.013
Finance	0.378	(0.049)	0.047	0.394	(0.066)	0.048
Region:						
South-East	0.063	(0.053)	0.006	0.082	(0.070)	0.008
South-West	-0.039	(0.066)	-0.004	-0.138	(0.091)	-0.012
Wales	-0.048	(0.081)	-0.004	-0.022	(0.108)	-0.002
West Midlands	0.014	(0.063)	0.001	-0.072	(0.086)	-0.006
East Midlands	0.066	(0.065)	0.007	0.065	(0.086)	0.006
East Anglia	0.136	(0.078)	0.015	0.209	(0.100)	0.023
Yorkshire and Humberside	0.092	(0.062)	0.009	0.043	(0.084)	0.004
North-West	0.085	(0.059)	0.009	0.083	(0.079)	0.008
North	0.104	(0.072)	0.011	0.109	(0.095)	0.011
Scotland	0.057	(0.062)	0.006	0.088	(0.082)	0.009
Age	-0.032	(0.008)	-0.003	-0.040	(0.010)	-0.004
Age^2/100	0.019	(0.010)	0.002	0.032	(0.013)	0.003
Part-time	0.484	(0.066)	0.067	0.433	(0.090)	0.057
Non-white	-0.209	(0.085)	-0.017	-0.189	(0.111)	-0.015
Employer size 25+	-0.157	(0.030)	-0.016	-0.157	(0.040)	-0.016
Number of observations		26232			15131	
Pseudo R^2		0.055			0.053	

TABLE B.14

Training and the Determinants of Male Mobility III: QLFS

Variable	Coef.	(S.E.)	Marg. effect	Coef.	(S.E.)	Marg. effect
Constant	-0.924	(0.213)		-0.900	(0.215)	
Non-qualification training	-0.099	(0.067)	-0.009	-0.097	(0.067)	-0.008
Qualification training	-0.006	(0.075)	-0.001			
Other				-0.053	(0.128)	-0.005
Lower vocational				0.416	(0.446)	0.054
Middle vocational				-0.033	(0.134)	-0.003
Higher vocational				-0.539	(0.273)	-0.032
Degree				0.258	(0.136)	0.030
Panel dummies:						
Jun 1992	0.095	(0.051)	0.009	0.094	(0.051)	0.009
Sep 1992	0.089	(0.051)	0.009	0.089	(0.051)	0.009
Dec 1992	0.105	(0.051)	0.010	0.104	(0.051)	0.010
Highest education qualification:						
Degree	0.200	(0.066)	0.021	0.192	(0.066)	0.020
Higher vocational	0.160	(0.074)	0.017	0.158	(0.075)	0.016
Middle vocational	0.098	(0.055)	0.010	0.101	(0.055)	0.010
Lower vocational	-0.011	(0.060)	-0.001	-0.007	(0.060)	-0.001
Other	0.212	(0.074)	0.023	0.211	(0.074)	0.023
Industry:						
Energy and water	0.142	(0.103)	0.015	0.147	(0.104)	0.015
Minerals	-0.026	(0.104)	-0.002	-0.021	(0.104)	-0.002
Metals	0.235	(0.062)	0.025	0.236	(0.062)	0.025
Other manufacturing	0.043	(0.077)	0.004	0.041	(0.077)	0.004
Construction	0.164	(0.082)	0.017	0.164	(0.082)	0.017
Wholesale and retail trade	0.366	(0.064)	0.043	0.366	(0.064)	0.043
Transport and communication	0.126	(0.076)	0.013	0.128	(0.076)	0.013
Finance	0.393	(0.066)	0.048	0.387	(0.066)	0.047
Region:						
South-East	0.083	(0.069)	0.008	0.084	(0.070)	0.008
South-West	-0.138	(0.091)	-0.012	-0.138	(0.091)	-0.012
Wales	-0.020	(0.108)	-0.002	-0.015	(0.108)	-0.001
West Midlands	-0.073	(0.086)	-0.006	-0.068	(0.086)	-0.006
East Midland	0.064	(0.086)	0.006	0.065	(0.086)	0.006
East Anglia	0.208	(0.100)	0.023	0.209	(0.100)	0.023
Yorkshire and Humberside	0.044	(0.084)	0.004	0.043	(0.084)	0.004
North-West	0.084	(0.079)	0.008	0.087	(0.079)	0.009
North	0.109	(0.095)	0.011	0.110	(0.095)	0.011
Scotland	0.090	(0.082)	0.009	0.092	(0.082)	0.009
Age	-0.040	(0.010)	-0.004	-0.041	(0.011)	-0.004
Age^2/100	0.031	(0.014)	0.003	0.033	(0.014)	0.003
Part-time	0.431	(0.091)	0.056	0.431	(0.091)	0.056
Non-white	-0.188	(0.111)	-0.015	-0.192	(0.111)	-0.015
Employer size 25+	-0.158	(0.040)	-0.016	-0.157	(0.040)	-0.016
Number of observations	15131			15131		
Pseudo R^2	0.053			0.055		

TABLE B.15

Training and the Determinants of Male Mobility IV: QLFS

Variable	Coef.	(S.E.)	Marg. effect	Coef.	(S.E.)	Marg. effect
Constant	-0.900	(0.214)		-0.911	(0.212)	
Employer qualification training	-0.243	(0.108)	-0.019			
Employer non-qualification training	-0.062	(0.084)	-0.005			
Other qualification training	0.243	(0.100)	0.027			
Other non-qualification training	-0.159	(0.104)	-0.013			
Employer continuing training				-0.088	(0.076)	-0.008
Employer completed training				-0.279	(0.139)	-0.021
Other continuing training				0.054	(0.081)	0.005
Other completed training				-0.033	(0.154)	-0.003
Panel dummies:						
Jun 1992	0.098	(0.051)	0.009	0.096	(0.051)	0.009
Sep 1992	0.091	(0.051)	0.009	0.089	(0.051)	0.009
Dec 1992	0.108	(0.051)	0.010	0.107	(0.051)	0.010
Highest education qualification:						
Degree	0.199	(0.066)	0.021	0.201	(0.066)	0.021
Higher vocational	0.164	(0.074)	0.017	0.164	(0.074)	0.017
Middle vocational	0.098	(0.055)	0.009	0.098	(0.055)	0.010
Lower vocational	-0.014	(0.060)	-0.001	-0.012	(0.060)	-0.001
Other	0.212	(0.074)	0.023	0.211	(0.074)	0.023
Industry:						
Energy and water	0.147	(0.104)	0.015	0.148	(0.103)	0.015
Minerals	-0.021	(0.104)	-0.002	-0.023	(0.104)	-0.002
Metals	0.238	(0.062)	0.025	0.237	(0.062)	0.025
Other manufacturing	0.040	(0.077)	0.004	0.043	(0.077)	0.004
Construction	0.165	(0.082)	0.017	0.167	(0.082)	0.018
Wholesale and retail trade	0.361	(0.064)	0.042	0.366	(0.064)	0.043
Transport and communication	0.125	(0.076)	0.013	0.128	(0.076)	0.013
Finance	0.392	(0.066)	0.047	0.395	(0.066)	0.048
Region:						
South-East	0.084	(0.070)	0.008	0.082	(0.070)	0.008
South-West	-0.129	(0.091)	-0.011	-0.138	(0.091)	-0.012
Wales	-0.019	(0.108)	-0.002	-0.019	(0.108)	-0.002
West Midlands	-0.069	(0.086)	-0.006	-0.072	(0.086)	-0.006
East Midlands	0.065	(0.086)	0.006	0.066	(0.086)	0.006
East Anglia	0.211	(0.100)	0.023	0.209	(0.100)	0.023
Yorkshire and Humberside	0.045	(0.084)	0.004	0.041	(0.084)	0.004
North-West	0.084	(0.079)	0.008	0.081	(0.079)	0.008
North	0.117	(0.095)	0.012	0.109	(0.095)	0.011
Scotland	0.092	(0.082)	0.009	0.086	(0.082)	0.008
Age	-0.041	(0.010)	-0.004	-0.040	(0.010)	-0.004
$Age^2/100$	0.033	(0.014)	0.003	0.032	(0.013)	0.003
Part-time	0.396	(0.092)	0.050	0.422	(0.091)	0.055
Non-white	-0.188	(0.111)	-0.015	-0.188	(0.111)	-0.015
Employer size 25+	-0.154	(0.040)	-0.015	-0.157	(0.040)	-0.016
Number of observations		15131			15131	
Pseudo R^2		0.055			0.054	

TABLE B.16

Training and the Determinants of Young Male Mobility I: QLFS

Variable	Coef.	(S.E.)	Marg. effect	Coef.	(S.E.)	Marg. effect
Constant	-0.283	(0.972)		-0.099	(0.979)	
Any training in last 4 weeks				-0.101	(0.060)	-0.015
Panel dummies:						
Jun 1992	0.010	(0.087)	0.002	0.003	(0.087)	0.000
Sep 1992	0.134	(0.083)	0.022	0.129	(0.083)	0.021
Dec 1992	0.040	(0.086)	0.006	0.037	(0.086)	0.006
Mar 1993	-0.073	(0.089)	-0.011	-0.073	(0.089)	-0.011
Jun 1993	0.129	(0.084)	0.021	0.121	(0.084)	0.020
Sep 1993	0.246	(0.083)	0.043	0.247	(0.083)	0.043
Highest education qualification:						
Degree	0.307	(0.104)	0.055	0.330	(0.105)	0.060
Higher vocational	0.303	(0.104)	0.055	0.323	(0.104)	0.059
Middle vocational	0.129	(0.085)	0.021	0.141	(0.086)	0.023
Lower vocational	0.083	(0.080)	0.013	0.092	(0.080)	0.014
Other	0.465	(0.135)	0.094	0.474	(0.135)	0.097
Industry:						
Energy and water	-0.141	(0.190)	-0.020	-0.137	(0.190)	-0.019
Minerals	-0.092	(0.145)	-0.013	-0.101	(0.145)	-0.014
Metals	0.135	(0.087)	0.022	0.126	(0.087)	0.020
Other manufacturing	0.102	(0.098)	0.017	0.086	(0.098)	0.014
Construction	0.134	(0.106)	0.022	0.127	(0.106)	0.021
Wholesale and retail trade	0.317	(0.081)	0.055	0.305	(0.081)	0.052
Transport and communication	0.091	(0.106)	0.015	0.082	(0.106)	0.013
Finance	0.279	(0.089)	0.049	0.278	(0.089)	0.049
Region:						
South-East	0.237	(0.090)	0.040	0.239	(0.090)	0.040
South-West	0.074	(0.112)	0.012	0.078	(0.112)	0.012
Wales	0.096	(0.133)	0.016	0.101	(0.133)	0.016
West Midlands	0.125	(0.106)	0.020	0.128	(0.106)	0.021
East Midlands	0.017	(0.115)	0.003	0.021	(0.115)	0.003
East Anglia	0.212	(0.135)	0.037	0.213	(0.135)	0.037
Yorkshire and Humberside	0.101	(0.107)	0.016	0.108	(0.108)	0.018
North-West	0.130	(0.100)	0.021	0.132	(0.100)	0.022
North	0.178	(0.123)	0.030	0.188	(0.123)	0.032
Scotland	0.046	(0.108)	0.007	0.045	(0.108)	0.007
Age	-0.096	(0.084)	-0.015	-0.108	(0.084)	-0.017
Age²/100	0.146	(0.179)	0.022	0.169	(0.180)	0.026
Part-time	0.453	(0.092)	0.090	0.453	(0.092)	0.090
Non-white	-0.203	(0.143)	-0.027	-0.199	(0.143)	-0.027
Employer size 25+	-0.217	(0.049)	-0.035	-0.213	(0.049)	-0.035
Number of observations		6474			6474	
Pseudo R²		0.052			0.053	

TABLE B.17

Training and the Determinants of Young Male Mobility II: QLFS

Variable	Coef.	(S.E.)	Marg. effect	Coef.	(S.E.)	Marg. effect
Constant	-0.072	(0.980)		-0.988	(1.303)	
Employer-funded training	-0.228	(0.081)	-0.031			
Other training	0.029	(0.079)	0.005			
Completed training				-0.118	(0.181)	-0.016
Continuing training				-0.138	(0.087)	-0.019
Panel dummies:						
Jun 1992	0.004	(0.087)	0.001	0.001	(0.088)	0.000
Sep 1992	0.132	(0.083)	0.021	0.130	(0.083)	0.020
Dec 1992	0.044	(0.086)	0.007	0.035	(0.086)	0.005
Mar 1993	-0.071	(0.090)	-0.010			
Jun 1993	0.124	(0.084)	0.020			
Sep 1993	0.249	(0.084)	0.043			
Highest education qualification:						
Degree	0.338	(0.105)	0.061	0.173	(0.141)	0.028
Higher vocational	0.334	(0.105)	0.061	0.244	(0.133)	0.041
Middle vocational	0.146	(0.086)	0.023	0.047	(0.107)	0.007
Lower vocational	0.089	(0.081)	0.014	-0.050	(0.104)	-0.007
Other	0.471	(0.136)	0.096	0.412	(0.197)	0.078
Industry:						
Energy and water	-0.129	(0.190)	-0.018	-0.288	(0.264)	-0.034
Minerals	-0.098	(0.145)	-0.014	-0.142	(0.191)	-0.019
Metals	0.125	(0.087)	0.020	0.147	(0.116)	0.023
Other manufacturing	0.082	(0.098)	0.013	-0.073	(0.138)	-0.010
Construction	0.118	(0.106)	0.019	0.095	(0.142)	0.015
Wholesale and retail trade	0.296	(0.081)	0.050	0.344	(0.108)	0.057
Transport and communication	0.079	(0.106)	0.013	0.212	(0.135)	0.035
Finance	0.275	(0.089)	0.048	0.277	(0.121)	0.047
Region:						
South-East	0.236	(0.090)	0.040	0.273	(0.118)	0.045
South-West	0.078	(0.112)	0.012	0.108	(0.146)	0.017
Wales	0.103	(0.133)	0.017	0.340	(0.170)	0.061
West Midlands	0.127	(0.107)	0.021	-0.072	(0.151)	-0.010
East Midlands	0.017	(0.116)	0.003	0.023	(0.152)	0.003
East Anglia	0.210	(0.135)	0.037	0.213	(0.172)	0.035
Yorkshire and Humberside	0.105	(0.108)	0.017	0.066	(0.144)	0.010
North-West	0.127	(0.100)	0.021	0.130	(0.132)	0.020
North	0.185	(0.123)	0.032	0.263	(0.159)	0.045
Scotland	0.038	(0.108)	0.006	0.045	(0.145)	0.007
Age	-0.110	(0.084)	-0.017	-0.023	(0.112)	-0.003
Age^2/100	0.172	(0.180)	0.026	-0.015	(0.240)	-0.002
Part-time	0.424	(0.093)	0.083	0.420	(0.127)	0.079
Non-white	-0.201	(0.143)	-0.027	-0.061	(0.185)	-0.008
Employer size 25+	-0.212	(0.049)	-0.034	-0.190	(0.066)	-0.029
Number of observations	6474			3776		
Pseudo R^2	0.054			0.054		

123

TABLE B.18

Training and the Determinants of Young Male Mobility III: QLFS

Variable	Coef.	(S.E.)	Marg. effect	Coef.	(S.E.)	Marg. effect
Constant	-1.026	(1.305)		-0.858	(1.327)	
Non-qualification training	-0.161	(0.123)	-0.021	-0.155	(0.123)	-0.020
Qualification training	-0.118	(0.099)	-0.016			
Other				-0.188	(0.190)	-0.024
Lower vocational				-0.024	(0.657)	-0.003
Middle vocational				-0.126	(0.152)	-0.017
Higher vocational				-0.524	(0.293)	-0.052
Degree				0.151	(0.190)	0.024
Panel dummies:						
Jun 1992	0.003	(0.088)	0.000	0.000	(0.088)	0.000
Sep 1992	0.132	(0.083)	0.020	0.131	(0.084)	0.020
Dec 1992	0.036	(0.086)	0.005	0.037	(0.086)	0.005
Highest education qualification:						
Degree	0.173	(0.141)	0.028	0.153	(0.142)	0.024
Higher vocational	0.243	(0.133)	0.040	0.242	(0.133)	0.040
Middle vocational	0.046	(0.107)	0.007	0.051	(0.107)	0.008
Lower vocational	-0.051	(0.104)	-0.007	-0.043	(0.104)	-0.006
Other	0.412	(0.197)	0.078	0.411	(0.198)	0.077
Industry:						
Energy and water	-0.290	(0.264)	-0.034	-0.289	(0.264)	-0.034
Minerals	-0.143	(0.191)	-0.019	-0.140	(0.192)	-0.018
Metals	0.145	(0.115)	0.022	0.139	(0.116)	0.021
Other manufacturing	-0.074	(0.138)	-0.010	-0.080	(0.138)	-0.011
Construction	0.093	(0.142)	0.014	0.084	(0.143)	0.013
Wholesale and retail trade	0.344	(0.108)	0.057	0.336	(0.109)	0.055
Transport and communication	0.211	(0.135)	0.035	0.210	(0.136)	0.034
Finance	0.276	(0.121)	0.046	0.259	(0.122)	0.043
Region:						
South-East	0.272	(0.118)	0.044	0.269	(0.118)	0.044
South-West	0.105	(0.146)	0.016	0.108	(0.146)	0.017
Wales	0.338	(0.170)	0.061	0.342	(0.170)	0.061
West Midlands	-0.073	(0.151)	-0.010	-0.069	(0.151)	-0.010
East Midlands	0.022	(0.152)	0.003	0.029	(0.152)	0.004
East Anglia	0.213	(0.172)	0.035	0.208	(0.172)	0.034
Yorkshire and Humberside	0.064	(0.144)	0.010	0.064	(0.144)	0.010
North-West	0.129	(0.132)	0.020	0.129	(0.132)	0.020
North	0.261	(0.159)	0.044	0.261	(0.160)	0.044
Scotland	0.043	(0.145)	0.006	0.042	(0.145)	0.006
Age	-0.020	(0.113)	-0.003	-0.033	(0.114)	-0.005
$Age^2/100$	-0.020	(0.240)	-0.003	0.007	(0.244)	0.001
Part-time	0.419	(0.127)	0.079	0.417	(0.128)	0.078
Non-white	-0.061	(0.184)	-0.008	-0.070	(0.185)	-0.010
Employer size 25+	-0.190	(0.066)	-0.029	-0.191	(0.066)	-0.029
Number of observations	3776			3776		
Pseudo R^2	0.054			0.056		

TABLE B.19

Training and the Determinants of Young Male Mobility IV: QLFS

Variable	Coef.	(S.E.)	Marg. effect	Coef.	(S.E.)	Marg. effect
Constant	-1.014	(1.308)		-0.990	(1.304)	
Employer qualification training	-0.342	(0.139)	-0.040			
Employer non-qualification training	-0.085	(0.160)	-0.012			
Other qualification training	0.114	(0.132)	0.018			
Other non-qualification training	-0.261	(0.184)	-0.032			
Employer continuing training				-0.279	(0.120)	-0.034
Employer completed training				-0.079	(0.222)	-0.011
Other continuing training				0.005	(0.115)	0.001
Other completed training				-0.193	(0.304)	-0.024
Panel dummies:						
Jun 1992	0.007	(0.088)	0.001	0.001	(0.088)	0.000
Sep 1992	0.138	(0.084)	0.021	0.134	(0.083)	0.020
Dec 1992	0.040	(0.087)	0.006	0.039	(0.086)	0.006
Highest education qualification:						
Degree	0.173	(0.141)	0.027	0.176	(0.141)	0.028
Higher vocational	0.254	(0.133)	0.042	0.250	(0.133)	0.042
Middle vocational	0.047	(0.107)	0.007	0.046	(0.107)	0.007
Lower vocational	-0.051	(0.104)	-0.007	-0.055	(0.104)	-0.008
Other	0.411	(0.198)	0.077	0.409	(0.197)	0.077
Industry:						
Energy and water	-0.294	(0.267)	-0.035	-0.294	(0.265)	-0.035
Minerals	-0.138	(0.192)	-0.018	-0.141	(0.191)	-0.019
Metals	0.147	(0.116)	0.023	0.145	(0.116)	0.022
Other manufacturing	-0.081	(0.138)	-0.011	-0.079	(0.138)	-0.011
Construction	0.095	(0.143)	0.014	0.091	(0.143)	0.014
Wholesale and retail trade	0.334	(0.109)	0.055	0.336	(0.109)	0.055
Transport and communication	0.204	(0.136)	0.033	0.205	(0.136)	0.033
Finance	0.268	(0.121)	0.045	0.269	(0.121)	0.045
Region:						
South-East	0.272	(0.118)	0.044	0.273	(0.118)	0.044
South-West	0.119	(0.146)	0.018	0.111	(0.146)	0.017
Wales	0.339	(0.170)	0.060	0.341	(0.170)	0.061
West Midlands	-0.071	(0.151)	-0.010	-0.075	(0.151)	-0.010
East Midlands	0.019	(0.152)	0.003	0.021	(0.152)	0.003
East Anglia	0.216	(0.172)	0.036	0.210	(0.172)	0.035
Yorkshire and Humberside	0.063	(0.144)	0.009	0.066	(0.144)	0.010
North-West	0.126	(0.133)	0.019	0.123	(0.132)	0.019
North	0.275	(0.160)	0.047	0.267	(0.160)	0.046
Scotland	0.048	(0.146)	0.007	0.045	(0.145)	0.007
Age	-0.019	(0.113)	-0.003	-0.021	(0.113)	-0.003
$Age^2/100$	-0.025	(0.241)	-0.004	-0.019	(0.240)	-0.003
Part-time	0.369	(0.129)	0.067	0.388	(0.129)	0.071
Non-white	-0.056	(0.184)	-0.008	-0.062	(0.184)	-0.009
Employer size 25+	-0.180	(0.067)	-0.027	-0.184	(0.067)	-0.028
Number of observations		3776			3776	
Pseudo R^2		0.058			0.056	

TABLE B.20

Training and the Determinants of Female Mobility I: QLFS

Variable	Coef.	(S.E.)	Marg. effect	Coef.	(S.E.)	Marg. effect
Constant	-0.270	(0.153)		-0.269	(0.153)	
Any training in last 4 weeks				-0.004	(0.035)	0.000
Panel dummies:						
Jun 1992	-0.022	(0.047)	-0.003	-0.023	(0.047)	-0.003
Sep 1992	0.073	(0.046)	0.009	0.073	(0.046)	0.009
Dec 1992	-0.017	(0.047)	-0.002	-0.017	(0.047)	-0.002
Mar 1993	-0.024	(0.047)	-0.003	-0.024	(0.047)	-0.003
Jun 1993	0.086	(0.046)	0.011	0.086	(0.046)	0.011
Sep 1993	0.085	(0.046)	0.011	0.085	(0.046)	0.011
Highest education qualification:						
Degree	0.212	(0.051)	0.029	0.213	(0.051)	0.029
Higher vocational	0.069	(0.049)	0.009	0.070	(0.050)	0.009
Middle vocational	0.041	(0.046)	0.005	0.042	(0.046)	0.005
Lower vocational	0.017	(0.036)	0.002	0.017	(0.036)	0.002
Other	-0.007	(0.063)	-0.001	-0.007	(0.063)	-0.001
Industry:						
Energy and water	-0.140	(0.152)	-0.015	-0.140	(0.152)	-0.015
Minerals	0.017	(0.106)	0.002	0.017	(0.106)	0.002
Metals	0.248	(0.058)	0.036	0.248	(0.058)	0.036
Other manufacturing	0.271	(0.051)	0.039	0.271	(0.051)	0.039
Construction	0.216	(0.094)	0.031	0.216	(0.094)	0.031
Wholesale and retail trade	0.269	(0.033)	0.037	0.269	(0.033)	0.037
Transport and communication	0.102	(0.071)	0.013	0.102	(0.071)	0.013
Finance	0.070	(0.041)	0.009	0.070	(0.041)	0.009
Region:						
South-East	-0.018	(0.049)	-0.002	-0.018	(0.049)	-0.002
South-West	-0.005	(0.058)	-0.001	-0.005	(0.058)	-0.001
Wales	-0.182	(0.074)	-0.019	-0.182	(0.074)	-0.019
West Midlands	-0.068	(0.057)	-0.008	-0.068	(0.057)	-0.008
East Midlands	-0.040	(0.060)	-0.005	-0.040	(0.060)	-0.005
East Anglia	-0.058	(0.075)	-0.007	-0.058	(0.075)	-0.007
Yorkshire and Humberside	-0.084	(0.057)	-0.010	-0.084	(0.057)	-0.010
North-West	-0.039	(0.054)	-0.005	-0.039	(0.054)	-0.005
North	-0.151	(0.067)	-0.017	-0.151	(0.067)	-0.017
Scotland	-0.075	(0.058)	-0.009	-0.076	(0.058)	-0.009
Age	-0.048	(0.008)	-0.006	-0.048	(0.008)	-0.006
Age²/100	0.029	(0.011)	0.004	0.029	(0.011)	0.004
Part-time	0.201	(0.028)	0.025	0.200	(0.028)	0.025
Non-white	-0.210	(0.081)	-0.022	-0.210	(0.081)	-0.022
Employer size 25+	-0.143	(0.026)	-0.018	-0.143	(0.026)	-0.018
Number of observations		25060			25060	
Pseudo R²		0.060			0.060	

TABLE B.21

Training and the Determinants of Female Mobility II: QLFS

Variable	Coef.	(S.E.)	Marg. effect	Coef.	(S.E.)	Marg. effect
Constant	-0.287	(0.153)		-0.540	(0.205)	
Employer-funded training	-0.146	(0.051)	-0.016			
Other training	0.110	(0.044)	0.014			
Completed training				-0.115	(0.094)	-0.012
Continuing training				0.029	(0.052)	0.003
Panel dummies:						
Jun 1992	-0.021	(0.047)	-0.003	-0.017	(0.047)	-0.002
Sep 1992	0.074	(0.046)	0.009	0.070	(0.046)	0.009
Dec 1992	-0.017	(0.047)	-0.002	-0.017	(0.047)	-0.002
Mar 1993	-0.025	(0.047)	-0.003			
Jun 1993	0.085	(0.046)	0.011			
Sep 1993	0.085	(0.046)	0.011			
Highest education qualification:						
Degree	0.220	(0.051)	0.031	0.283	(0.068)	0.040
Higher vocational	0.073	(0.050)	0.009	0.164	(0.065)	0.021
Middle vocational	0.043	(0.046)	0.005	0.120	(0.058)	0.015
Lower vocational	0.014	(0.036)	0.002	0.013	(0.048)	0.002
Other	-0.011	(0.063)	-0.001	-0.052	(0.093)	-0.006
Industry:						
Energy and water	-0.129	(0.151)	-0.014	-0.025	(0.199)	-0.003
Minerals	0.018	(0.106)	0.002	0.070	(0.138)	0.009
Metals	0.245	(0.058)	0.035	0.320	(0.074)	0.047
Other manufacturing	0.267	(0.051)	0.038	0.343	(0.067)	0.051
Construction	0.218	(0.094)	0.031	0.278	(0.126)	0.040
Wholesale and retail trade	0.265	(0.033)	0.036	0.290	(0.045)	0.039
Transport and communication	0.102	(0.071)	0.013	0.202	(0.093)	0.028
Finance	0.071	(0.041)	0.009	0.038	(0.057)	0.005
Region:						
South-East	-0.017	(0.049)	-0.002	-0.012	(0.065)	-0.001
South-West	-0.004	(0.058)	0.000	-0.055	(0.080)	-0.006
Wales	-0.179	(0.074)	-0.019	-0.046	(0.095)	-0.005
West Midlands	-0.068	(0.058)	-0.008	-0.076	(0.079)	-0.009
East Midlands	-0.040	(0.060)	-0.005	-0.005	(0.080)	-0.001
East Anglia	-0.058	(0.075)	-0.007	-0.059	(0.102)	-0.007
Yorkshire and Humberside	-0.083	(0.057)	-0.010	0.017	(0.075)	0.002
North-West	-0.040	(0.054)	-0.005	0.002	(0.073)	0.000
North	-0.150	(0.067)	-0.016	-0.113	(0.090)	-0.012
Scotland	-0.074	(0.058)	-0.009	0.020	(0.076)	0.002
Age	-0.047	(0.008)	-0.006	-0.038	(0.011)	-0.005
Age^2/100	0.027	(0.011)	0.003	0.018	(0.015)	0.002
Part-time	0.193	(0.028)	0.024	0.235	(0.037)	0.029
Non-white	-0.211	(0.081)	-0.022	-0.215	(0.108)	-0.022
Employer size 25+	-0.145	(0.026)	-0.018	-0.170	(0.035)	-0.021
Number of observations	25060			14357		
Pseudo R^2	0.061			0.059		

TABLE B.22

Training and the Determinants of Female Mobility III: QLFS

Variable	Coef.	(S.E.)	Marg. effect	Coef.	(S.E.)	Marg. effect
Constant	-0.573	(0.206)		-0.557	(0.207)	
Non-qualification training	-0.100	(0.063)	-0.011	-0.098	(0.063)	-0.011
Qualification training	0.109	(0.065)	0.014			
Other				0.091	(0.105)	0.011
Lower vocational				0.402	(0.186)	0.064
Middle vocational				-0.014	(0.167)	-0.002
Higher vocational				0.247	(0.132)	0.035
Degree				0.007	(0.157)	0.001
Panel dummies:						
Jun 1992	-0.016	(0.047)	-0.002	-0.014	(0.048)	-0.002
Sep 1992	0.074	(0.046)	0.009	0.074	(0.046)	0.009
Dec 1992	-0.017	(0.047)	-0.002	-0.016	(0.047)	-0.002
Highest education qualification:						
Degree	0.287	(0.068)	0.041	0.291	(0.068)	0.041
Higher vocational	0.164	(0.065)	0.021	0.159	(0.065)	0.021
Middle vocational	0.121	(0.058)	0.015	0.122	(0.058)	0.015
Lower vocational	0.014	(0.048)	0.002	0.011	(0.048)	0.001
Other	-0.056	(0.093)	-0.006	-0.057	(0.093)	-0.006
Industry:						
Energy and water	-0.027	(0.199)	-0.005	-0.042	(0.201)	-0.005
Minerals	0.071	(0.138)	0.009	0.073	(0.138)	0.009
Metals	0.321	(0.074)	0.047	0.323	(0.074)	0.047
Other manufacturing	0.346	(0.067)	0.051	0.346	(0.067)	0.051
Construction	0.275	(0.126)	0.040	0.279	(0.126)	0.040
Wholesale and retail trade	0.292	(0.045)	0.039	0.294	(0.045)	0.039
Transport and communication	0.207	(0.093)	0.028	0.203	(0.093)	0.028
Finance	0.038	(0.057)	0.005	0.041	(0.057)	0.005
Region:						
South-East	-0.012	(0.065)	-0.001	-0.013	(0.065)	-0.002
South-West	-0.057	(0.080)	-0.006	-0.061	(0.080)	-0.007
Wales	-0.052	(0.095)	-0.006	-0.055	(0.095)	-0.006
West Midlands	-0.080	(0.079)	-0.009	-0.084	(0.079)	-0.009
East Midlands	-0.009	(0.081)	-0.001	-0.012	(0.081)	-0.001
East Anglia	-0.059	(0.102)	-0.007	-0.060	(0.102)	-0.007
Yorkshire and Humberside	0.015	(0.075)	0.002	0.012	(0.075)	0.001
North-West	-0.001	(0.073)	0.000	-0.003	(0.073)	0.000
North	-0.115	(0.090)	-0.013	-0.120	(0.090)	-0.013
Scotland	0.019	(0.076)	0.002	0.017	(0.076)	0.002
Age	-0.037	(0.011)	-0.004	-0.038	(0.011)	-0.004
Age^2/100	0.016	(0.015)	0.002	0.018	(0.015)	0.002
Part-time	0.232	(0.037)	0.028	0.233	(0.037)	0.028
Non-white	-0.214	(0.108)	-0.022	-0.215	(0.108)	-0.022
Employer size 25+	-0.170	(0.035)	-0.021	-0.170	(0.035)	-0.021
Number of observations		14357			14357	
Pseudo R^2		0.060			0.061	

TABLE B.23

Training and the Determinants of Female Mobility IV: QLFS

Variable	Coef.	(S.E.)	Marg. effect	Coef.	(S.E.)	Marg. effect
Constant	-0.582	(0.206)		-0.552	(0.206)	
Employer qualification training	-0.052	(0.097)	-0.006			
Employer non-qualification training	-0.166	(0.087)	-0.017			
Other qualification training	0.239	(0.084)	0.033			
Other non-qualification training	-0.038	(0.085)	-0.004			
Employer continuing training				-0.118	(0.078)	-0.013
Employer completed training				-0.113	(0.116)	-0.012
Other continuing training				0.139	(0.066)	0.018
Other completed training				-0.126	(0.152)	-0.014
Panel dummies:						
Jun 1992	-0.013	(0.048)	-0.002	-0.016	(0.047)	-0.002
Sep 1992	0.074	(0.046)	0.009	0.071	(0.046)	0.009
Dec 1992	-0.017	(0.047)	-0.002	-0.018	(0.047)	-0.002
Highest education qualification:						
Degree	0.291	(0.068)	0.041	0.287	(0.068)	0.040
Higher vocational	0.165	(0.065)	0.021	0.166	(0.065)	0.022
Middle vocational	0.119	(0.058)	0.015	0.118	(0.058)	0.015
Lower vocational	0.011	(0.048)	0.001	0.009	(0.048)	0.001
Other	-0.057	(0.093)	-0.006	-0.053	(0.093)	-0.006
Industry:						
Energy and water	-0.011	(0.199)	-0.001	-0.010	(0.198)	-0.001
Minerals	0.075	(0.138)	0.009	0.076	(0.138)	0.010
Metals	0.318	(0.074)	0.046	0.315	(0.074)	0.046
Other manufacturing	0.343	(0.067)	0.051	0.338	(0.067)	0.050
Construction	0.279	(0.126)	0.040	0.279	(0.126)	0.040
Wholesale and retail trade	0.289	(0.045)	0.039	0.287	(0.045)	0.038
Transport and communication	0.207	(0.093)	0.028	0.201	(0.093)	0.027
Finance	0.039	(0.057)	0.005	0.037	(0.057)	0.004
Region:						
South-East	-0.011	(0.065)	-0.001	-0.012	(0.065)	-0.001
South-West	-0.056	(0.080)	-0.006	-0.055	(0.080)	-0.006
Wales	-0.049	(0.095)	-0.006	-0.044	(0.095)	-0.005
West Midlands	-0.082	(0.079)	-0.009	-0.079	(0.079)	-0.009
East Midlands	-0.010	(0.081)	-0.001	-0.007	(0.081)	-0.001
East Anglia	-0.058	(0.102)	-0.007	-0.059	(0.102)	-0.007
Yorkshire and Humberside	0.017	(0.075)	0.002	0.018	(0.075)	0.002
North-West	0.000	(0.073)	0.000	0.002	(0.073)	0.000
North	-0.114	(0.090)	-0.012	-0.113	(0.090)	-0.012
Scotland	0.021	(0.076)	0.002	0.020	(0.076)	0.002
Age	-0.036	(0.011)	-0.004	-0.037	(0.011)	-0.004
$Age^2/100$	0.016	(0.015)	0.002	0.017	(0.015)	0.002
Part-time	0.225	(0.037)	0.027	0.228	(0.037)	0.028
Non-white	-0.216	(0.108)	-0.022	-0.217	(0.108)	-0.022
Employer size 25+	-0.170	(0.035)	-0.021	-0.170	(0.035)	-0.021
Number of observations	14357			14357		
Pseudo R^2	0.060			0.060		

TABLE B.24

Training and the Determinants of Young Female Mobility I: QLFS

Variable	Coef.	(S.E.)	Marg. effect	Coef.	(S.E.)	Marg. effect
Constant	2.194	(0.892)		2.308	(0.897)	
Any training in last 4 weeks				-0.074	(0.054)	-0.014
Panel dummies:						
Jun 1992	0.005	(0.080)	0.001	0.001	(0.080)	0.000
Sep 1992	0.077	(0.079)	0.015	0.075	(0.079)	0.015
Dec 1992	0.144	(0.077)	0.029	0.143	(0.077)	0.029
Mar 1993	0.139	(0.078)	0.028	0.139	(0.078)	0.028
Jun 1993	0.166	(0.078)	0.034	0.163	(0.078)	0.033
Sep 1993	0.197	(0.077)	0.041	0.196	(0.077)	0.041
Highest education qualification:						
Degree	0.342	(0.101)	0.077	0.358	(0.102)	0.081
Higher vocational	0.152	(0.102)	0.031	0.165	(0.103)	0.034
Middle vocational	0.080	(0.087)	0.016	0.088	(0.087)	0.017
Lower vocational	-0.010	(0.079)	-0.002	-0.007	(0.079)	-0.001
Other	0.114	(0.153)	0.023	0.119	(0.153)	0.024
Industry:						
Energy and water	-0.072	(0.217)	-0.013	-0.069	(0.218)	-0.013
Minerals	0.209	(0.150)	0.045	0.209	(0.150)	0.045
Metals	0.205	(0.099)	0.044	0.203	(0.099)	0.043
Other manufacturing	0.212	(0.084)	0.045	0.206	(0.084)	0.043
Construction	0.244	(0.160)	0.054	0.240	(0.161)	0.052
Wholesale and retail trade	0.306	(0.057)	0.064	0.304	(0.057)	0.064
Transport and communication	0.152	(0.105)	0.031	0.150	(0.105)	0.031
Finance	0.056	(0.064)	0.011	0.057	(0.064)	0.011
Region:						
South-East	-0.070	(0.078)	-0.013	-0.070	(0.079)	-0.013
South-West	-0.137	(0.097)	-0.024	-0.137	(0.097)	-0.024
Wales	-0.208	(0.122)	-0.035	-0.213	(0.122)	-0.036
West Midlands	-0.104	(0.093)	-0.019	-0.105	(0.093)	-0.019
East Midlands	-0.132	(0.101)	-0.024	-0.134	(0.101)	-0.024
East Anglia	-0.167	(0.129)	-0.029	-0.165	(0.129)	-0.029
Yorkshire and Humberside	-0.131	(0.092)	-0.023	-0.129	(0.092)	-0.023
North-West	-0.033	(0.086)	-0.006	-0.034	(0.086)	-0.006
North	-0.229	(0.108)	-0.039	-0.231	(0.108)	-0.039
Scotland	-0.128	(0.093)	-0.023	-0.134	(0.093)	-0.024
Age	-0.249	(0.078)	-0.048	-0.257	(0.078)	-0.049
Age^2/100	0.418	(0.168)	0.080	0.433	(0.168)	0.083
Part-time	0.249	(0.052)	0.052	0.248	(0.052)	0.051
Non-white	-0.145	(0.120)	-0.026	-0.144	(0.120)	-0.025
Employer size 25+	-0.193	(0.044)	-0.038	-0.190	(0.044)	-0.038
Number of observations	6548			6548		
Pseudo R^2	0.052			0.052		

130

TABLE B.25

Training and the Determinants of Young Female Mobility II: QLFS

Variable	Coef.	(S.E.)	Marg. effect	Coef.	(S.E.)	Marg. effect
Constant	2.247	(0.898)		2.638	(1.214)	
Employer-funded training	-0.197	(0.080)	-0.034			
Other training	0.019	(0.068)	0.004			
Completed training				-0.258	(0.170)	-0.039
Continuing training				-0.131	(0.082)	-0.022
Panel dummies:						
Jun 1992	0.001	(0.080)	0.000	0.004	(0.081)	0.001
Sep 1992	0.072	(0.079)	0.014	0.081	(0.080)	0.015
Dec 1992	0.140	(0.078)	0.028	0.143	(0.078)	0.026
Mar 1993	0.134	(0.079)	0.027			
Jun 1993	0.159	(0.078)	0.033			
Sep 1993	0.195	(0.077)	0.040			
Highest education qualification:						
Degree	0.365	(0.102)	0.083	0.457	(0.135)	0.101
Higher vocational	0.166	(0.103)	0.034	0.158	(0.137)	0.030
Middle vocational	0.090	(0.087)	0.018	0.147	(0.112)	0.027
Lower vocational	-0.009	(0.079)	-0.002	-0.029	(0.105)	-0.005
Other	0.114	(0.154)	0.023	-0.056	(0.235)	-0.010
Industry:						
Energy and water	-0.061	(0.218)	-0.011	-0.002	(0.313)	0.000
Minerals	0.216	(0.150)	0.047	0.360	(0.192)	0.078
Metals	0.200	(0.099)	0.042	0.310	(0.125)	0.065
Other manufacturing	0.204	(0.084)	0.043	0.254	(0.115)	0.051
Construction	0.243	(0.161)	0.053	0.253	(0.237)	0.052
Wholesale and retail trade	0.301	(0.057)	0.063	0.363	(0.077)	0.072
Transport and communication	0.150	(0.105)	0.031	0.317	(0.138)	0.067
Finance	0.059	(0.064)	0.012	0.014	(0.090)	0.002
Region:						
South-East	-0.069	(0.079)	-0.013	-0.180	(0.106)	-0.030
South-West	-0.133	(0.097)	-0.024	-0.266	(0.134)	-0.041
Wales	-0.210	(0.122)	-0.036	-0.217	(0.160)	-0.034
West Midlands	-0.106	(0.093)	-0.019	-0.246	(0.129)	-0.038
East Midlands	-0.135	(0.101)	-0.024	-0.104	(0.133)	-0.017
East Anglia	-0.164	(0.129)	-0.028	-0.301	(0.173)	-0.044
Yorkshire and Humberside	-0.127	(0.092)	-0.023	-0.117	(0.121)	-0.019
North-West	-0.035	(0.086)	-0.007	-0.173	(0.120)	-0.028
North	-0.227	(0.108)	-0.038	-0.305	(0.147)	-0.045
Scotland	-0.131	(0.093)	-0.023	-0.066	(0.121)	-0.011
Age	-0.252	(0.078)	-0.048	-0.288	(0.106)	-0.051
Age^2/100	0.425	(0.168)	0.081	0.504	(0.228)	0.089
Part-time	0.239	(0.052)	0.049	0.322	(0.070)	0.064
Non-white	-0.146	(0.120)	-0.026	-0.342	(0.177)	-0.049
Employer size 25+	-0.191	(0.044)	-0.038	-0.192	(0.060)	-0.035
Number of observations		6548			3785	
Pseudo R^2		0.053			0.064	

TABLE B.26

Training and the Determinants of Young Female Mobility III: QLFS

Variable	Coef.	(S.E.)	Marg. effect	Coef.	(S.E.)	Marg. effect
Constant	2.634	(1.215)		2.813	(1.227)	
Non-qualification training	-0.190	(0.110)	-0.030	-0.189	(0.110)	-0.030
Qualification training	-0.125	(0.096)	-0.021			
Other				-0.016	(0.150)	-0.003
Lower vocational				0.007	(0.347)	0.001
Middle vocational				-0.400	(0.218)	-0.055
Higher vocational				0.029	(0.193)	0.005
Degree				-0.283	(0.238)	-0.042
Panel dummies:						
Jun 1992	0.004	(0.081)	0.001	0.002	(0.081)	0.000
Sep 1992	0.082	(0.080)	0.015	0.082	(0.080)	0.015
Dec 1992	0.142	(0.078)	0.026	0.141	(0.078)	0.026
Highest education qualification:						
Degree	0.457	(0.135)	0.101	0.467	(0.136)	0.103
Higher vocational	0.158	(0.137)	0.030	0.155	(0.137)	0.030
Middle vocational	0.147	(0.112)	0.027	0.149	(0.112)	0.028
Lower vocational	-0.029	(0.105)	-0.005	-0.031	(0.105)	-0.005
Other	-0.058	(0.235)	-0.010	-0.058	(0.235)	-0.010
Industry:						
Energy and water	-0.004	(0.313)	-0.001	-0.026	(0.315)	-0.005
Minerals	0.362	(0.192)	0.079	0.374	(0.193)	0.082
Metals	0.312	(0.125)	0.065	0.314	(0.125)	0.066
Other manufacturing	0.253	(0.115)	0.051	0.260	(0.115)	0.052
Construction	0.252	(0.237)	0.052	0.259	(0.237)	0.053
Wholesale and retail trade	0.363	(0.077)	0.072	0.370	(0.077)	0.074
Transport and communication	0.318	(0.138)	0.067	0.321	(0.139)	0.068
Finance	0.013	(0.090)	0.002	0.017	(0.090)	0.003
Region:						
South-East	-0.179	(0.106)	-0.030	-0.182	(0.106)	-0.030
South-West	-0.267	(0.134)	-0.041	-0.271	(0.135)	-0.041
Wales	-0.217	(0.160)	-0.034	-0.222	(0.160)	-0.034
West Midlands	-0.247	(0.129)	-0.038	-0.258	(0.129)	-0.040
East Midlands	-0.104	(0.133)	-0.017	-0.117	(0.133)	-0.019
East Anglia	-0.299	(0.173)	-0.044	-0.311	(0.173)	-0.045
Yorkshire and Humberside	-0.116	(0.121)	-0.019	-0.127	(0.122)	-0.021
North-West	-0.172	(0.120)	-0.028	-0.179	(0.120)	-0.029
North	-0.304	(0.147)	-0.045	-0.315	(0.147)	-0.046
Scotland	-0.067	(0.121)	-0.011	-0.074	(0.121)	-0.013
Age	-0.288	(0.106)	-0.051	-0.302	(0.107)	-0.053
Age^2/100	0.504	(0.228)	0.089	0.533	(0.230)	0.094
Part-time	0.321	(0.070)	0.064	0.331	(0.070)	0.066
Non-white	-0.339	(0.177)	-0.049	-0.341	(0.177)	-0.049
Employer size 25+	-0.193	(0.060)	-0.035	-0.194	(0.060)	-0.036
Number of observations	3785			3785		
Pseudo R^2	0.064			0.065		

TABLE B.27

Training and the Determinants of Young Female Mobility IV: QLFS

Variable	Coef.	(S.E.)	Marg. effect	Coef.	(S.E.)	Marg. effect
Constant	2.600	(1.216)		2.601	(1.215)	
Employer qualification training	-0.235	(0.142)	-0.036			
Employer non-qualification training	-0.215	(0.153)	-0.033			
Other qualification training	-0.036	(0.124)	-0.006			
Other non-qualification training	-0.171	(0.149)	-0.027			
Employer continuing training				-0.286	(0.125)	-0.043
Employer completed training				-0.066	(0.193)	-0.011
Other continuing training				-0.024	(0.101)	-0.004
Other completed training				-0.857	(0.423)	-0.086
Panel dummies:						
Jun 1992	0.005	(0.081)	0.001	0.002	(0.081)	0.000
Sep 1992	0.082	(0.080)	0.015	0.083	(0.080)	0.015
Dec 1992	0.140	(0.078)	0.026	0.138	(0.078)	0.025
Highest education qualification:						
Degree	0.461	(0.135)	0.102	0.458	(0.135)	0.100
Higher vocational	0.159	(0.137)	0.030	0.162	(0.137)	0.031
Middle vocational	0.146	(0.112)	0.027	0.144	(0.112)	0.026
Lower vocational	-0.031	(0.105)	-0.005	-0.031	(0.105)	-0.005
Other	-0.061	(0.235)	-0.010	-0.062	(0.235)	-0.010
Industry:						
Energy and water	0.007	(0.312)	0.001	0.028	(0.314)	0.005
Minerals	0.367	(0.192)	0.080	0.372	(0.192)	0.081
Metals	0.308	(0.125)	0.064	0.298	(0.125)	0.061
Other manufacturing	0.253	(0.115)	0.051	0.246	(0.115)	0.049
Construction	0.254	(0.237)	0.052	0.246	(0.237)	0.050
Wholesale and retail trade	0.360	(0.077)	0.072	0.356	(0.077)	0.070
Transport and communication	0.316	(0.138)	0.067	0.316	(0.138)	0.066
Finance	0.015	(0.090)	0.003	0.015	(0.090)	0.003
Region:						
South-East	-0.178	(0.106)	-0.029	-0.181	(0.106)	-0.030
South-West	-0.263	(0.135)	-0.040	-0.268	(0.135)	-0.041
Wales	-0.215	(0.160)	-0.033	-0.218	(0.161)	-0.034
West Midlands	-0.248	(0.129)	-0.038	-0.250	(0.129)	-0.038
East Midlands	-0.104	(0.133)	-0.017	-0.108	(0.133)	-0.018
East Anglia	-0.298	(0.173)	-0.044	-0.301	(0.174)	-0.044
Yorkshire and Humberside	-0.112	(0.121)	-0.019	-0.109	(0.122)	-0.018
North-West	-0.169	(0.120)	-0.027	-0.174	(0.120)	-0.028
North	-0.300	(0.147)	-0.045	-0.309	(0.147)	-0.045
Scotland	-0.065	(0.121)	-0.011	-0.070	(0.121)	-0.012
Age	-0.285	(0.106)	-0.050	-0.285	(0.106)	-0.050
Age^2/100	0.500	(0.228)	0.088	0.501	(0.228)	0.088
Part-time	0.313	(0.070)	0.062	0.313	(0.070)	0.061
Non-white	-0.340	(0.178)	-0.049	-0.346	(0.178)	-0.049
Employer size 25+	-0.191	(0.060)	-0.035	-0.190	(0.060)	-0.035
Number of observations		3785			3785	
Pseudo R^2		0.064			0.066	

TABLE B.28

Mobility and the Determinants of Male Training: NCDS

Variable	Probit			IV-Probit		
	Coef.	(S.E.)	Marg. effect	Coef.	(S.E.)	Marg. effect
Constant	-2.039	(0.058)		-1.513	(0.182)	
Moved job last year	-0.051	(0.023)	-0.006	0.423	(0.137)	0.006
Year dummies:						
1982	0.073	(0.041)	0.010	0.156	(0.049)	0.022
1983	0.080	(0.041)	0.011	0.161	(0.048)	0.023
1984	0.099	(0.041)	0.014	0.166	(0.046)	0.024
1985	0.141	(0.040)	0.020	0.198	(0.044)	0.029
1986	0.183	(0.040)	0.027	0.224	(0.042)	0.034
1987	0.163	(0.040)	0.024	0.214	(0.043)	0.032
1988	0.209	(0.039)	0.031	0.261	(0.042)	0.040
1989	0.330	(0.038)	0.052	0.367	(0.040)	0.059
1990	0.464	(0.038)	0.080	0.494	(0.040)	0.086
Quarter dummies:						
2nd quarter	0.035	(0.022)	0.005	0.031	(0.022)	0.004
3rd quarter	0.085	(0.022)	0.012	0.081	(0.022)	0.011
4th quarter	0.020	(0.023)	0.003	0.013	(0.023)	0.002
Highest education qualification:						
Other	0.245	(0.043)	0.038	0.199	(0.045)	0.030
O levels	0.307	(0.033)	0.048	0.303	(0.033)	0.047
Lower vocational	0.257	(0.035)	0.039	0.205	(0.038)	0.030
5+ O levels	0.483	(0.036)	0.085	0.460	(0.036)	0.080
Middle vocational	0.537	(0.029)	0.090	0.493	(0.032)	0.081
A levels	0.773	(0.036)	0.161	0.693	(0.044)	0.138
Higher vocational	0.685	(0.032)	0.133	0.623	(0.038)	0.117
Degree	0.695	(0.033)	0.135	0.482	(0.075)	0.084
Industry 1981 job:						
Energy and water	-0.120	(0.040)	-0.015	-0.172	(0.043)	-0.020
Minerals	-0.023	(0.045)	-0.003	-0.060	(0.046)	-0.008
Metals	0.056	(0.027)	0.008	-0.016	(0.036)	-0.002
Other manufacturing	-0.041	(0.036)	-0.005	-0.087	(0.039)	-0.011
Construction	-0.168	(0.038)	-0.020	-0.252	(0.047)	-0.028
Wholesale and retail trade	-0.067	(0.033)	-0.008	-0.188	(0.051)	-0.022
Transport and communication	0.022	(0.034)	0.003	-0.049	(0.041)	-0.006
Finance	0.187	(0.033)	0.028	0.126	(0.038)	0.018
Other services	0.146	(0.027)	0.021	0.024	(0.047)	0.003
1981 region:						
South-East	0.001	(0.029)	0.000	0.003	(0.029)	0.000
South-West	-0.203	(0.039)	-0.024	-0.170	(0.040)	-0.020
Wales	-0.196	(0.045)	-0.023	-0.128	(0.050)	-0.015
West Midlands	-0.008	(0.035)	-0.001	0.026	(0.037)	0.004
East Midlands	-0.086	(0.037)	-0.011	-0.038	(0.040)	-0.005
East Anglia	0.040	(0.049)	0.005	0.095	(0.052)	0.013
Yorkshire and Humberside	0.153	(0.034)	0.022	0.158	(0.034)	0.023
North-West	-0.043	(0.033)	-0.006	-0.042	(0.033)	-0.005
North	0.222	(0.036)	0.034	0.223	(0.036)	0.034
Scotland	-0.180	(0.037)	-0.021	-0.159	(0.037)	-0.019
Employer size 1981 job:						
10–24	0.121	(0.033)	0.017	0.123	(0.033)	0.017
25–99	0.112	(0.029)	0.015	0.123	(0.029)	0.017
100–500	0.195	(0.029)	0.028	0.226	(0.031)	0.033
500+	0.132	(0.030)	0.018	0.187	(0.035)	0.026
Union member 1981	0.035	(0.019)	0.005	0.074	(0.022)	0.010
Private sector 1981	-0.249	(0.022)	-0.035	-0.333	(0.035)	-0.048
Part-time 1981	-0.124	(0.073)	-0.015	-0.085	(0.074)	-0.011
Number of observations	59957			59957		
Pseudo R^2	0.0704			0.0706		

Detailed results

TABLE B.29

Determinants of Male Employer Training I: NCDS

Variable	Probit			IV-Probit		
	Coef.	(S.E.)	Marg. effect	Coef.	(S.E.)	Marg. effect
Constant	0.574	(0.171)		0.657	(0.534)	
Moved job last year	-0.194	(0.063)	-0.054	0.087	(0.405)	0.002
Year dummies:						
1982	0.000	(0.117)	0.000	0.020	(0.139)	0.005
1983	0.112	(0.117)	0.028	0.129	(0.138)	0.032
1984	0.187	(0.117)	0.045	0.198	(0.134)	0.048
1985	0.217	(0.116)	0.052	0.236	(0.129)	0.056
1986	0.268	(0.115)	0.062	0.282	(0.122)	0.065
1987	0.338	(0.117)	0.077	0.342	(0.127)	0.077
1988	0.322	(0.114)	0.074	0.325	(0.125)	0.074
1989	0.366	(0.110)	0.082	0.376	(0.116)	0.084
1990	0.571	(0.112)	0.117	0.578	(0.115)	0.118
Quarter dummies:						
2nd quarter	0.066	(0.065)	0.017	0.064	(0.065)	0.016
3rd quarter	-0.087	(0.062)	-0.023	-0.087	(0.062)	-0.023
4th quarter	0.012	(0.067)	0.003	0.010	(0.067)	0.002
Highest education qualification:						
Other	-0.123	(0.132)	-0.033	-0.146	(0.137)	-0.040
O levels	0.148	(0.107)	0.036	0.139	(0.107)	0.034
Lower vocational	0.156	(0.113)	0.038	0.137	(0.124)	0.034
5+ O levels	0.017	(0.109)	0.004	0.004	(0.110)	0.001
Middle vocational	0.313	(0.093)	0.074	0.301	(0.101)	0.071
A levels	-0.075	(0.106)	-0.020	-0.095	(0.126)	-0.026
Higher vocational	0.105	(0.098)	0.026	0.098	(0.113)	0.025
Degree	0.240	(0.099)	0.057	0.183	(0.221)	0.044
Industry 1981 job:						
Energy and water	1.003	(0.169)	0.160	1.001	(0.175)	0.160
Minerals	-0.043	(0.136)	-0.011	-0.047	(0.138)	-0.012
Metals	-0.025	(0.082)	-0.007	-0.039	(0.104)	-0.010
Other manufacturing	0.117	(0.112)	0.029	0.097	(0.119)	0.024
Construction	-0.177	(0.112)	-0.051	-0.193	(0.135)	-0.055
Wholesale and retail trade	-0.216	(0.099)	-0.060	-0.238	(0.150)	-0.067
Transport and communication	0.253	(0.104)	0.059	0.246	(0.124)	0.057
Finance	0.422	(0.099)	0.091	0.406	(0.114)	0.088
Other services	0.234	(0.074)	0.056	0.211	(0.134)	0.051
1981 region:						
South-East	0.183	(0.087)	0.045	0.177	(0.087)	0.043
South-West	-0.049	(0.118)	-0.013	-0.029	(0.121)	-0.008
Wales	-0.189	(0.131)	-0.053	-0.175	(0.146)	-0.048
West Midlands	-0.437	(0.096)	-0.131	-0.435	(0.102)	-0.130
East Midlands	0.275	(0.117)	0.064	0.277	(0.125)	0.064
East Anglia	0.086	(0.151)	0.021	0.101	(0.160)	0.025
Yorkshire and Humberside	-0.083	(0.096)	-0.022	-0.086	(0.096)	-0.023
North-West	-0.306	(0.093)	-0.088	-0.309	(0.093)	-0.089
North	0.067	(0.102)	0.017	0.075	(0.102)	0.019
Scotland	-0.354	(0.104)	-0.104	-0.353	(0.106)	-0.103
Employer size 1981 job:						
10–24	-0.064	(0.098)	-0.017	-0.065	(0.098)	-0.017
25–99	0.222	(0.089)	0.054	0.228	(0.089)	0.056
100–500	0.032	(0.086)	0.008	0.032	(0.090)	0.008
500+	0.134	(0.089)	0.034	0.142	(0.100)	0.036
Union member 1981	-0.194	(0.054)	-0.050	-0.178	(0.067)	-0.046
Private sector 1981	0.000	(0.067)	0.000	-0.014	(0.103)	-0.004
Part-time 1981	0.707	(0.276)	0.127	0.698	(0.275)	0.126
Number of observations	4940			4940		
Pseudo R^2	0.0795			0.0774		

Note: Estimation of this equation is on the sub-sample of men who undertook some form of training in the quarter.

135

TABLE B.30

Determinants of Male Completed Training: NCDS

Variable	Probit			IV-Probit		
	Coef.	(S.E.)	Marg. effect	Coef.	(S.E.)	Marg. effect
Constant	-0.832	(0.153)		-2.040	(0.447)	
Moved job last year	-0.027	(0.055)	-0.010	-0.957	(0.333)	-0.031
Year dummies:						
1982	0.139	(0.111)	0.054	-0.037	(0.127)	-0.014
1983	0.380	(0.110)	0.150	0.212	(0.125)	0.083
1984	0.374	(0.109)	0.148	0.228	(0.121)	0.090
1985	0.393	(0.108)	0.155	0.270	(0.116)	0.106
1986	0.544	(0.106)	0.214	0.454	(0.110)	0.179
1987	0.678	(0.106)	0.265	0.563	(0.113)	0.222
1988	0.714	(0.104)	0.279	0.599	(0.111)	0.235
1989	0.827	(0.100)	0.320	0.749	(0.104)	0.292
1990	1.011	(0.100)	0.383	0.950	(0.102)	0.362
Quarter dummies:						
2nd quarter	0.170	(0.054)	0.066	0.181	(0.054)	0.071
3rd quarter	0.293	(0.053)	0.115	0.305	(0.053)	0.119
4th quarter	0.093	(0.056)	0.036	0.108	(0.057)	0.042
Highest education qualification:						
Other	0.095	(0.116)	0.037	0.189	(0.121)	0.074
O levels	-0.024	(0.090)	-0.009	-0.013	(0.091)	-0.005
Lower vocational	0.126	(0.098)	0.049	0.243	(0.107)	0.095
5+ O levels	0.115	(0.094)	0.045	0.160	(0.095)	0.063
Middle vocational	-0.145	(0.080)	-0.055	-0.049	(0.087)	-0.019
A levels	-0.080	(0.093)	-0.031	0.082	(0.109)	0.032
Higher vocational	-0.020	(0.085)	-0.008	0.115	(0.097)	0.045
Degree	0.150	(0.085)	0.059	0.618	(0.184)	0.243
Industry 1981 job:						
Energy and water	0.091	(0.098)	0.036	0.206	(0.106)	0.081
Minerals	0.031	(0.114)	0.012	0.099	(0.117)	0.039
Metals	-0.126	(0.071)	-0.048	0.026	(0.088)	0.010
Other manufacturing	-0.189	(0.096)	-0.071	-0.097	(0.101)	-0.037
Construction	-0.377	(0.107)	-0.138	-0.195	(0.124)	-0.074
Wholesale and retail trade	0.352	(0.089)	0.139	0.619	(0.129)	0.243
Transport and communication	0.163	(0.084)	0.064	0.330	(0.102)	0.130
Finance	-0.060	(0.077)	-0.023	0.071	(0.090)	0.028
Other services	-0.184	(0.063)	-0.070	0.082	(0.112)	0.032
1981 region:						
South-East	-0.049	(0.069)	-0.019	-0.050	(0.069)	-0.019
South-West	0.285	(0.095)	0.112	0.218	(0.098)	0.086
Wales	0.242	(0.113)	0.095	0.088	(0.125)	0.034
West Midlands	-0.215	(0.085)	-0.081	-0.299	(0.089)	-0.111
East Midlands	0.009	(0.090)	0.003	-0.103	(0.098)	-0.039
East Anglia	0.143	(0.117)	0.056	0.015	(0.125)	0.006
Yorkshire and Humberside	-0.297	(0.081)	-0.110	-0.297	(0.081)	-0.110
North-West	-0.051	(0.080)	-0.019	-0.058	(0.080)	-0.022
North	-0.542	(0.084)	-0.191	-0.543	(0.084)	-0.191
Scotland	-0.081	(0.092)	-0.031	-0.128	(0.093)	-0.049
Employer size 1981 job:						
10–24	-0.013	(0.087)	-0.005	-0.014	(0.087)	-0.005
25–99	0.010	(0.077)	0.004	-0.013	(0.078)	-0.005
100–500	0.064	(0.076)	0.025	-0.005	(0.080)	-0.002
500+	0.124	(0.077)	0.048	0.010	(0.087)	0.004
Union member 1981	-0.092	(0.045)	-0.035	-0.182	(0.055)	-0.070
Private sector 1981	0.014	(0.056)	0.005	0.204	(0.086)	0.078
Part-time 1981	0.267	(0.178)	0.105	0.189	(0.181)	0.075
Number of observations	4940			4940		
Pseudo R^2	0.0744			0.0756		

Note: Estimation of this equation is on the sub-sample of men who undertook some form of training in the quarter.

TABLE B.31

Determinants of Male Qualification Training: NCDS

Variable	Probit			IV-Probit		
	Coef.	(S.E.)	Marg. effect	Coef.	(S.E.)	Marg. effect
Constant	0.115	(0.151)		0.896	(0.443)	
Moved job last year	-0.041	(0.056)	-0.016	0.625	(0.331)	0.020
Year dummies:						
1982	-0.186	(0.111)	-0.073	-0.069	(0.127)	-0.027
1983	-0.291	(0.110)	-0.115	-0.182	(0.125)	-0.072
1984	-0.309	(0.110)	-0.122	-0.214	(0.121)	-0.085
1985	-0.451	(0.108)	-0.178	-0.369	(0.116)	-0.146
1986	-0.529	(0.106)	-0.209	-0.469	(0.111)	-0.185
1987	-0.634	(0.106)	-0.248	-0.560	(0.113)	-0.221
1988	-0.902	(0.104)	-0.344	-0.829	(0.111)	-0.319
1989	-0.958	(0.101)	-0.363	-0.906	(0.104)	-0.346
1990	-1.169	(0.101)	-0.428	-1.129	(0.103)	-0.416
Quarter dummies:						
2nd quarter	-0.026	(0.054)	-0.010	-0.034	(0.054)	-0.013
3rd quarter	0.011	(0.053)	0.004	0.004	(0.053)	0.002
4th quarter	-0.021	(0.056)	-0.008	-0.032	(0.056)	-0.012
Highest education qualification:						
Other	0.301	(0.118)	0.113	0.236	(0.123)	0.090
O levels	-0.029	(0.092)	-0.011	-0.041	(0.092)	-0.016
Lower vocational	0.209	(0.098)	0.080	0.128	(0.107)	0.050
5+ O levels	0.216	(0.094)	0.082	0.182	(0.095)	0.070
Middle vocational	0.265	(0.080)	0.101	0.198	(0.087)	0.076
A levels	-0.106	(0.093)	-0.042	-0.216	(0.109)	-0.085
Higher vocational	0.163	(0.085)	0.062	0.074	(0.097)	0.029
Degree	0.000	(0.085)	0.000	-0.312	(0.185)	-0.124
Industry 1981 job:						
Energy and water	-0.229	(0.099)	-0.091	-0.301	(0.107)	-0.120
Minerals	0.249	(0.119)	0.094	0.205	(0.121)	0.078
Metals	0.041	(0.071)	0.016	-0.058	(0.088)	-0.023
Other manufacturing	-0.272	(0.097)	-0.108	-0.338	(0.102)	-0.134
Construction	0.198	(0.109)	0.071	0.079	(0.126)	0.029
Wholesale and retail trade	0.161	(0.089)	0.062	-0.012	(0.128)	-0.005
Transport and communication	-0.070	(0.085)	-0.028	-0.178	(0.103)	-0.070
Finance	0.036	(0.078)	0.014	-0.049	(0.090)	-0.019
Other services	-0.318	(0.064)	-0.126	-0.491	(0.112)	-0.194
1981 region:						
South-East	0.371	(0.070)	0.140	0.373	(0.070)	0.141
South-West	0.448	(0.096)	0.164	0.498	(0.099)	0.181
Wales	0.257	(0.114)	0.097	0.362	(0.126)	0.134
West Midlands	0.571	(0.086)	0.205	0.628	(0.091)	0.223
East Midlands	0.746	(0.093)	0.256	0.822	(0.101)	0.277
East Anglia	0.462	(0.118)	0.167	0.550	(0.127)	0.195
Yorkshire and Humberside	0.799	(0.083)	0.272	0.803	(0.083)	0.273
North-West	0.209	(0.081)	0.080	0.218	(0.081)	0.083
North	0.862	(0.085)	0.286	0.869	(0.085)	0.288
Scotland	0.589	(0.093)	0.210	0.622	(0.095)	0.220
Employer size 1981 job:						
10–24	0.186	(0.085)	0.071	0.184	(0.085)	0.071
25–99	0.225	(0.076)	0.087	0.240	(0.076)	0.092
100–500	0.307	(0.074)	0.117	0.351	(0.078)	0.133
500+	0.271	(0.076)	0.104	0.344	(0.086)	0.131
Union member 1981	0.048	(0.046)	0.019	0.108	(0.055)	0.042
Private sector 1981	-0.183	(0.057)	-0.071	-0.307	(0.087)	-0.118
Part-time 1981	-0.079	(0.171)	-0.031	-0.028	(0.174)	-0.011
Number of observations	4940			4940		
Pseudo R^2	0.1006			0.1010		

Note: Estimation of this equation is on the sub-sample of men who undertook some form of training in the quarter.

TABLE B.32

Determinants of Male Employer Training II: NCDS

Variable	Probit			IV-Probit		
	Coef.	(S.E.)	Marg. effect	Coef.	(S.E.)	Marg. effect
Constant	-2.168	(0.063)		-1.653	(0.193)	
Moved job last year	-0.085	(0.025)	-0.009	0.417	(0.145)	0.005
Year dummies:						
1982	0.056	(0.045)	0.006	0.140	(0.053)	0.017
1983	0.079	(0.045)	0.009	0.160	(0.052)	0.020
1984	0.112	(0.044)	0.013	0.179	(0.049)	0.022
1985	0.159	(0.044)	0.020	0.216	(0.047)	0.028
1986	0.211	(0.043)	0.027	0.253	(0.045)	0.033
1987	0.196	(0.043)	0.025	0.248	(0.046)	0.032
1988	0.241	(0.042)	0.031	0.293	(0.046)	0.039
1989	0.361	(0.041)	0.050	0.399	(0.043)	0.057
1990	0.518	(0.041)	0.079	0.549	(0.042)	0.086
Quarter dummies:						
2nd quarter	0.045	(0.023)	0.005	0.041	(0.023)	0.005
3rd quarter	0.064	(0.023)	0.007	0.060	(0.023)	0.007
4th quarter	0.019	(0.024)	0.002	0.013	(0.024)	0.001
Highest education qualification:						
Other	0.205	(0.046)	0.026	0.160	(0.049)	0.020
O levels	0.307	(0.036)	0.041	0.303	(0.036)	0.040
Lower vocational	0.251	(0.037)	0.033	0.198	(0.041)	0.025
5+ O levels	0.459	(0.038)	0.069	0.435	(0.039)	0.064
Middle vocational	0.547	(0.031)	0.080	0.504	(0.034)	0.072
A levels	0.718	(0.039)	0.128	0.636	(0.047)	0.108
Higher vocational	0.652	(0.035)	0.108	0.590	(0.040)	0.095
Degree	0.687	(0.035)	0.116	0.472	(0.079)	0.070
Industry 1981 job:						
Energy and water	0.001	(0.041)	0.000	-0.050	(0.045)	-0.005
Minerals	-0.026	(0.048)	-0.003	-0.063	(0.050)	-0.007
Metals	0.056	(0.029)	0.006	-0.016	(0.038)	-0.002
Other manufacturing	-0.015	(0.038)	-0.002	-0.061	(0.041)	-0.006
Construction	-0.162	(0.042)	-0.016	-0.246	(0.050)	-0.023
Wholesale and retail trade	-0.104	(0.036)	-0.011	-0.225	(0.055)	-0.022
Transport and communication	0.074	(0.036)	0.009	0.003	(0.044)	0.000
Finance	0.235	(0.034)	0.031	0.174	(0.040)	0.022
Other services	0.193	(0.029)	0.024	0.071	(0.050)	0.008
1981 region:						
South-East	0.017	(0.030)	0.002	0.020	(0.030)	0.002
South-West	-0.195	(0.041)	-0.019	-0.161	(0.042)	-0.016
Wales	-0.220	(0.048)	-0.021	-0.152	(0.053)	-0.015
West Midlands	-0.095	(0.038)	-0.010	-0.061	(0.040)	-0.007
East Midlands	-0.062	(0.038)	-0.007	-0.014	(0.041)	-0.002
East Anglia	0.043	(0.051)	0.005	0.099	(0.054)	0.012
Yorkshire and Humberside	0.125	(0.036)	0.015	0.129	(0.036)	0.016
North-West	-0.096	(0.036)	-0.010	-0.094	(0.036)	-0.010
North	0.228	(0.037)	0.029	0.229	(0.037)	0.030
Scotland	-0.238	(0.040)	-0.023	-0.216	(0.040)	-0.021
Employer size 1981 job:						
10–24	0.095	(0.036)	0.011	0.097	(0.036)	0.011
25–99	0.146	(0.031)	0.017	0.158	(0.031)	0.019
100–500	0.201	(0.031)	0.024	0.232	(0.033)	0.028
500+	0.150	(0.032)	0.018	0.205	(0.037)	0.025
Union member 1981	0.005	(0.020)	0.001	0.043	(0.024)	0.005
Private sector 1981	-0.222	(0.023)	-0.026	-0.306	(0.037)	-0.037
Part-time 1981	-0.018	(0.074)	-0.002	0.022	(0.076)	0.002
Number of observations	59957			59957		
Pseudo R^2	0.0748			0.0747		

TABLE B.33

Determinants of Male Non-Employer Training: NCDS

Variable	Probit			IV-Probit		
	Coef.	(S.E.)	Marg. effect	Coef.	(S.E.)	Marg. effect
Constant	-2.525	(0.105)		-2.244	(0.340)	
Moved job last year	0.077	(0.039)	0.002	0.214	(0.258)	0.001
Year dummies:						
1982	0.079	(0.069)	0.003	0.117	(0.085)	0.004
1983	0.048	(0.070)	0.002	0.084	(0.085)	0.003
1984	0.026	(0.070)	0.001	0.056	(0.081)	0.002
1985	0.037	(0.070)	0.001	0.062	(0.078)	0.002
1986	0.027	(0.070)	0.001	0.045	(0.074)	0.001
1987	-0.011	(0.071)	0.000	0.012	(0.077)	0.000
1988	0.022	(0.069)	0.001	0.046	(0.076)	0.001
1989	0.097	(0.067)	0.003	0.113	(0.071)	0.004
1990	0.085	(0.070)	0.003	0.098	(0.072)	0.003
Quarter dummies:						
2nd quarter	-0.018	(0.042)	-0.001	-0.020	(0.042)	-0.001
3rd quarter	0.128	(0.040)	0.004	0.126	(0.040)	0.004
4th quarter	0.013	(0.042)	0.000	0.010	(0.042)	0.000
Highest education qualification:						
Other	0.280	(0.074)	0.011	0.261	(0.079)	0.010
O levels	0.187	(0.062)	0.007	0.186	(0.062)	0.007
Lower vocational	0.179	(0.063)	0.006	0.155	(0.070)	0.005
5+ O levels	0.396	(0.064)	0.018	0.388	(0.065)	0.017
Middle vocational	0.294	(0.054)	0.011	0.274	(0.060)	0.010
A levels	0.673	(0.064)	0.040	0.636	(0.080)	0.037
Higher vocational	0.549	(0.059)	0.028	0.520	(0.070)	0.026
Degree	0.474	(0.061)	0.022	0.378	(0.141)	0.016
Industry 1981 job:						
Energy and water	-0.740	(0.120)	-0.011	-0.765	(0.124)	-0.011
Minerals	-0.020	(0.080)	-0.001	-0.036	(0.083)	-0.001
Metals	0.041	(0.048)	0.001	0.007	(0.065)	0.000
Other manufacturing	-0.107	(0.066)	-0.003	-0.128	(0.072)	-0.003
Construction	-0.110	(0.065)	-0.003	-0.150	(0.082)	-0.004
Wholesale and retail trade	0.050	(0.055)	0.002	-0.007	(0.091)	0.000
Transport and communication	-0.175	(0.067)	-0.004	-0.208	(0.079)	-0.005
Finance	-0.075	(0.068)	-0.002	-0.103	(0.077)	-0.003
Other services	-0.067	(0.049)	-0.002	-0.124	(0.088)	-0.003
1981 region:						
South-East	-0.081	(0.058)	-0.002	-0.081	(0.058)	-0.002
South-West	-0.157	(0.076)	-0.004	-0.144	(0.078)	-0.004
Wales	-0.043	(0.081)	-0.001	-0.011	(0.090)	0.000
West Midlands	0.238	(0.061)	0.009	0.254	(0.064)	0.010
East Midlands	-0.174	(0.076)	-0.004	-0.152	(0.081)	-0.004
East Anglia	0.002	(0.098)	0.000	0.027	(0.103)	0.001
Yorkshire and Humberside	0.182	(0.063)	0.007	0.186	(0.063)	0.007
North-West	0.134	(0.060)	0.005	0.134	(0.060)	0.005
North	0.107	(0.070)	0.004	0.106	(0.070)	0.004
Scotland	0.070	(0.064)	0.002	0.079	(0.065)	0.003
Employer size 1981 job:						
10–24	0.160	(0.057)	0.006	0.161	(0.057)	0.006
25–99	-0.041	(0.053)	-0.001	-0.036	(0.054)	-0.001
100–500	0.108	(0.052)	0.003	0.123	(0.055)	0.004
500+	0.023	(0.055)	0.001	0.049	(0.064)	0.002
Union member 1981	0.133	(0.034)	0.004	0.150	(0.042)	0.005
Private sector 1981	-0.239	(0.039)	-0.008	-0.279	(0.064)	-0.010
Part-time 1981	-0.559	(0.197)	-0.009	-0.540	(0.198)	-0.009
Number of observations	55848			55848		
Pseudo R^2	0.0580			0.0576		

Note: Estimation of this equation is on the sub-sample of men who did not undertake employer training in the quarter.

139

TABLE B.34

Mobility and the Determinants of Female Training: NCDS

Variable	Probit			IV-Probit		
	Coef.	(S.E.)	Marg. effect	Coef.	(S.E.)	Marg. effect
Constant	-2.111	(0.063)		-1.747	(0.297)	
Moved job last year	0.137	(0.022)	0.017	0.389	(0.343)	0.004
Year dummies:						
1982	0.093	(0.041)	0.012	0.152	(0.073)	0.020
1983	0.106	(0.041)	0.013	0.181	(0.088)	0.024
1984	0.029	(0.043)	0.004	0.090	(0.076)	0.011
1985	0.058	(0.043)	0.007	0.102	(0.064)	0.013
1986	0.130	(0.042)	0.016	0.181	(0.070)	0.024
1987	0.160	(0.042)	0.021	0.186	(0.052)	0.024
1988	0.169	(0.042)	0.022	0.183	(0.047)	0.024
1989	0.283	(0.040)	0.039	0.279	(0.040)	0.039
1990	0.406	(0.041)	0.061	0.401	(0.041)	0.061
Quarter dummies:						
2nd quarter	-0.003	(0.025)	-0.001	-0.002	(0.025)	0.000
3rd quarter	0.099	(0.025)	0.012	0.104	(0.025)	0.013
4th quarter	-0.017	(0.026)	-0.002	-0.019	(0.026)	-0.002
Highest education qualification:						
Other	0.270	(0.056)	0.038	0.237	(0.063)	0.033
O levels	0.245	(0.037)	0.032	0.222	(0.044)	0.029
Lower vocational	0.491	(0.044)	0.079	0.457	(0.054)	0.072
5+ O levels	0.378	(0.040)	0.055	0.374	(0.040)	0.055
Middle vocational	0.543	(0.044)	0.090	0.579	(0.057)	0.099
A levels	0.776	(0.041)	0.146	0.726	(0.063)	0.134
Higher vocational	0.696	(0.038)	0.119	0.593	(0.107)	0.096
Degree	0.689	(0.039)	0.120	0.555	(0.135)	0.090
Industry 1981 job:						
Energy and water	0.043	(0.078)	0.005	0.047	(0.078)	0.006
Minerals	0.120	(0.066)	0.015	0.053	(0.090)	0.006
Metals	0.072	(0.049)	0.009	-0.004	(0.088)	0.000
Other manufacturing	-0.156	(0.050)	-0.016	-0.249	(0.104)	-0.025
Construction	-0.237	(0.164)	-0.023	-0.333	(0.189)	-0.030
Wholesale and retail trade	0.111	(0.037)	0.014	0.027	(0.090)	0.003
Transport and communication	0.143	(0.050)	0.019	0.090	(0.071)	0.011
Finance	0.250	(0.034)	0.034	0.244	(0.034)	0.033
Other services	0.194	(0.026)	0.024	0.133	(0.064)	0.016
1981 region:						
South-East	-0.125	(0.030)	-0.014	-0.085	(0.048)	-0.010
South-West	-0.134	(0.040)	-0.014	-0.093	(0.057)	-0.010
Wales	0.098	(0.045)	0.012	0.189	(0.099)	0.025
West Midlands	-0.080	(0.037)	-0.009	-0.045	(0.051)	-0.005
East Midlands	-0.142	(0.041)	-0.015	-0.111	(0.049)	-0.012
East Anglia	-0.250	(0.053)	-0.024	-0.200	(0.071)	-0.020
Yorkshire and Humberside	-0.129	(0.038)	-0.014	-0.047	(0.088)	-0.005
North-West	0.007	(0.034)	0.001	0.038	(0.044)	0.005
North	-0.199	(0.050)	-0.020	-0.126	(0.086)	-0.014
Scotland	-0.122	(0.036)	-0.013	-0.094	(0.045)	-0.010
Employer size 1981 job:						
10–24	-0.103	(0.033)	-0.011	-0.088	(0.036)	-0.010
25–99	0.015	(0.029)	0.002	0.051	(0.045)	0.006
100–500	0.039	(0.030)	0.005	0.069	(0.042)	0.008
500+	0.013	(0.031)	0.001	0.055	(0.050)	0.007
Union member 1981	-0.004	(0.020)	-0.001	0.058	(0.064)	0.007
Private sector 1981	-0.071	(0.026)	-0.008	-0.086	(0.030)	-0.010
Part-time 1981	-0.156	(0.034)	-0.017	-0.164	(0.034)	-0.017
Number of observations		51162			51162	
Pseudo R^2		0.0625			0.0611	

TABLE B.35

Determinants of Female Employer Training I: NCDS

Variable	Probit			IV-Probit		
	Coef.	(S.E.)	Marg. effect	Coef.	(S.E.)	Marg. effect
Constant	0.736	(0.178)		3.101	(0.797)	
Moved job last year	-0.263	(0.056)	-0.096	2.851	(0.913)	0.064
Year dummies:						
1982	-0.186	(0.119)	-0.068	0.347	(0.200)	0.115
1983	-0.356	(0.120)	-0.133	0.307	(0.234)	0.103
1984	-0.290	(0.126)	-0.107	0.235	(0.204)	0.080
1985	-0.204	(0.126)	-0.075	0.206	(0.175)	0.071
1986	-0.343	(0.122)	-0.128	0.150	(0.188)	0.052
1987	-0.514	(0.120)	-0.195	-0.220	(0.145)	-0.082
1988	-0.392	(0.120)	-0.147	-0.180	(0.132)	-0.066
1989	-0.419	(0.115)	-0.158	-0.347	(0.115)	-0.131
1990	-0.355	(0.114)	-0.133	-0.325	(0.114)	-0.122
Quarter dummies:						
2nd quarter	0.012	(0.068)	0.004	0.017	(0.068)	0.006
3rd quarter	-0.161	(0.064)	-0.058	-0.126	(0.065)	-0.046
4th quarter	-0.128	(0.070)	-0.046	-0.136	(0.070)	-0.049
Highest education qualification:						
Other	-0.871	(0.163)	-0.335	-1.099	(0.181)	-0.417
O levels	-0.135	(0.115)	-0.049	-0.340	(0.131)	-0.126
Lower vocational	-0.256	(0.130)	-0.095	-0.529	(0.156)	-0.203
5+ O levels	-0.148	(0.119)	-0.054	-0.208	(0.120)	-0.077
Middle vocational	-0.001	(0.129)	0.000	0.327	(0.161)	0.108
A levels	0.293	(0.120)	0.097	-0.111	(0.172)	-0.040
Higher vocational	0.171	(0.116)	0.059	-0.678	(0.288)	-0.259
Degree	0.205	(0.116)	0.069	-0.889	(0.362)	-0.341
Industry 1981 job:						
Energy and water	-0.717	(0.213)	-0.277	-0.689	(0.212)	-0.267
Minerals	-0.366	(0.167)	-0.138	-0.862	(0.233)	-0.333
Metals	-0.553	(0.138)	-0.212	-1.173	(0.239)	-0.442
Other manufacturing	0.018	(0.143)	0.006	-0.765	(0.281)	-0.295
Wholesale and retail trade	-0.247	(0.101)	-0.091	-0.943	(0.235)	-0.360
Transport and communication	-0.497	(0.128)	-0.190	-0.946	(0.190)	-0.364
Finance	0.470	(0.095)	0.149	0.446	(0.095)	0.144
Other services	0.103	(0.071)	0.036	-0.390	(0.170)	-0.143
1981 region:						
South-East	0.510	(0.084)	0.164	0.803	(0.128)	0.244
South-West	0.161	(0.104)	0.055	0.474	(0.146)	0.150
Wales	-0.369	(0.108)	-0.139	0.352	(0.255)	0.115
West Midlands	0.046	(0.097)	0.016	0.322	(0.133)	0.107
East Midlands	0.483	(0.116)	0.151	0.666	(0.132)	0.198
East Anglia	0.136	(0.151)	0.046	0.537	(0.196)	0.165
Yorkshire and Humberside	-0.290	(0.099)	-0.108	0.403	(0.237)	0.131
North-West	0.408	(0.090)	0.132	0.618	(0.116)	0.190
North	0.663	(0.148)	0.193	1.207	(0.236)	0.289
Scotland	0.291	(0.099)	0.097	0.479	(0.118)	0.153
Employer size 1981 job:						
10–24	-0.097	(0.094)	-0.035	0.035	(0.104)	0.013
25–99	-0.167	(0.079)	-0.060	0.117	(0.122)	0.041
100–500	-0.298	(0.081)	-0.109	-0.044	(0.115)	-0.016
500+	-0.005	(0.087)	-0.002	0.312	(0.138)	0.106
Union member 1981	0.302	(0.053)	0.106	0.807	(0.168)	0.279
Private sector 1981	-0.013	(0.070)	-0.005	-0.170	(0.084)	-0.060
Part-time 1981	-0.309	(0.094)	-0.115	-0.340	(0.095)	-0.128
Number of observations	3623			3623		
Pseudo R^2	0.1175			0.1149		

Note: Estimation of this equation is on the sub-sample of women who undertook some form of training in the quarter.

TABLE B.36

Determinants of Female Completed Training: NCDS

Variable	Probit			IV-Probit		
	Coef.	(S.E.)	Marg. effect	Coef.	(S.E.)	Marg. effect
Constant	-0.755	(0.172)		-1.803	(0.702)	
Moved job last year	-0.153	(0.055)	-0.057	-1.190	(0.802)	-0.034
Year dummies:						
1982	0.016	(0.114)	0.006	-0.174	(0.182)	-0.064
1983	0.322	(0.113)	0.126	0.080	(0.211)	0.031
1984	0.414	(0.117)	0.162	0.216	(0.185)	0.083
1985	0.532	(0.116)	0.209	0.392	(0.158)	0.153
1986	0.452	(0.115)	0.177	0.291	(0.171)	0.113
1987	0.530	(0.114)	0.208	0.450	(0.133)	0.176
1988	0.562	(0.113)	0.220	0.513	(0.123)	0.201
1989	0.618	(0.108)	0.242	0.636	(0.108)	0.249
1990	0.687	(0.107)	0.268	0.709	(0.106)	0.277
Quarter dummies:						
2nd quarter	0.101	(0.063)	0.039	0.098	(0.063)	0.037
3rd quarter	0.142	(0.060)	0.054	0.126	(0.061)	0.048
4th quarter	-0.165	(0.067)	-0.062	-0.158	(0.067)	-0.059
Highest education qualification:						
Other	-0.284	(0.160)	-0.102	-0.172	(0.175)	-0.063
O levels	-0.123	(0.110)	-0.046	-0.046	(0.123)	-0.017
Lower vocational	-0.569	(0.126)	-0.191	-0.455	(0.148)	-0.157
5+ O levels	-0.202	(0.114)	-0.074	-0.195	(0.115)	-0.072
Middle vocational	-0.258	(0.122)	-0.093	-0.369	(0.148)	-0.130
A levels	-0.494	(0.113)	-0.169	-0.339	(0.159)	-0.120
Higher vocational	-0.444	(0.109)	-0.157	-0.114	(0.256)	-0.042
Degree	-0.078	(0.109)	-0.029	0.358	(0.321)	0.140
Industry 1981 job:						
Energy and water	0.410	(0.207)	0.161	0.390	(0.207)	0.153
Minerals	0.142	(0.173)	0.055	0.349	(0.222)	0.137
Metals	-0.298	(0.138)	-0.107	-0.057	(0.219)	-0.021
Other manufacturing	-0.103	(0.140)	-0.038	0.188	(0.252)	0.073
Wholesale and retail trade	-0.075	(0.100)	-0.028	0.179	(0.209)	0.069
Transport and communication	0.136	(0.125)	0.053	0.310	(0.175)	0.121
Finance	0.049	(0.086)	0.019	0.061	(0.086)	0.023
Other services	0.008	(0.067)	0.003	0.201	(0.151)	0.077
1981 region:						
South-East	0.017	(0.077)	0.007	-0.110	(0.114)	-0.041
South-West	0.066	(0.100)	0.025	-0.066	(0.133)	-0.025
Wales	-0.315	(0.111)	-0.112	-0.614	(0.230)	-0.201
West Midlands	0.032	(0.093)	0.012	-0.090	(0.122)	-0.033
East Midlands	0.088	(0.105)	0.034	0.004	(0.117)	0.001
East Anglia	0.135	(0.142)	0.052	-0.029	(0.181)	-0.011
Yorkshire and Humberside	-0.086	(0.098)	-0.032	-0.356	(0.213)	-0.126
North-West	-0.012	(0.085)	-0.005	-0.114	(0.106)	-0.042
North	0.192	(0.133)	0.074	-0.064	(0.209)	-0.024
Scotland	-0.141	(0.092)	-0.052	-0.228	(0.108)	-0.083
Employer size 1981 job:						
10–24	0.287	(0.087)	0.111	0.229	(0.096)	0.088
25–99	0.256	(0.075)	0.099	0.133	(0.111)	0.051
100–500	0.206	(0.077)	0.079	0.100	(0.106)	0.038
500+	0.277	(0.081)	0.107	0.129	(0.125)	0.049
Union member 1981	0.052	(0.051)	0.020	-0.151	(0.150)	-0.057
Private sector 1981	0.112	(0.067)	0.042	0.167	(0.079)	0.063
Part-time 1981	-0.230	(0.092)	-0.084	-0.210	(0.092)	-0.077
Number of observations	3623			3623		
Pseudo R^2	0.0554			0.0542		

Note: Estimation of this equation is on the sub-sample of women who undertook some form of training in the quarter.

TABLE B.37

Determinants of Female Qualification Training: NCDS

Variable	Probit			IV-Probit		
	Coef.	(S.E.)	Marg. effect	Coef.	(S.E.)	Marg. effect
Constant	0.710	(0.169)		0.235	(0.710)	
Moved job last year	0.130	(0.054)	0.049	-0.595	(0.811)	-0.017
Year dummies:						
1982	0.026	(0.109)	0.010	-0.099	(0.180)	-0.038
1983	-0.035	(0.110)	-0.014	-0.188	(0.212)	-0.073
1984	-0.402	(0.113)	-0.158	-0.522	(0.184)	-0.205
1985	-0.462	(0.113)	-0.182	-0.561	(0.157)	-0.221
1986	-0.562	(0.111)	-0.221	-0.680	(0.169)	-0.266
1987	-0.493	(0.110)	-0.194	-0.570	(0.131)	-0.224
1988	-0.435	(0.110)	-0.172	-0.496	(0.120)	-0.195
1989	-0.587	(0.105)	-0.231	-0.619	(0.105)	-0.243
1990	-0.853	(0.104)	-0.329	-0.872	(0.103)	-0.336
Quarter dummies:						
2nd quarter	-0.005	(0.063)	-0.002	-0.007	(0.063)	-0.003
3rd quarter	0.108	(0.061)	0.041	0.102	(0.062)	0.039
4th quarter	0.019	(0.066)	0.007	0.019	(0.066)	0.007
Highest education qualification:						
Other	0.499	(0.163)	0.174	0.544	(0.179)	0.187
O levels	-0.134	(0.111)	-0.052	-0.088	(0.124)	-0.034
Lower vocational	0.187	(0.125)	0.070	0.246	(0.147)	0.091
5+ O levels	0.168	(0.115)	0.063	0.188	(0.116)	0.070
Middle vocational	-0.324	(0.124)	-0.128	-0.398	(0.150)	-0.157
A levels	-0.020	(0.113)	-0.008	0.073	(0.159)	0.028
Higher vocational	0.118	(0.109)	0.045	0.304	(0.259)	0.112
Degree	-0.164	(0.110)	-0.064	0.072	(0.325)	0.027
Industry 1981 job:						
Energy and water	-0.510	(0.211)	-0.201	-0.507	(0.211)	-0.200
Minerals	-0.620	(0.170)	-0.244	-0.522	(0.220)	-0.206
Metals	0.424	(0.146)	0.151	0.566	(0.227)	0.194
Other manufacturing	0.338	(0.145)	0.123	0.513	(0.258)	0.179
Wholesale and retail trade	-0.113	(0.100)	-0.044	0.041	(0.212)	0.016
Transport and communication	-0.153	(0.124)	-0.060	-0.052	(0.176)	-0.020
Finance	-0.462	(0.086)	-0.182	-0.457	(0.086)	-0.180
Other services	-0.158	(0.068)	-0.061	-0.051	(0.152)	-0.020
1981 region:						
South-East	-0.016	(0.076)	-0.006	-0.077	(0.114)	-0.030
South-West	0.352	(0.101)	0.128	0.293	(0.133)	0.107
Wales	-0.071	(0.106)	-0.028	-0.219	(0.230)	-0.086
West Midlands	0.105	(0.094)	0.040	0.051	(0.123)	0.019
East Midlands	0.312	(0.106)	0.114	0.280	(0.119)	0.103
East Anglia	-0.317	(0.143)	-0.125	-0.402	(0.183)	-0.159
Yorkshire and Humberside	0.109	(0.096)	0.041	-0.039	(0.213)	-0.015
North-West	0.062	(0.085)	0.024	0.024	(0.106)	0.009
North	0.122	(0.134)	0.046	0.018	(0.210)	0.007
Scotland	0.472	(0.093)	0.168	0.438	(0.108)	0.157
Employer size 1981 job:						
10–24	-0.531	(0.087)	-0.209	-0.558	(0.096)	-0.219
25–99	-0.204	(0.074)	-0.079	-0.262	(0.111)	-0.102
100–500	-0.083	(0.077)	-0.032	-0.136	(0.105)	-0.053
500+	-0.173	(0.080)	-0.067	-0.235	(0.124)	-0.091
Union member 1981	-0.013	(0.051)	-0.005	-0.124	(0.152)	-0.047
Private sector 1981	0.073	(0.067)	0.028	0.110	(0.079)	0.042
Part-time 1981	-0.003	(0.091)	-0.001	0.001	(0.092)	0.000
Number of observations	3623			3623		
Pseudo R^2	0.0857			0.0846		

Note: Estimation of this equation is on the sub-sample of women who undertook some form of training in the quarter.

143

TABLE B.38

Determinants of Female Employer Training II: NCDS

Variable	Probit Coef.	(S.E.)	Marg. effect	IV-Probit Coef.	(S.E.)	Marg. effect
Constant	-2.216	(0.072)		-1.557	(0.333)	
Moved job last year	0.063	(0.025)	0.005	0.760	(0.384)	0.006
Year dummies:						
1982	0.036	(0.045)	0.003	0.166	(0.082)	0.015
1983	0.015	(0.046)	0.001	0.180	(0.098)	0.017
1984	-0.030	(0.048)	-0.002	0.104	(0.085)	0.009
1985	0.015	(0.047)	0.001	0.116	(0.071)	0.010
1986	0.034	(0.047)	0.003	0.152	(0.078)	0.014
1987	0.025	(0.047)	0.002	0.089	(0.059)	0.008
1988	0.074	(0.046)	0.006	0.115	(0.052)	0.010
1989	0.178	(0.045)	0.017	0.181	(0.045)	0.017
1990	0.288	(0.045)	0.029	0.286	(0.045)	0.029
Quarter dummies:						
2nd quarter	0.004	(0.028)	0.000	0.007	(0.028)	0.001
3rd quarter	0.047	(0.028)	0.004	0.056	(0.028)	0.005
4th quarter	-0.046	(0.029)	-0.004	-0.049	(0.030)	-0.004
Highest education qualification:						
Other	-0.005	(0.077)	0.000	-0.069	(0.084)	-0.005
O levels	0.204	(0.044)	0.019	0.154	(0.051)	0.014
Lower vocational	0.401	(0.051)	0.045	0.330	(0.063)	0.035
5+ O levels	0.291	(0.047)	0.029	0.282	(0.047)	0.028
Middle vocational	0.528	(0.050)	0.065	0.606	(0.064)	0.078
A levels	0.770	(0.046)	0.111	0.664	(0.071)	0.089
Higher vocational	0.675	(0.044)	0.085	0.459	(0.120)	0.051
Degree	0.682	(0.045)	0.089	0.401	(0.152)	0.043
Industry 1981 job:						
Energy and water	-0.199	(0.105)	-0.014	-0.191	(0.105)	-0.013
Minerals	0.044	(0.077)	0.004	-0.092	(0.104)	-0.007
Metals	-0.095	(0.062)	-0.007	-0.255	(0.103)	-0.017
Other manufacturing	-0.172	(0.058)	-0.012	-0.369	(0.117)	-0.023
Construction	-0.007	(0.166)	-0.001	-0.210	(0.196)	-0.014
Wholesale and retail trade	0.005	(0.045)	0.000	-0.174	(0.102)	-0.013
Transport and communication	0.001	(0.060)	0.000	-0.110	(0.083)	-0.008
Finance	0.326	(0.037)	0.033	0.315	(0.038)	0.032
Other services	0.198	(0.030)	0.017	0.072	(0.072)	0.006
1981 region:						
South-East	-0.010	(0.034)	-0.001	0.071	(0.054)	0.006
South-West	-0.070	(0.045)	-0.005	0.018	(0.064)	0.001
Wales	-0.021	(0.055)	-0.002	0.169	(0.112)	0.016
West Midlands	-0.051	(0.043)	-0.004	0.023	(0.058)	0.002
East Midlands	0.000	(0.046)	0.000	0.059	(0.054)	0.005
East Anglia	-0.212	(0.061)	-0.015	-0.107	(0.082)	-0.008
Yorkshire and Humberside	-0.197	(0.046)	-0.014	-0.025	(0.100)	-0.002
North-West	0.114	(0.039)	0.010	0.176	(0.050)	0.016
North	-0.068	(0.056)	-0.005	0.082	(0.096)	0.007
Scotland	-0.021	(0.040)	-0.002	0.038	(0.051)	0.003
Employer size 1981 job:						
10–24	-0.098	(0.037)	-0.008	-0.065	(0.041)	-0.005
25–99	-0.006	(0.033)	0.000	0.068	(0.051)	0.006
100–500	-0.012	(0.034)	-0.001	0.052	(0.047)	0.004
500+	0.022	(0.035)	0.002	0.109	(0.057)	0.010
Union member 1981	0.054	(0.023)	0.004	0.185	(0.071)	0.015
Private sector 1981	-0.066	(0.030)	-0.006	-0.100	(0.034)	-0.008
Part-time 1981	-0.221	(0.041)	-0.016	-0.235	(0.041)	-0.016
Number of observations	51162			51162		
Pseudo R^2	0.0726			0.0725		

TABLE B.39

Determinants of Female Non-Employer Training: NCDS

Variable	Probit			IV-Probit		
	Coef.	(S.E.)	Marg. effect	Coef.	(S.E.)	Marg. effect
Constant	-2.662	(0.097)		-3.521	(0.411)	
Moved job last year	0.208	(0.031)	0.010	-1.075	(0.472)	-0.005
Year dummies:						
1982	0.191	(0.068)	0.010	-0.011	(0.107)	0.000
1983	0.267	(0.067)	0.014	0.012	(0.126)	0.001
1984	0.153	(0.070)	0.007	-0.055	(0.111)	-0.002
1985	0.137	(0.071)	0.007	-0.021	(0.097)	-0.001
1986	0.306	(0.068)	0.017	0.120	(0.102)	0.006
1987	0.386	(0.066)	0.023	0.279	(0.079)	0.015
1988	0.342	(0.067)	0.020	0.270	(0.073)	0.015
1989	0.431	(0.065)	0.027	0.415	(0.065)	0.026
1990	0.539	(0.065)	0.037	0.533	(0.065)	0.037
Quarter dummies:						
2nd quarter	-0.020	(0.039)	-0.001	-0.024	(0.039)	-0.001
3rd quarter	0.165	(0.036)	0.008	0.151	(0.037)	0.007
4th quarter	0.038	(0.039)	0.002	0.043	(0.039)	0.002
Highest education qualification:						
Other	0.507	(0.070)	0.036	0.601	(0.081)	0.047
O levels	0.269	(0.054)	0.014	0.349	(0.062)	0.019
Lower vocational	0.529	(0.063)	0.037	0.639	(0.077)	0.050
5+ O levels	0.450	(0.058)	0.028	0.464	(0.058)	0.030
Middle vocational	0.449	(0.067)	0.029	0.332	(0.083)	0.020
A levels	0.550	(0.063)	0.039	0.705	(0.091)	0.058
Higher vocational	0.524	(0.058)	0.034	0.850	(0.150)	0.072
Degree	0.518	(0.060)	0.034	0.940	(0.187)	0.089
Industry 1981 job:						
Energy and water	0.315	(0.097)	0.019	0.300	(0.097)	0.018
Minerals	0.254	(0.090)	0.014	0.447	(0.123)	0.031
Metals	0.293	(0.065)	0.017	0.528	(0.118)	0.038
Other manufacturing	-0.062	(0.073)	-0.003	0.235	(0.143)	0.013
Wholesale and retail trade	0.246	(0.052)	0.013	0.515	(0.123)	0.034
Transport and communication	0.321	(0.066)	0.019	0.481	(0.095)	0.033
Finance	0.016	(0.055)	0.001	0.022	(0.055)	0.001
Other services	0.135	(0.041)	0.006	0.323	(0.089)	0.016
1981 region:						
South-East	-0.322	(0.046)	-0.011	-0.443	(0.069)	-0.015
South-West	-0.207	(0.059)	-0.007	-0.352	(0.083)	-0.011
Wales	0.243	(0.058)	0.013	-0.051	(0.135)	-0.002
West Midlands	-0.111	(0.053)	-0.004	-0.228	(0.072)	-0.008
East Midlands	-0.377	(0.068)	-0.012	-0.471	(0.078)	-0.014
East Anglia	-0.260	(0.077)	-0.009	-0.421	(0.101)	-0.012
Yorkshire and Humberside	-0.007	(0.052)	0.000	-0.268	(0.121)	-0.009
North-West	-0.165	(0.051)	-0.006	-0.261	(0.065)	-0.009
North	-0.375	(0.080)	-0.011	-0.609	(0.127)	-0.015
Scotland	-0.281	(0.055)	-0.010	-0.372	(0.067)	-0.012
Employer size 1981 job:						
10–24	-0.097	(0.050)	-0.004	-0.143	(0.054)	-0.006
25–99	0.054	(0.043)	0.002	-0.054	(0.063)	-0.002
100–500	0.125	(0.043)	0.006	0.028	(0.059)	0.001
500+	-0.013	(0.047)	-0.001	-0.141	(0.072)	-0.006
Union member 1981	-0.133	(0.030)	-0.006	-0.329	(0.088)	-0.014
Private sector 1981	-0.090	(0.038)	-0.004	-0.033	(0.044)	-0.001
Part-time 1981	-0.030	(0.047)	-0.001	-0.012	(0.048)	0.000
Number of observations	48653			48653		
Pseudo R^2	0.0637			0.0602		

Note: Estimation of this equation is on the sub-sample of women who did not undertake employer training in the quarter.

TABLE B.40

Mobility and the Determinants of Male Training: QLFS

Variable	Males			Young Males		
	Coef.	(S.E.)	Marg. effect	Coef.	(S.E.)	Marg. effect
Constant	-0.658	(0.135)		6.962	(1.033)	
Moved job last year	-0.044	(0.040)	-0.008	-0.170	(0.061)	-0.036
Panel dummies:						
Jun 1992	-0.144	(0.039)	-0.024	-0.368	(0.078)	-0.072
Sep 1992	-0.079	(0.038)	-0.014	-0.194	(0.073)	-0.041
Dec 1992	-0.065	(0.038)	-0.011	-0.152	(0.073)	-0.032
Mar 1993	0.009	(0.038)	0.002	-0.067	(0.073)	-0.015
Jun 1993	-0.199	(0.040)	-0.032	-0.358	(0.076)	-0.071
Sep 1993	-0.089	(0.039)	-0.015	-0.247	(0.077)	-0.051
Highest education qualification:						
Degree	0.766	(0.044)	0.182	1.193	(0.127)	0.384
Higher vocational	0.765	(0.049)	0.194	1.046	(0.130)	0.333
Middle vocational	0.665	(0.046)	0.156	0.984	(0.119)	0.288
Lower vocational	0.475	(0.042)	0.094	0.742	(0.114)	0.169
Other	0.377	(0.051)	0.080	0.526	(0.171)	0.149
Industry:						
Energy and water	-0.041	(0.056)	-0.007	-0.031	(0.138)	-0.007
Minerals	-0.173	(0.051)	-0.028	-0.144	(0.112)	-0.030
Metals	-0.294	(0.034)	-0.046	-0.144	(0.071)	-0.031
Other manufacturing	-0.416	(0.043)	-0.060	-0.451	(0.086)	-0.084
Construction	-0.376	(0.048)	-0.054	-0.300	(0.090)	-0.059
Wholesale and retail trade	-0.327	(0.037)	-0.050	-0.450	(0.071)	-0.089
Transport and communication	-0.299	(0.042)	-0.046	-0.349	(0.091)	-0.067
Finance	-0.138	(0.036)	-0.023	-0.101	(0.073)	-0.022
Region:						
South-East	0.030	(0.041)	0.005	0.029	(0.081)	0.007
South-West	0.056	(0.050)	0.010	0.117	(0.098)	0.028
Wales	0.059	(0.059)	0.011	0.119	(0.117)	0.029
West Midlands	0.056	(0.048)	0.010	0.079	(0.093)	0.019
East Midlands	0.046	(0.050)	0.008	0.045	(0.100)	0.010
East Anglia	-0.055	(0.066)	-0.010	0.155	(0.122)	0.038
Yorkshire and Humberside	0.068	(0.048)	0.013	0.119	(0.094)	0.028
North-West	-0.020	(0.046)	-0.004	-0.013	(0.089)	-0.003
North	0.022	(0.057)	0.004	-0.076	(0.113)	-0.017
Scotland	-0.048	(0.049)	-0.008	-0.056	(0.095)	-0.012
Age	-0.031	(0.006)	-0.006	-0.653	(0.088)	-0.148
Age^2/100	0.019	(0.008)	0.003	1.231	(0.184)	0.279
Part-time	0.066	(0.064)	0.012	0.059	(0.094)	0.014
Non-white	-0.069	(0.063)	-0.012	0.103	(0.118)	0.025
Employer size 25+	0.152	(0.026)	0.026	0.117	(0.048)	0.026
Number of observations	26638			5903		
Pseudo R^2	0.068			0.083		

TABLE B.41

Determinants of Male Employer Training I: QLFS

Variable	Males			Young Males		
	Coef.	(S.E.)	Marg. effect	Coef.	(S.E.)	Marg. effect
Constant	-0.081	(0.298)		4.703	(2.310)	
Moved job last year	-0.072	(0.089)	-0.028	-0.194	(0.140)	-0.076
Panel dummies:						
Jun 1992	-0.078	(0.087)	-0.030	-0.049	(0.178)	-0.019
Sep 1992	0.021	(0.084)	0.008	0.083	(0.161)	0.032
Dec 1992	-0.001	(0.084)	0.000	0.151	(0.162)	0.058
Mar 1993	0.008	(0.082)	0.003	-0.002	(0.157)	-0.001
Jun 1993	-0.019	(0.089)	-0.007	-0.019	(0.180)	-0.008
Sep 1993	0.150	(0.086)	0.057	0.124	(0.172)	0.048
Highest education qualification:						
Degree	0.354	(0.117)	0.133	0.819	(0.365)	0.286
Higher vocational	0.208	(0.125)	0.079	0.455	(0.375)	0.167
Middle vocational	0.332	(0.121)	0.124	0.536	(0.352)	0.201
Lower vocational	0.121	(0.115)	0.047	0.386	(0.344)	0.150
Other	0.048	(0.135)	0.019			
Industry:						
Energy and water	0.431	(0.119)	0.155			
Minerals	0.172	(0.111)	0.065	0.382	(0.236)	0.141
Metals	0.338	(0.076)	0.126	0.391	(0.145)	0.148
Other manufacturing	0.027	(0.100)	0.010	-0.239	(0.193)	-0.094
Construction	0.219	(0.109)	0.082			
Wholesale and retail trade	0.043	(0.085)	0.017	-0.185	(0.159)	-0.073
Transport and communication	0.416	(0.096)	0.151	0.561	(0.207)	0.201
Finance	0.298	(0.076)	0.112	0.291	(0.147)	0.111
Region:						
South-East	0.067	(0.090)	0.026	0.029	(0.180)	0.011
South-West	0.022	(0.110)	0.009	0.073	(0.224)	0.028
Wales	0.008	(0.130)	0.003	0.126	(0.262)	0.048
West Midlands	0.112	(0.106)	0.043	0.117	(0.207)	0.045
East Midlands	0.050	(0.111)	0.019	-0.208	(0.226)	-0.082
East Anglia	-0.130	(0.147)	-0.051	-0.466	(0.266)	-0.184
Yorkshire and Humberside	-0.057	(0.106)	-0.022	-0.264	(0.211)	-0.105
North-West	-0.060	(0.103)	-0.024	-0.061	(0.204)	-0.024
North	0.196	(0.126)	0.074	0.090	(0.266)	0.035
Scotland	0.025	(0.108)	0.010	-0.028	(0.219)	-0.011
Age	0.000	(0.014)	0.000	-0.411	(0.198)	-0.161
Age^2/100	-0.003	(0.019)	-0.001	0.825	(0.418)	0.322
Part-time	-1.236	(0.160)	-0.441	-1.462	(0.222)	-0.501
Non-white	0.051	(0.140)	0.020	-0.173	(0.238)	-0.069
Employer size 25+	-0.007	(0.060)	-0.003	0.015	(0.115)	0.006
Number of observations	3179			867		
Pseudo R^2	0.044			0.129		

Note: Estimation of this equation is on the sub-sample of men who undertook some form of training in the quarter. The other qualification, energy and water, and construction dummies have been excluded from the young male equation because they completely determine employer training outcomes.

TABLE B.42

Determinants of Male Employer Training II: QLFS

Variable	Males			Young Males		
	Coef.	(S.E.)	Marg. effect	Coef.	(S.E.)	Marg. effect
Constant	-1.212	(0.154)		7.257	(1.205)	
Moved job last year	-0.066	(0.047)	-0.008	-0.258	(0.075)	-0.033
Panel dummies:						
Jun 1992	-0.149	(0.046)	-0.017	-0.325	(0.093)	-0.041
Sep 1992	-0.055	(0.044)	-0.007	-0.106	(0.085)	-0.015
Dec 1992	-0.051	(0.045)	-0.006	-0.064	(0.085)	-0.009
Mar 1993	0.009	(0.044)	0.001	-0.032	(0.085)	-0.005
Jun 1993	0.270	(0.042)	0.039	0.041	(0.083)	0.006
Sep 1993	-0.026	(0.045)	-0.003	-0.173	(0.090)	-0.023
Highest education qualification:						
Degree	0.808	(0.052)	0.149	1.353	(0.164)	0.359
Higher vocational	0.757	(0.058)	0.148	1.104	(0.168)	0.279
Middle vocational	0.699	(0.054)	0.127	1.052	(0.158)	0.233
Lower vocational	0.451	(0.051)	0.065	0.781	(0.153)	0.119
Other	0.333	(0.060)	0.051	0.422	(0.230)	0.081
Industry:						
Energy and water	0.089	(0.061)	0.012	0.082	(0.149)	0.013
Minerals	-0.103	(0.058)	-0.012	-0.001	(0.121)	0.000
Metals	-0.143	(0.038)	-0.017	-0.002	(0.078)	0.000
Other manufacturing	-0.369	(0.050)	-0.037	-0.550	(0.108)	-0.060
Construction	-0.267	(0.053)	-0.028	-0.244	(0.103)	-0.031
Wholesale and retail trade	-0.295	(0.044)	-0.032	-0.496	(0.087)	-0.061
Transport and communication	-0.129	(0.046)	-0.015	-0.102	(0.099)	-0.014
Finance	-0.017	(0.040)	-0.002	-0.020	(0.081)	-0.003
Region:						
South-East	0.048	(0.046)	0.006	0.034	(0.093)	0.005
South-West	0.067	(0.056)	0.009	0.223	(0.111)	0.037
Wales	0.059	(0.067)	0.008	0.085	(0.135)	0.013
West Midlands	0.074	(0.054)	0.010	0.168	(0.105)	0.027
East Midlands	0.045	(0.057)	0.006	-0.020	(0.117)	-0.003
East Anglia	-0.083	(0.076)	-0.010	-0.031	(0.149)	-0.004
Yorkshire and Humberside	0.051	(0.055)	0.007	0.010	(0.110)	0.001
North-West	-0.037	(0.053)	-0.005	0.027	(0.102)	0.004
North	0.061	(0.063)	0.008	-0.003	(0.129)	0.000
Scotland	-0.034	(0.055)	-0.004	0.001	(0.108)	0.000
Age	-0.025	(0.007)	-0.003	-0.721	(0.102)	-0.106
Age^2/100	0.014	(0.009)	0.002	1.370	(0.214)	0.202
Part-time	-0.548	(0.102)	-0.046	-0.918	(0.159)	-0.075
Non-white	-0.058	(0.071)	-0.007	0.072	(0.135)	0.011
Employer size 25+	0.137	(0.030)	0.016	0.136	(0.057)	0.019
Number of observations	26638			5903		
Pseudo R^2	0.068			0.105		

TABLE B.43

Determinants of Male Non-Employer Training: QLFS

Variable	Males			Young Males		
	Coef.	(S.E.)	Marg. effect	Coef.	(S.E.)	Marg. effect
Constant	-1.083	(0.177)		2.874	(1.312)	
Moved job last year	0.027	(0.051)	0.003	-0.062	(0.076)	-0.008
Panel dummies:						
Jun 1992	-0.097	(0.051)	-0.009	-0.295	(0.099)	-0.032
Sep 1992	-0.083	(0.051)	-0.007	-0.221	(0.095)	-0.025
Dec 1992	-0.055	(0.051)	-0.005	-0.191	(0.096)	-0.022
Mar 1993	0.008	(0.050)	0.001	-0.071	(0.094)	-0.009
Jun 1993	-0.033	(0.051)	-0.003	-0.137	(0.095)	-0.016
Sep 1993	-0.148	(0.052)	-0.013	-0.247	(0.100)	-0.028
Highest education qualification:						
Degree	0.566	(0.058)	0.074	0.785	(0.160)	0.155
Higher vocational	0.622	(0.064)	0.090	0.796	(0.162)	0.160
Middle vocational	0.478	(0.060)	0.060	0.741	(0.146)	0.132
Lower vocational	0.400	(0.054)	0.043	0.594	(0.138)	0.077
Other	0.346	(0.065)	0.041	0.522	(0.203)	0.094
Industry:						
Energy and water	-0.249	(0.079)	-0.019	-0.289	(0.203)	-0.030
Minerals	-0.227	(0.067)	-0.018	-0.301	(0.156)	-0.031
Metals	-0.409	(0.046)	-0.031	-0.308	(0.095)	-0.033
Other manufacturing	-0.394	(0.054)	-0.029	-0.347	(0.105)	-0.036
Construction	-0.426	(0.063)	-0.029	-0.283	(0.115)	-0.030
Wholesale and retail trade	-0.304	(0.047)	-0.024	-0.331	(0.086)	-0.037
Transport and communication	-0.463	(0.058)	-0.032	-0.640	(0.136)	-0.055
Finance	-0.277	(0.049)	-0.022	-0.246	(0.097)	-0.027
Region:						
South-East	-0.010	(0.053)	-0.001	-0.001	(0.105)	0.000
South-West	0.015	(0.065)	0.001	-0.005	(0.131)	-0.001
Wales	0.047	(0.077)	0.005	0.115	(0.149)	0.016
West Midlands	-0.014	(0.064)	-0.001	-0.059	(0.125)	-0.007
East Midlands	-0.016	(0.066)	-0.002	0.068	(0.128)	0.009
East Anglia	-0.002	(0.083)	0.000	0.301	(0.146)	0.047
Yorkshire and Humberside	0.084	(0.062)	0.008	0.209	(0.118)	0.030
North-West	-0.007	(0.060)	-0.001	-0.019	(0.115)	-0.002
North	-0.085	(0.077)	-0.007	-0.242	(0.156)	-0.026
Scotland	-0.073	(0.064)	-0.007	-0.116	(0.125)	-0.014
Age	-0.024	(0.008)	-0.002	-0.340	(0.112)	-0.043
Age²/100	0.012	(0.011)	0.000	0.609	(0.235)	0.001
Part-time	0.414	(0.069)	0.054	0.533	(0.101)	0.095
Non-white	-0.120	(0.084)	-0.010	0.072	(0.153)	0.010
Employer size 25+	0.125	(0.034)	0.011	0.070	(0.060)	0.009
Number of observations	24497			5281		
Pseudo R²	0.060			0.080		

Note: Estimation of this equation is on the sub-sample of men who did not undertake employer training in the quarter.

TABLE B.44

Mobility and the Determinants of Female Training: QLFS

Variable	Females			Young Females		
	Coef.	(S.E.)	Marg. effect	Coef.	(S.E.)	Marg. effect
Constant	-1.239	(0.144)		4.004	(1.024)	
Moved job last year	0.123	(0.034)	0.024	0.093	(0.052)	0.023
Panel dummies:						
Jun 1992	-0.159	(0.040)	-0.028	-0.319	(0.076)	-0.067
Sep 1992	-0.044	(0.039)	-0.008	-0.016	(0.072)	-0.004
Dec 1992	-0.058	(0.039)	-0.011	-0.125	(0.073)	-0.029
Mar 1993	0.003	(0.038)	0.001	-0.076	(0.073)	-0.018
Jun 1993	-0.216	(0.040)	-0.037	-0.284	(0.076)	-0.061
Sep 1993	-0.051	(0.039)	-0.009	-0.096	(0.073)	-0.022
Highest education qualification:						
Degree	0.919	(0.044)	0.249	0.999	(0.125)	0.322
Higher vocational	0.886	(0.043)	0.237	0.846	(0.128)	0.266
Middle vocational	0.700	(0.046)	0.178	0.685	(0.120)	0.197
Lower vocational	0.447	(0.038)	0.090	0.325	(0.115)	0.076
Other	0.342	(0.054)	0.076	0.600	(0.175)	0.182
Industry:						
Energy and water	-0.128	(0.109)	-0.022	-0.066	(0.178)	-0.015
Minerals	-0.263	(0.086)	-0.042	-0.262	(0.155)	-0.054
Metals	-0.339	(0.056)	-0.052	-0.346	(0.101)	-0.070
Other manufacturing	-0.510	(0.054)	-0.072	-0.496	(0.089)	-0.094
Construction	-0.076	(0.085)	-0.014	-0.166	(0.165)	-0.036
Wholesale and retail trade	-0.218	(0.032)	-0.038	-0.237	(0.057)	-0.053
Transport and communication	-0.149	(0.061)	-0.026	-0.051	(0.100)	-0.012
Finance	-0.204	(0.033)	-0.035	-0.163	(0.056)	-0.037
Region:						
South-East	0.079	(0.041)	0.015	0.026	(0.076)	0.006
South-West	0.113	(0.049)	0.023	0.162	(0.093)	0.041
Wales	0.070	(0.060)	0.014	0.258	(0.109)	0.069
West Midlands	0.050	(0.049)	0.010	0.066	(0.090)	0.016
East Midlands	0.141	(0.051)	0.028	0.072	(0.098)	0.018
East Anglia	0.164	(0.063)	0.034	0.128	(0.119)	0.032
Yorkshire and Humberside	0.114	(0.048)	0.023	0.068	(0.089)	0.017
North-West	0.047	(0.046)	0.009	0.106	(0.084)	0.026
North	0.052	(0.056)	0.010	-0.015	(0.104)	-0.003
Scotland	-0.038	(0.049)	-0.007	-0.165	(0.092)	-0.037
Age	-0.007	(0.007)	-0.001	-0.414	(0.087)	-0.099
Age^2/100	-0.001	(0.009)	0.000	0.792	(0.182)	0.189
Part-time	-0.237	(0.024)	-0.044	-0.159	(0.054)	-0.036
Non-white	-0.086	(0.063)	-0.015	-0.045	(0.114)	-0.010
Employer size 25+	0.113	(0.023)	0.021	0.061	(0.044)	0.015
Number of observations	25198			5995		
Pseudo R^2	0.088			0.065		

TABLE B.45

Determinants of Female Employer Training I: QLFS

Variable	Females			Young Females		
	Coef.	(S.E.)	Marg. effect	Coef.	(S.E.)	Marg. effect
Constant	-0.572	(0.313)		-2.545	(2.343)	
Moved job last year	-0.233	(0.072)	-0.093	-0.289	(0.119)	-0.114
Panel dummies:						
Jun 1992	0.006	(0.086)	0.002	0.000	(0.181)	0.000
Sep 1992	-0.075	(0.080)	-0.030	-0.015	(0.161)	-0.006
Dec 1992	-0.134	(0.081)	-0.053	-0.200	(0.165)	-0.079
Mar 1993	-0.005	(0.079)	-0.002	-0.111	(0.162)	-0.044
Jun 1993	-0.043	(0.087)	-0.017	0.130	(0.176)	0.052
Sep 1993	0.067	(0.081)	0.027	0.172	(0.163)	0.068
Highest education qualification:						
Degree	0.176	(0.105)	0.070	-0.478	(0.354)	-0.186
Higher vocational	0.186	(0.105)	0.074	-0.227	(0.359)	-0.090
Middle vocational	0.108	(0.112)	0.043	-0.579	(0.349)	-0.225
Lower vocational	0.046	(0.099)	0.018	-0.583	(0.340)	-0.229
Other	-0.078	(0.138)	-0.031			
Industry:						
Energy and water						
Minerals	0.182	(0.194)	0.072			
Metals	-0.023	(0.129)	-0.009			
Other manufacturing	-0.031	(0.133)	-0.012			
Construction	-0.199	(0.183)	-0.079	0.217	(0.413)	0.086
Wholesale and retail trade	-0.298	(0.075)	-0.118	-0.059	(0.134)	-0.024
Transport and communication	0.114	(0.133)	0.045	0.119	(0.221)	0.047
Finance	0.027	(0.071)	0.011	0.226	(0.121)	0.090
Region:						
South-East	-0.049	(0.086)	-0.019	0.077	(0.168)	0.031
South-West	-0.050	(0.104)	-0.020	-0.366	(0.201)	-0.143
Wales	0.100	(0.125)	0.040	0.005	(0.227)	0.002
West Midlands	-0.076	(0.105)	-0.030	0.032	(0.194)	0.013
East Midlands	-0.201	(0.108)	-0.080	-0.275	(0.221)	-0.108
East Anglia	-0.113	(0.131)	-0.045	-0.008	(0.254)	-0.003
Yorkshire and Humberside	-0.151	(0.101)	-0.060	-0.328	(0.194)	-0.129
North-West	-0.156	(0.097)	-0.062	-0.348	(0.182)	-0.137
North	-0.057	(0.121)	-0.023	-0.079	(0.234)	-0.032
Scotland	-0.188	(0.104)	-0.075			
Age	0.040	(0.016)	0.016	0.231	(0.199)	0.092
$Age^2/100$	-0.050	(0.021)	-0.020	-0.403	(0.419)	-0.161
Part-time	-0.288	(0.052)	-0.114	-0.460	(0.133)	-0.180
Non-white	0.034	(0.135)	0.014	-0.273	(0.114)	-0.108
Employer size 25+	0.018	(0.050)	0.007	0.150	(0.104)	0.060
Number of observations	3303			822		
Pseudo R^2	0.032			0.086		

Note: Estimation of this equation is on the sub-sample of women who undertook some form of training in the quarter. The energy and water dummy is excluded from the female and young female equations because it completely determines employer training outcomes. The other qualification, minerals, metals, and other manufacturing dummies have been excluded from the young female equation because they completely determine employer training outcomes.

TABLE B.46

Determinants of Female Employer Training II: QLFS

Variable	Females			Young Females		
	Coef.	(S.E.)	Marg. effect	Coef.	(S.E.)	Marg. effect
Constant	-1.984	(0.177)		0.948	(1.273)	
Moved job last year	-0.025	(0.043)	-0.003	-0.072	(0.066)	-0.010
Panel dummies:						
Jun 1992	-0.128	(0.049)	-0.013	-0.291	(0.093)	-0.037
Sep 1992	-0.062	(0.047)	-0.007	-0.025	(0.087)	-0.004
Dec 1992	-0.098	(0.048)	-0.011	-0.237	(0.090)	-0.031
Mar 1993	0.002	(0.047)	0.000	-0.107	(0.088)	-0.015
Jun 1993	0.274	(0.044)	0.036	0.265	(0.082)	0.045
Sep 1993	-0.013	(0.047)	-0.001	-0.040	(0.087)	-0.006
Highest education qualification:						
Degree	0.875	(0.053)	0.164	0.727	(0.146)	0.156
Higher vocational	0.838	(0.053)	0.153	0.720	(0.147)	0.156
Middle vocational	0.668	(0.057)	0.113	0.460	(0.141)	0.083
Lower vocational	0.433	(0.048)	0.054	0.152	(0.135)	0.022
Other	0.279	(0.069)	0.038	0.300	(0.215)	0.054
Industry:						
Energy and water	0.137	(0.112)	0.017	0.078	(0.193)	0.012
Minerals	-0.184	(0.098)	-0.018	0.062	(0.160)	0.010
Metals	-0.349	(0.068)	-0.031	-0.351	(0.121)	-0.042
Other manufacturing	-0.465	(0.065)	-0.038	-0.438	(0.108)	-0.050
Construction	-0.141	(0.103)	-0.014	-0.102	(0.192)	-0.014
Wholesale and retail trade	-0.367	(0.041)	-0.035	-0.295	(0.071)	-0.039
Transport and communication	-0.127	(0.071)	-0.013	0.011	(0.114)	0.002
Finance	-0.170	(0.039)	-0.017	-0.029	(0.064)	-0.004
Region:						
South-East	0.054	(0.047)	0.006	0.061	(0.087)	0.009
South-West	0.086	(0.057)	0.010	0.016	(0.110)	0.002
Wales	0.135	(0.067)	0.017	0.241	(0.125)	0.042
West Midlands	0.013	(0.057)	0.001	0.057	(0.103)	0.009
East Midlands	0.007	(0.061)	0.001	-0.073	(0.117)	-0.010
East Anglia	0.073	(0.075)	0.009	0.083	(0.139)	0.013
Yorkshire and Humberside	0.068	(0.056)	0.008	0.011	(0.104)	0.002
North-West	-0.020	(0.054)	-0.002	-0.016	(0.099)	-0.002
North	-0.015	(0.066)	-0.002	-0.095	(0.124)	-0.013
Scotland	-0.078	(0.057)	-0.008	-0.189	(0.107)	-0.025
Age	0.016	(0.009)	0.002	-0.201	(0.107)	-0.030
Age^2/100	-0.027	(0.012)	-0.003	0.406	(0.223)	0.060
Part-time	-0.347	(0.029)	-0.038	-0.410	(0.071)	-0.052
Non-white	-0.037	(0.072)	-0.004	-0.008	(0.130)	-0.001
Employer size 25+	0.088	(0.028)	0.010	0.121	(0.054)	0.017
Number of observations	25198			5995		
Pseudo R^2	0.102			0.084		

TABLE B.47

Determinants of Female Non-Employer Training: QLFS

Variable	Females			Young Females		
	Coef.	(S.E.)	Marg. effect	Coef.	(S.E.)	Marg. effect
Constant	-1.222	(0.172)		4.258	(1.213)	
Moved job last year	0.210	(0.040)	0.028	0.182	(0.060)	0.030
Panel dummies:						
Jun 1992	-0.151	(0.050)	-0.016	-0.282	(0.096)	-0.038
Sep 1992	-0.019	(0.048)	-0.002	-0.007	(0.090)	-0.001
Dec 1992	-0.013	(0.048)	-0.002	-0.019	(0.089)	-0.003
Mar 1993	-0.002	(0.048)	0.000	-0.035	(0.090)	-0.005
Jun 1993	0.019	(0.048)	0.002	-0.063	(0.092)	-0.009
Sep 1993	-0.078	(0.048)	-0.009	-0.131	(0.092)	-0.019
Highest education qualification:						
Degree	0.789	(0.054)	0.148	1.084	(0.168)	0.277
Higher vocational	0.776	(0.052)	0.143	0.828	(0.171)	0.194
Middle vocational	0.616	(0.056)	0.106	0.773	(0.160)	0.163
Lower vocational	0.411	(0.046)	0.053	0.469	(0.154)	0.070
Other	0.352	(0.064)	0.052	0.676	(0.223)	0.154
Industry:						
Energy and water	-0.612	(0.191)	-0.045	-0.267	(0.247)	-0.034
Minerals	-0.288	(0.113)	-0.027	-0.495	(0.236)	-0.054
Metals	-0.281	(0.069)	-0.027	-0.332	(0.127)	-0.041
Other manufacturing	-0.454	(0.067)	-0.040	-0.440	(0.109)	-0.052
Construction	-0.020	(0.101)	-0.002	-0.299	(0.216)	-0.037
Wholesale and retail trade	-0.117	(0.037)	-0.013	-0.199	(0.067)	-0.028
Transport and communication	-0.204	(0.079)	-0.021	-0.154	(0.128)	-0.021
Finance	-0.206	(0.042)	-0.022	-0.279	(0.072)	-0.038
Region:						
South-East	0.079	(0.051)	0.010	-0.059	(0.097)	-0.009
South-West	0.113	(0.061)	0.014	0.200	(0.112)	0.034
Wales	0.006	(0.077)	0.001	0.152	(0.138)	0.026
West Midlands	0.059	(0.061)	0.007	0.017	(0.113)	0.003
East Midlands	0.190	(0.062)	0.026	0.118	(0.118)	0.019
East Anglia	0.189	(0.076)	0.026	0.015	(0.150)	0.002
Yorkshire and Humberside	0.133	(0.060)	0.017	0.075	(0.109)	0.012
North-West	0.071	(0.057)	0.009	0.135	(0.103)	0.022
North	0.043	(0.070)	0.005	-0.011	(0.127)	-0.002
Scotland	0.002	(0.061)	0.000	-0.132	(0.113)	-0.019
Age	-0.029	(0.009)	-0.003	-0.456	(0.103)	-0.070
Age^2/100	0.026	(0.011)	0.000	0.838	(0.219)	0.001
Part-time	-0.104	(0.028)	-0.012	0.024	(0.062)	0.004
Non-white	-0.090	(0.080)	-0.010	0.008	(0.140)	0.001
Employer size 25+	0.093	(0.028)	0.011	0.017	(0.054)	0.003
Number of observations		23247			5409	
Pseudo R^2		0.066			0.072	

Note: Estimation of this equation is on the sub-sample of women who did not undertake employer training in the quarter.

TABLE B.48

Poisson Model of Training and Male Job Changes: NCDS

Variable	Coef.	(S.E.)	Marg. effect	Coef.	(S.E.)	Marg. effect
Constant	0.412	(0.018)		0.500	(0.018)	
Training last quarter				0.002	(0.009)	0.009
Number of other training						
courses since 1981				0.002	(0.001)	0.003
Employer-provided training 1981				-0.232	(0.005)	-0.641
Year dummies:						
1982	0.055	(0.013)	0.156	0.055	(0.013)	0.153
1983	0.113	(0.013)	0.325	0.112	(0.013)	0.323
1984	0.173	(0.013)	0.512	0.174	(0.013)	0.514
1985	0.223	(0.013)	0.673	0.224	(0.013)	0.674
1986	0.274	(0.013)	0.846	0.278	(0.013)	0.855
1987	0.331	(0.012)	1.046	0.334	(0.012)	1.049
1988	0.388	(0.012)	1.254	0.389	(0.012)	1.252
1989	0.447	(0.012)	1.478	0.448	(0.012)	1.478
1990	0.495	(0.012)	1.682	0.497	(0.012)	1.683
Quarter dummies:						
2nd quarter	0.016	(0.007)	0.044	0.016	(0.007)	0.043
3rd quarter	0.029	(0.007)	0.081	0.029	(0.007)	0.081
4th quarter	0.038	(0.007)	0.105	0.038	(0.007)	0.105
Highest education qualification:						
Other	0.005	(0.011)	0.015	0.067	(0.011)	0.189
O levels	0.002	(0.009)	0.005	0.050	(0.009)	0.141
Lower vocational	-0.016	(0.009)	-0.044	0.044	(0.009)	0.123
5 + O levels	-0.061	(0.010)	-0.163	-0.015	(0.010)	-0.039
Middle vocational	-0.085	(0.008)	-0.227	-0.011	(0.008)	-0.030
A levels	-0.008	(0.012)	-0.022	0.047	(0.012)	0.133
Higher vocational	-0.140	(0.010)	-0.366	-0.053	(0.011)	-0.140
Degree	0.023	(0.010)	0.064	0.074	(0.010)	0.209
Industry 1981 job:						
Energy and water	0.345	(0.014)	1.115	0.344	(0.014)	1.105
Minerals	0.339	(0.014)	1.098	0.325	(0.014)	1.039
Metals	0.341	(0.009)	1.067	0.287	(0.009)	0.873
Other manufacturing	0.388	(0.010)	1.262	0.334	(0.011)	1.056
Construction	0.383	(0.011)	1.248	0.307	(0.011)	0.961
Wholesale and retail trade	0.502	(0.009)	1.694	0.448	(0.009)	1.472
Transport and communication	0.462	(0.011)	1.568	0.425	(0.011)	1.412
Finance	0.348	(0.011)	1.121	0.305	(0.012)	0.957
Other services	0.408	(0.010)	1.321	0.393	(0.010)	1.257
1981 region:						
South-East	0.040	(0.009)	0.111	0.028	(0.009)	0.077
South-West	-0.052	(0.012)	-0.141	-0.068	(0.012)	-0.180
Wales	-0.130	(0.014)	-0.338	-0.137	(0.014)	-0.355
West Midlands	-0.034	(0.011)	-0.092	-0.036	(0.011)	-0.097
East Midlands	-0.045	(0.012)	-0.122	-0.048	(0.012)	-0.128
East Anglia	-0.034	(0.016)	-0.092	-0.045	(0.016)	-0.121
Yorkshire and Humberside	0.045	(0.011)	0.126	0.029	(0.011)	0.080
North-West	0.046	(0.011)	0.128	0.043	(0.011)	0.119
North	0.048	(0.012)	0.134	0.052	(0.012)	0.145
Scotland	0.004	(0.011)	0.010	-0.011	(0.011)	-0.030
Employer size 1981 job:						
10–24	0.000	(0.009)	0.000	0.007	(0.009)	0.020
25–99	-0.038	(0.008)	-0.103	-0.030	(0.008)	-0.081
100–500	-0.064	(0.008)	-0.172	-0.039	(0.008)	-0.107
500+	-0.095	(0.009)	-0.256	-0.060	(0.009)	-0.162
Union member 1981	-0.052	(0.006)	-0.144	-0.048	(0.006)	-0.132
Private sector 1981	0.075	(0.007)	0.203	0.072	(0.007)	0.195
Part-time 1981	-0.059	(0.023)	-0.158	-0.093	(0.023)	-0.243
Times moved 1958 to 1974	0.026	(0.001)	0.071	0.025	(0.001)	0.069
Mother employed 1974	0.042	(0.005)	0.114	0.043	(0.005)	0.118
Number of observations	59957			59957		
Pseudo R^2	0.0474			0.0558		

TABLE B.49

Poisson Model of Training and Female Job Changes: NCDS

Variable	Coef.	(S.E.)	Marg. effect	Coef.	(S.E.)	Marg. effect
Constant	0.599	(0.018)		0.627	(0.019)	
Training last quarter				0.062	(0.010)	0.188
Number of other training courses since 1981				0.006	(0.001)	0.019
Employer-provided training 1981				-0.079	(0.006)	-0.231
Year dummies:						
1982	0.060	(0.012)	0.182	0.059	(0.012)	0.177
1983	0.126	(0.012)	0.389	0.124	(0.012)	0.382
1984	0.193	(0.012)	0.613	0.191	(0.012)	0.607
1985	0.240	(0.012)	0.781	0.238	(0.012)	0.771
1986	0.286	(0.012)	0.950	0.282	(0.012)	0.935
1987	0.343	(0.012)	1.167	0.338	(0.012)	1.146
1988	0.416	(0.012)	1.458	0.410	(0.012)	1.433
1989	0.474	(0.012)	1.704	0.466	(0.012)	1.670
1990	0.520	(0.012)	1.921	0.510	(0.012)	1.873
Quarter dummies:						
2nd quarter	0.016	(0.007)	0.047	0.015	(0.007)	0.045
3rd quarter	0.034	(0.007)	0.101	0.033	(0.007)	0.098
4th quarter	0.042	(0.007)	0.124	0.040	(0.007)	0.119
Highest education qualification:						
Other	-0.006	(0.014)	-0.018	0.003	(0.014)	0.010
O levels	0.103	(0.008)	0.312	0.108	(0.008)	0.328
Lower vocational	0.194	(0.011)	0.623	0.188	(0.011)	0.601
5+ O levels	0.040	(0.010)	0.118	0.046	(0.010)	0.137
Middle vocational	-0.006	(0.012)	-0.017	0.004	(0.012)	0.012
A levels	0.119	(0.012)	0.368	0.115	(0.012)	0.355
Higher vocational	0.196	(0.010)	0.621	0.213	(0.010)	0.677
Degree	0.082	(0.011)	0.249	0.078	(0.011)	0.236
Industry 1981 job:						
Energy and water	0.274	(0.025)	0.924	0.278	(0.025)	0.939
Minerals	0.396	(0.019)	1.419	0.397	(0.019)	1.423
Metals	0.620	(0.013)	2.446	0.613	(0.013)	2.406
Other manufacturing	0.584	(0.012)	2.230	0.571	(0.012)	2.169
Construction	0.493	(0.032)	1.872	0.487	(0.032)	1.840
Wholesale and retail trade	0.567	(0.010)	2.077	0.562	(0.010)	2.054
Transport and communication	0.545	(0.014)	2.091	0.543	(0.014)	2.078
Finance	0.280	(0.011)	0.919	0.285	(0.011)	0.937
Other services	0.512	(0.009)	1.672	0.510	(0.009)	1.661
1981 region:						
South-East	-0.091	(0.009)	-0.260	-0.095	(0.009)	-0.271
South-West	-0.217	(0.012)	-0.584	-0.219	(0.012)	-0.587
Wales	-0.273	(0.015)	-0.712	-0.284	(0.015)	-0.736
West Midlands	-0.186	(0.011)	-0.509	-0.193	(0.011)	-0.524
East Midlands	-0.102	(0.012)	-0.288	-0.104	(0.012)	-0.292
East Anglia	-0.170	(0.014)	-0.463	-0.172	(0.014)	-0.468
Yorkshire and Humberside	-0.177	(0.011)	-0.485	-0.181	(0.011)	-0.494
North-West	-0.143	(0.010)	-0.399	-0.146	(0.010)	-0.406
North	-0.231	(0.014)	-0.616	-0.236	(0.014)	-0.627
Scotland	-0.139	(0.010)	-0.388	-0.145	(0.010)	-0.405
Employer size 1981 job:						
10–24	0.004	(0.009)	0.012	0.004	(0.009)	0.011
25–99	-0.144	(0.008)	-0.408	-0.141	(0.008)	-0.401
100–500	-0.056	(0.008)	-0.163	-0.052	(0.008)	-0.150
500+	-0.101	(0.009)	-0.290	-0.094	(0.009)	-0.271
Union member 1981	-0.200	(0.006)	-0.586	-0.192	(0.006)	-0.564
Private sector 1981	-0.024	(0.008)	-0.070	-0.026	(0.008)	-0.076
Part-time 1981	0.003	(0.009)	0.010	-0.011	(0.009)	-0.033
Times moved 1958 to 1974	0.019	(0.001)	0.057	0.019	(0.001)	0.056
Mother employed 1974	0.006	(0.006)	0.017	0.004	(0.006)	0.011
Number of observations		51162			51162	
Pseudo R^2		0.0744			0.0756	

TABLE B.50

Job Changes and Male Training: NCDS

Variable	Probit			IV-Probit		
	Coef.	(S.E.)	Marg. effect	Coef.	(S.E.)	Marg. effect
Constant	-2.047	(0.058)		-2.118	(0.064)	
Number of jobs	0.002	(0.004)	0.000	0.147	(0.053)	0.019
Year dummies:						
1982	0.075	(0.041)	0.010	0.056	(0.042)	0.008
1983	0.081	(0.041)	0.011	0.043	(0.043)	0.006
1984	0.100	(0.041)	0.014	0.040	(0.046)	0.005
1985	0.142	(0.040)	0.020	0.062	(0.050)	0.008
1986	0.183	(0.040)	0.027	0.082	(0.054)	0.011
1987	0.162	(0.040)	0.023	0.038	(0.060)	0.005
1988	0.209	(0.040)	0.031	0.059	(0.067)	0.008
1989	0.329	(0.039)	0.052	0.151	(0.075)	0.022
1990	0.462	(0.039)	0.080	0.260	(0.083)	0.040
Quarter dummies:						
2nd quarter	0.035	(0.022)	0.005	0.028	(0.022)	0.004
3rd quarter	0.085	(0.022)	0.012	0.073	(0.022)	0.010
4th quarter	0.019	(0.023)	0.003	0.004	(0.024)	0.001
Highest education qualification:						
Other	0.244	(0.043)	0.038	0.239	(0.043)	0.037
O levels	0.307	(0.033)	0.048	0.305	(0.033)	0.048
Lower vocational	0.255	(0.035)	0.039	0.263	(0.035)	0.040
5+ O levels	0.483	(0.036)	0.085	0.508	(0.037)	0.091
Middle vocational	0.536	(0.029)	0.090	0.572	(0.031)	0.097
A levels	0.771	(0.036)	0.160	0.778	(0.036)	0.162
Higher vocational	0.685	(0.032)	0.133	0.739	(0.038)	0.147
Degree	0.690	(0.033)	0.133	0.680	(0.033)	0.131
Industry 1981 job:						
Energy and water	-0.123	(0.040)	-0.015	-0.245	(0.060)	-0.027
Minerals	-0.026	(0.045)	-0.003	-0.147	(0.063)	-0.017
Metals	0.053	(0.028)	0.007	-0.068	(0.052)	-0.009
Other manufacturing	-0.044	(0.036)	-0.006	-0.186	(0.063)	-0.022
Construction	-0.172	(0.039)	-0.020	-0.312	(0.064)	-0.034
Wholesale and retail trade	-0.073	(0.034)	-0.009	-0.278	(0.082)	-0.031
Transport and communication	0.018	(0.035)	0.002	-0.159	(0.073)	-0.019
Finance	0.184	(0.033)	0.027	0.058	(0.056)	0.008
Other services	0.141	(0.028)	0.020	-0.010	(0.061)	-0.001
1981 region:						
South-East	0.001	(0.029)	0.000	-0.015	(0.030)	-0.002
South-West	-0.201	(0.039)	-0.023	-0.185	(0.039)	-0.022
Wales	-0.193	(0.045)	-0.022	-0.136	(0.049)	-0.016
West Midlands	-0.008	(0.035)	-0.001	0.006	(0.036)	0.001
East Midlands	-0.085	(0.037)	-0.011	-0.063	(0.037)	-0.008
East Anglia	0.042	(0.049)	0.006	0.061	(0.049)	0.008
Yorkshire and Humberside	0.153	(0.034)	0.022	0.134	(0.035)	0.019
North-West	-0.043	(0.033)	-0.006	-0.059	(0.034)	-0.007
North	0.224	(0.036)	0.034	0.210	(0.036)	0.031
Scotland	-0.179	(0.037)	-0.021	-0.181	(0.037)	-0.021
Employer size 1981 job:						
10–24	0.121	(0.033)	0.017	0.120	(0.033)	0.017
25–99	0.112	(0.029)	0.015	0.129	(0.030)	0.018
100–500	0.196	(0.029)	0.028	0.221	(0.031)	0.032
500+	0.134	(0.030)	0.018	0.172	(0.033)	0.024
Union member 1981	0.036	(0.019)	0.005	0.057	(0.020)	0.008
Private sector 1981	-0.251	(0.022)	-0.035	-0.281	(0.024)	-0.040
Part-time 1981	-0.123	(0.073)	-0.015	-0.097	(0.074)	-0.012
Number of observations		59957			59957	
Pseudo R^2		0.0703			0.0705	

TABLE B.51

Job Changes and Female Training: NCDS

Variable	Probit			IV-Probit		
	Coef.	(S.E.)	Marg. effect	Coef.	(S.E.)	Marg. effect
Constant	-2.104	(0.063)		-1.991	(0.097)	
Number of jobs	0.027	(0.005)	0.003	-0.088	(0.076)	-0.010
Year dummies:						
1982	0.078	(0.041)	0.010	0.097	(0.042)	0.012
1983	0.084	(0.041)	0.010	0.122	(0.048)	0.015
1984	0.003	(0.043)	0.000	0.064	(0.058)	0.008
1985	0.028	(0.043)	0.003	0.105	(0.065)	0.013
1986	0.095	(0.042)	0.012	0.188	(0.074)	0.024
1987	0.122	(0.042)	0.015	0.235	(0.085)	0.032
1988	0.125	(0.042)	0.016	0.267	(0.102)	0.037
1989	0.235	(0.041)	0.032	0.401	(0.116)	0.060
1990	0.356	(0.041)	0.052	0.542	(0.129)	0.089
Quarter dummies:						
2nd quarter	-0.004	(0.025)	-0.001	0.002	(0.025)	0.000
3rd quarter	0.096	(0.025)	0.012	0.108	(0.026)	0.013
4th quarter	-0.021	(0.026)	-0.002	-0.006	(0.028)	-0.001
Highest education qualification:						
Other	0.269	(0.056)	0.038	0.268	(0.056)	0.038
O levels	0.240	(0.037)	0.032	0.275	(0.044)	0.037
Lower vocational	0.478	(0.044)	0.076	0.544	(0.062)	0.090
5+ O levels	0.375	(0.040)	0.055	0.388	(0.040)	0.057
Middle vocational	0.539	(0.044)	0.089	0.535	(0.044)	0.089
A levels	0.772	(0.041)	0.145	0.812	(0.049)	0.156
Higher vocational	0.690	(0.038)	0.118	0.759	(0.059)	0.134
Degree	0.696	(0.039)	0.121	0.721	(0.043)	0.128
Industry 1981 job:						
Energy and water	0.032	(0.078)	0.004	0.097	(0.091)	0.012
Minerals	0.098	(0.066)	0.012	0.212	(0.101)	0.029
Metals	0.037	(0.050)	0.004	0.227	(0.138)	0.031
Other manufacturing	-0.190	(0.050)	-0.020	-0.007	(0.130)	-0.001
Construction	-0.257	(0.164)	-0.025	-0.110	(0.193)	-0.012
Wholesale and retail trade	0.077	(0.038)	0.009	0.255	(0.123)	0.035
Transport and communication	0.109	(0.050)	0.014	0.278	(0.123)	0.040
Finance	0.232	(0.034)	0.031	0.304	(0.058)	0.043
Other services	0.164	(0.027)	0.020	0.319	(0.107)	0.041
1981 region:						
South-East	-0.121	(0.030)	-0.013	-0.153	(0.038)	-0.017
South-West	-0.120	(0.040)	-0.013	-0.198	(0.065)	-0.020
Wales	0.112	(0.045)	0.014	0.013	(0.080)	0.002
West Midlands	-0.066	(0.038)	-0.007	-0.139	(0.060)	-0.015
East Midlands	-0.136	(0.041)	-0.015	-0.172	(0.049)	-0.018
East Anglia	-0.240	(0.053)	-0.024	-0.305	(0.068)	-0.029
Yorkshire and Humberside	-0.119	(0.038)	-0.013	-0.188	(0.058)	-0.019
North-West	0.020	(0.034)	0.002	-0.038	(0.051)	-0.004
North	-0.183	(0.050)	-0.019	-0.269	(0.075)	-0.026
Scotland	-0.111	(0.036)	-0.012	-0.165	(0.050)	-0.018
Employer size 1981 job:						
10–24	-0.103	(0.033)	-0.011	-0.104	(0.033)	-0.012
25–99	0.026	(0.029)	0.003	-0.025	(0.043)	-0.003
100–500	0.042	(0.030)	0.005	0.020	(0.032)	0.002
500+	0.019	(0.031)	0.002	-0.018	(0.039)	-0.002
Union member 1981	0.007	(0.020)	0.001	-0.063	(0.050)	-0.007
Private sector 1981	-0.068	(0.026)	-0.008	-0.074	(0.026)	-0.009
Part-time 1981	-0.155	(0.034)	-0.016	-0.157	(0.034)	-0.017
Number of observations		51162			51162	
Pseudo R^2		0.0623			0.0611	

TABLE B.52

Job Changes and Male Employer Training: NCDS

Variable	Probit Coef.	(S.E.)	Marg. effect	IV-Probit Coef.	(S.E.)	Marg. effect
Constant	0.561	(0.171)		0.517	(0.189)	
Number of jobs	-0.021	(0.013)	-0.005	0.060	(0.156)	0.015
Year dummies:						
1982	0.007	(0.116)	0.002	-0.004	(0.118)	-0.001
1983	0.120	(0.117)	0.030	0.097	(0.125)	0.024
1984	0.196	(0.118)	0.047	0.161	(0.133)	0.039
1985	0.239	(0.116)	0.056	0.193	(0.143)	0.046
1986	0.292	(0.116)	0.067	0.233	(0.156)	0.055
1987	0.354	(0.118)	0.080	0.281	(0.176)	0.065
1988	0.338	(0.115)	0.077	0.253	(0.195)	0.060
1989	0.397	(0.112)	0.088	0.296	(0.219)	0.068
1990	0.605	(0.114)	0.122	0.489	(0.243)	0.104
Quarter dummies:						
2nd quarter	0.066	(0.065)	0.017	0.062	(0.066)	0.016
3rd quarter	-0.083	(0.062)	-0.022	-0.091	(0.064)	-0.024
4th quarter	0.012	(0.067)	0.003	0.004	(0.069)	0.001
Highest education qualification:						
Other	-0.124	(0.131)	-0.034	-0.139	(0.131)	-0.038
O levels	0.143	(0.107)	0.035	0.139	(0.107)	0.034
Lower vocational	0.141	(0.113)	0.035	0.150	(0.114)	0.037
5+ O levels	0.002	(0.108)	0.000	0.020	(0.113)	0.005
Middle vocational	0.301	(0.093)	0.071	0.325	(0.101)	0.076
A levels	-0.087	(0.106)	-0.023	-0.075	(0.108)	-0.020
Higher vocational	0.096	(0.098)	0.024	0.134	(0.116)	0.033
Degree	0.222	(0.099)	0.053	0.223	(0.099)	0.053
Industry 1981 job:						
Energy and water	1.016	(0.169)	0.161	0.962	(0.213)	0.157
Minerals	-0.027	(0.136)	-0.007	-0.088	(0.183)	-0.024
Metals	-0.012	(0.082)	-0.003	-0.073	(0.151)	-0.019
Other manufacturing	0.111	(0.112)	0.027	0.049	(0.187)	0.012
Construction	-0.157	(0.112)	-0.043	-0.233	(0.185)	-0.066
Wholesale and retail trade	-0.184	(0.100)	-0.051	-0.298	(0.241)	-0.085
Transport and communication	0.277	(0.104)	0.064	0.187	(0.218)	0.045
Finance	0.429	(0.099)	0.092	0.367	(0.167)	0.081
Other services	0.256	(0.075)	0.060	0.174	(0.176)	0.042
1981 region:						
South-East	0.182	(0.087)	0.045	0.169	(0.089)	0.042
South-West	-0.045	(0.118)	-0.012	-0.030	(0.119)	-0.008
Wales	-0.195	(0.131)	-0.054	-0.165	(0.145)	-0.045
West Midlands	-0.444	(0.096)	-0.133	-0.436	(0.098)	-0.131
East Midlands	0.281	(0.117)	0.065	0.276	(0.119)	0.064
East Anglia	0.089	(0.150)	0.022	0.098	(0.152)	0.024
Yorkshire and Humberside	-0.086	(0.095)	-0.023	-0.095	(0.098)	-0.026
North-West	-0.309	(0.093)	-0.089	-0.315	(0.094)	-0.091
North	0.067	(0.102)	0.017	0.070	(0.103)	0.018
Scotland	-0.353	(0.104)	-0.103	-0.358	(0.104)	-0.105
Employer size 1981 job:						
10–24	-0.070	(0.098)	-0.018	-0.066	(0.098)	-0.018
25–99	0.218	(0.089)	0.053	0.232	(0.090)	0.057
100–500	0.027	(0.086)	0.007	0.035	(0.090)	0.009
500+	0.131	(0.089)	0.033	0.146	(0.096)	0.036
Union member 1981	-0.191	(0.054)	-0.049	-0.176	(0.060)	-0.045
Private sector 1981	0.008	(0.067)	0.002	-0.009	(0.074)	-0.002
Part-time 1981	0.705	(0.273)	0.126	0.700	(0.274)	0.126
Number of observations	4940			4940		
Pseudo R^2	0.0780			0.0775		

Note: Estimation of this equation is on the sub-sample of men who undertook some form of training in the quarter.

TABLE B.53

Job Changes and Female Employer Training: NCDS

Variable	Probit			IV-Probit		
	Coef.	(S.E.)	Marg. effect	Coef.	(S.E.)	Marg. effect
Constant	0.676	(0.178)		0.285	(0.252)	
Number of jobs	0.000	(0.013)	0.000	0.419	(0.192)	0.150
Year dummies:						
1982	-0.154	(0.119)	-0.056	-0.222	(0.123)	-0.082
1983	-0.322	(0.120)	-0.120	-0.466	(0.137)	-0.177
1984	-0.269	(0.126)	-0.100	-0.492	(0.162)	-0.187
1985	-0.173	(0.126)	-0.064	-0.459	(0.182)	-0.174
1986	-0.298	(0.122)	-0.112	-0.645	(0.200)	-0.248
1987	-0.474	(0.120)	-0.180	-0.898	(0.228)	-0.344
1988	-0.354	(0.121)	-0.133	-0.874	(0.267)	-0.335
1989	-0.372	(0.116)	-0.140	-0.983	(0.303)	-0.376
1990	-0.320	(0.115)	-0.120	-1.011	(0.337)	-0.386
Quarter dummies:						
2nd quarter	0.010	(0.068)	0.004	-0.014	(0.069)	-0.005
3rd quarter	-0.162	(0.064)	-0.059	-0.209	(0.068)	-0.076
4th quarter	-0.124	(0.070)	-0.045	-0.181	(0.075)	-0.066
Highest education qualification:						
Other	-0.850	(0.163)	-0.328	-0.821	(0.163)	-0.317
O levels	-0.143	(0.115)	-0.052	-0.276	(0.130)	-0.102
Lower vocational	-0.258	(0.130)	-0.096	-0.500	(0.171)	-0.191
5+ O levels	-0.168	(0.119)	-0.062	-0.223	(0.121)	-0.082
Middle vocational	0.025	(0.128)	0.009	0.043	(0.129)	0.015
A levels	0.274	(0.120)	0.092	0.138	(0.135)	0.048
Higher vocational	0.146	(0.116)	0.051	-0.098	(0.161)	-0.036
Degree	0.183	(0.116)	0.063	0.088	(0.124)	0.031
Industry 1981 job:						
Energy and water	-0.719	(0.212)	-0.279	-0.975	(0.243)	-0.374
Minerals	-0.359	(0.168)	-0.136	-0.773	(0.253)	-0.299
Metals	-0.565	(0.138)	-0.217	-1.265	(0.350)	-0.471
Other manufacturing	-0.014	(0.145)	-0.005	-0.678	(0.337)	-0.261
Wholesale and retail trade	-0.281	(0.104)	-0.105	-0.912	(0.307)	-0.348
Transport and communication	-0.510	(0.128)	-0.196	-1.141	(0.317)	-0.431
Finance	0.474	(0.095)	0.152	0.213	(0.153)	0.073
Other services	0.091	(0.073)	0.032	-0.482	(0.272)	-0.177
1981 region:						
South-East	0.501	(0.084)	0.163	0.616	(0.099)	0.195
South-West	0.159	(0.104)	0.055	0.430	(0.162)	0.138
Wales	-0.369	(0.108)	-0.140	-0.008	(0.198)	-0.003
West Midlands	0.036	(0.097)	0.013	0.295	(0.153)	0.098
East Midlands	0.474	(0.116)	0.150	0.605	(0.131)	0.183
East Anglia	0.142	(0.152)	0.049	0.367	(0.182)	0.119
Yorkshire and Humberside	-0.272	(0.099)	-0.101	-0.031	(0.148)	-0.011
North-West	0.391	(0.090)	0.128	0.593	(0.129)	0.183
North	0.631	(0.148)	0.188	0.946	(0.206)	0.250
Scotland	0.280	(0.099)	0.094	0.455	(0.128)	0.146
Employer size 1981 job:						
10–24	-0.100	(0.094)	-0.036	-0.101	(0.094)	-0.037
25–99	-0.173	(0.079)	-0.063	-0.002	(0.112)	-0.001
100–500	-0.296	(0.081)	-0.109	-0.223	(0.088)	-0.082
500+	-0.021	(0.087)	-0.008	0.110	(0.106)	0.038
Union member 1981	0.308	(0.054)	0.109	0.564	(0.129)	0.198
Private sector 1981	-0.023	(0.070)	-0.008	-0.005	(0.071)	-0.002
Part-time 1981	-0.301	(0.094)	-0.113	-0.300	(0.094)	-0.112
Number of observations	3623			3623		
Pseudo R^2	0.1127			0.1138		

Note: Estimation of this equation is on the sub-sample of women who undertook some form of training in the quarter.

159

TABLE B.54

Simultaneous Model of the Determinants of Training: NCDS

Variable	Males Coef.	(S.E.)	Marg. effect	Females Coef.	(S.E.)	Marg. effect
Constant	-0.882	(0.331)		0.392	(1.148)	
Moved job this quarter	0.653	(0.184)	0.005	1.646	(0.754)	0.008
Moved job last year	-0.053	(0.023)	-0.007	0.136	(0.022)	0.017
Year dummies:						
1982	0.116	(0.043)	0.016	-0.022	(0.067)	-0.003
1983	0.099	(0.041)	0.014	-0.016	(0.070)	-0.002
1984	0.105	(0.041)	0.015	-0.172	(0.102)	-0.018
1985	0.131	(0.040)	0.019	-0.123	(0.093)	-0.013
1986	0.181	(0.040)	0.027	-0.038	(0.087)	-0.004
1987	0.187	(0.040)	0.027	-0.026	(0.095)	-0.003
1988	0.200	(0.039)	0.030	-0.094	(0.127)	-0.010
1989	0.321	(0.038)	0.051	-0.009	(0.140)	-0.001
1990	0.508	(0.040)	0.089	0.229	(0.091)	0.031
Quarter dummies:						
2nd quarter	0.059	(0.023)	0.008	0.020	(0.027)	0.002
3rd quarter	0.096	(0.022)	0.013	0.006	(0.049)	0.001
4th quarter	0.094	(0.031)	0.013	0.124	(0.069)	0.015
Highest education qualification:						
Other	0.204	(0.044)	0.031	0.192	(0.066)	0.026
O levels	0.332	(0.034)	0.053	0.174	(0.049)	0.022
Lower vocational	0.226	(0.036)	0.034	0.379	(0.068)	0.057
5+ O levels	0.500	(0.036)	0.089	0.362	(0.040)	0.052
Middle vocational	0.546	(0.029)	0.092	0.713	(0.089)	0.131
A levels	0.716	(0.040)	0.145	0.719	(0.048)	0.132
Higher vocational	0.665	(0.033)	0.128	0.508	(0.094)	0.079
Degree	0.518	(0.060)	0.092	0.440	(0.121)	0.067
Industry 1981 job:						
Energy and water	-0.182	(0.044)	-0.021	0.194	(0.105)	0.026
Minerals	-0.122	(0.053)	-0.015	-0.189	(0.156)	-0.019
Metals	-0.042	(0.039)	-0.005	-0.094	(0.091)	-0.010
Other manufacturing	-0.104	(0.040)	-0.013	-0.342	(0.099)	-0.032
Construction	-0.282	(0.050)	-0.031	-0.370	(0.175)	-0.032
Wholesale and retail trade	-0.246	(0.060)	-0.028	-0.102	(0.104)	-0.011
Transport and communication	-0.057	(0.041)	-0.007	0.084	(0.056)	0.010
Finance	0.128	(0.037)	0.018	0.278	(0.036)	0.038
Other services	-0.012	(0.052)	-0.002	0.019	(0.085)	0.002
1981 region:						
South-East	-0.003	(0.029)	0.000	-0.101	(0.032)	-0.011
South-West	-0.210	(0.039)	-0.024	-0.053	(0.054)	-0.006
Wales	-0.179	(0.045)	-0.021	0.238	(0.078)	0.033
West Midlands	-0.022	(0.035)	-0.003	-0.011	(0.049)	-0.001
East Midlands	-0.055	(0.038)	-0.007	-0.147	(0.041)	-0.016
East Anglia	0.097	(0.052)	0.014	-0.133	(0.075)	-0.014
Yorkshire and Humberside	0.117	(0.036)	0.017	0.046	(0.088)	0.005
North-West	-0.076	(0.035)	-0.010	0.083	(0.049)	0.010
North	0.149	(0.041)	0.022	-0.091	(0.071)	-0.010
Scotland	-0.203	(0.037)	-0.024	-0.079	(0.041)	-0.009
Employer size 1981 job:						
10–24	0.122	(0.033)	0.017	-0.084	(0.034)	-0.009
25–99	0.145	(0.031)	0.020	0.113	(0.053)	0.014
100–500	0.239	(0.032)	0.035	0.074	(0.034)	0.009
500+	0.205	(0.036)	0.029	0.093	(0.048)	0.011
Union member 1981	0.059	(0.020)	0.008	0.141	(0.069)	0.017
Private sector 1981	-0.321	(0.030)	-0.046	-0.212	(0.070)	-0.025
Part-time 1981	-0.078	(0.074)	-0.010	-0.171	(0.035)	-0.018
Number of observations	59957			51162		
Pseudo R²	0.0708			0.0627		

APPENDIX C
Further Education College Questionnaire

Name of college:
Contact name:
Phone no:
Fax no:
Term dates in Academic Year 1991/92:
    Autumn term: Half term:
    Spring term: Half term:
    Summer term: Half term:
Term dates in Academic Year 1992/93:
    Autumn term: Half term:
    Spring term: Half term:
    Summer term: Half term:
Term dates in Academic Year 1993/94:
    Autumn term: Half term:
    Spring term: Half term:
    Summer term: Half term:
Term dates in Academic Year 1994/95:
    Autumn term: Half term:
    Spring term: Half term:
    Summer term: Half term:
Term dates in Academic Year 1995/96:
    Autumn term: Half term:
    Spring term: Half term:
    Summer term: Half term:
Do you ever offer courses during the vacation period?
    Yes/No
Were your term dates determined by the LEA before
    your incorporation?
What was the name of your LEA (before
    incorporation)?
Thank you for your time and co-operation!

APPENDIX D
Summary of Major Results

In this appendix, we summarise, in simple terms, the major findings of the report.

D.1 The Effect of Training on Mobility

In looking at the impact of training on mobility, we use a 'before-and-after' approach which involves estimating models that look at the impact of various types of training in an earlier period on the probability of moving jobs over the next year or at their impact on the number of jobs an individual has held at a particular point in time. In all our work looking at the impact of training on mobility, we assume that the unobserved individual characteristics that determine the probability of moving jobs or the number of jobs held are uncorrelated with previous training receipt (and, indeed, all our other explanatory variables); that is, we assume that lagged training is exogenous. If this condition does not hold, then our estimates of the impact of training on mobility will be biased, and instrumental variable techniques need to be employed.

In order to carry out instrumental variable estimation, we require at least one suitable instrument for training — that is, a variable that determines training receipt but not mobility controlling for training receipt. This is very difficult, as most characteristics that determine training receipt (such as employer characteristics, region and education) also determine the probability of a person moving jobs or the number of jobs a person has held. Training does, however, display marked weekly seasonal patterns and this appears to be closely related to term times of further education colleges in the person's local region. It is hoped in work arising out of this report to use information on further education term and holiday times as instruments for training in our QLFS sample to correct for the possible endogeneity of lagged training.

D.1.1 NCDS men

For men in our NCDS sample, the results concerning the effect of training on mobility are given in Tables 5.3, 5.9 and 5.23 of Chapter 5. The results from Table 5.3 show that, after controlling for other individual characteristics, receiving any training in the previous quarter reduces the probability of moving jobs in the current or next three quarters by 1.0 percentage point.

It is clear from Table 5.3, however, that it is important to distinguish between different types of training, particularly employer-funded versus other training and qualification versus non-qualification training. A man who receives employer-funded training in the previous quarter has a significantly lower probability of moving jobs in the following year (2.9 percentage points lower) than an individual who has not undertaken training in the previous quarter. On the other hand, a man who has undertaken other work-related training has a significantly higher probability of moving jobs (2.5 percentage points higher) than an individual who has not undertaken training in the previous quarter. If we further disaggregate employer-funded versus other training by whether a qualification was obtained (specification 6 in Table 5.3), we see that the positive impact on the probability of moving jobs of other training is confined to training involving a qualification. This suggests that men may undertake non-employer-funded qualification training courses with a view to changing jobs in the next year.

The NCDS, unlike the QLFS, also allows us to look at the impact of an individual's whole history of training on the probability of moving jobs and on the number of jobs held over their entire working life. By restricting ourselves to training in just one quarter and job moves over a relatively short period of time, we might be overlooking an important part of the relationship between training and mobility. We look at these possibilities in Tables 5.9 and 5.23 of the report.

In Table 5.9, we once again measure mobility in terms of the probability of moving jobs in the current or next three quarters. In our estimation procedure, we also include a variable identifying the number of work-related training courses the individual has undertaken since 1981 (excluding the previous quarter) and whether the individual received employer-provided training in their 1981 job. Those who did receive such training have a significantly lower probability of moving jobs (on average, 3.5 percentage points lower) than individuals who did not. This seems to indicate that training received early on in an individual's career (at the age of 23) may be a much more important determinant of mobility than training received after this time.

In Table 5.23, we use a different measure of mobility — namely, the number of jobs the person has held in the quarter of observation — and look at whether training affects this alternative measure of mobility positively or negatively. In this model, training received in the previous quarter has no significant impact on the number of jobs held. However, individuals who received employer-provided training in their 1981 job have held, on average, 2.5 jobs compared with the 3.1 jobs held by men who did not receive such training, a difference of 0.64 jobs (as measured by the marginal effect in Table 5.23) or just over 20 per cent. This again suggests that it may be training received early in a man's career which has the greatest impact on his future mobility.

D.1.2 NCDS women

The results that look at the effect of training on mobility for our NCDS women are given in Tables 5.4, 5.10 and 5.24 of Chapter 5. The results from Table 5.4 show that, after controlling for other individual characteristics, receiving any training in the previous quarter slightly increased the probability of moving jobs in the current or next three quarters, but this effect is not statistically significant.

For women, the impact of training on subsequent mobility seems to be related to whether or not a qualification was obtained as part of that training. When we distinguish between qualification and non-qualification training (specifications 5 and 7 in Table 5.4), we see that a woman undertaking a qualification training course in the previous quarter has a significantly higher probability of moving jobs (3.4 percentage points higher) than a woman who has not undertaken training in the previous quarter. On the other hand, a woman who has undertaken a non-qualification training course in the previous quarter has a significantly lower probability of moving jobs in the next year (3.4 percentage points lower). From specification 6, it appears that this result is driven by non-employer-funded qualification training courses with a view to changing jobs in the next year.

The results of Table 5.4 are robust to inclusion of earlier training variables, as shown in Table 5.10. As was the case for men, women who received employer-provided training in their 1981 job are much less likely to move jobs than women who did not receive such training (around 2.0 percentage points less likely). The number of work-related training courses undertaken since 1981 also appears to be an important determinant of mobility for women. For every additional course undertaken since 1981 (excluding courses undertaken in the previous quarter), the probability of moving jobs over the next year decreases, on average, by 0.4 percentage points. By simply looking at training in the previous quarter, we miss an important part of the relationship between training and mobility for women.

A slightly different story emerges when we instead measure mobility by the number of jobs a woman has held in a particular quarter (Table 5.24). As was the case with men, women who received employer-provided training in their 1981 job have held, on average, fewer jobs than women who did not receive such training (0.23 jobs fewer). However, while employer-provided training received early in a woman's career reduces job mobility, training received between the ages of 23 and 33 is associated with more job changes. This again suggests that the relationship between training and mobility is not straightforward, and misleading conclusions may be drawn if one only considers recent training episodes.

D.1.3 QLFS men

For our five-quarter QLFS panel, we look at what impact training received in the first quarter of the panel has on the probability of moving jobs in the following four quarters. For our QLFS panels, we do not have information on earlier training which was found to be important in our NCDS sample. Also, our QLFS sample contains men of all working ages, whereas our NCDS panel consists only of individuals aged between 23 and 32 (from 1981 to 1990). For this reason, we also split our QLFS panel into those aged under 30 and those aged 30 and above to see whether the relationship between training and mobility is different for younger and older workers.

The main results for our QLFS men are given in Tables 5.5 and 5.6 of the report. For some of the different training breakdowns (namely, whether or not a qualification was obtained, and whether the training was completed or continuing), we only have data for the panels commencing in 1992. For our panels commencing in Summer 1994 we have information on training received in the last 13 weeks.

From Table 5.5, we see that training received in the first quarter of the panel (whether in the last four weeks or in the last 13 weeks) has no significant impact on the probability of moving jobs in the next four quarters. As was the case for men in our NCDS sample, it is important to distinguish between types of training, particularly employer-funded versus other training and qualification versus non-qualification training. A man who receives employer-funded training in the previous quarter has a marginally significant lower probability of moving jobs in the following year (1.1 percentage points lower) than an individual who has not undertaken training in the previous quarter (specification 2). If this employer-funded training also involves a qualification (specification 6), then the probability of moving jobs in the next year is reduced by 4.0 percentage points. On the other hand, a person who has undertaken other work-related training with a qualification has a significantly higher probability of moving jobs (1.8 percentage points higher) than an individual who has not undertaken training in the previous quarter.

If we just look at men aged under 30 (Table 5.6), then the impact of training on future mobility is stronger, particularly when we use the 13-week training question. For our Summer 1994 panel, those who received training in Summer 1994 (based on the 13-week question) are much less likely to move jobs between Autumn 1994 and Summer 1995 than individuals who did not undertake such training (a difference of 4.4 percentage points). The results from the seven earlier panels suggest that employer-funded training leads to a significantly lower probability of moving jobs in the next year than for individuals who did not undertake training in the first quarter (a difference of 3.1 percentage points based on the four-week training question — see specification 2). These results are very similar to those obtained for our NCDS male sample.

D.1.4 QLFS women

For women in our QLFS panel, undertaking employer-funded training and undertaking other work-related training have opposing effects on mobility. Undertaking employer-funded training in the first quarter reduces the probability of moving jobs in the subsequent year by an average of 1.6 percentage points. Undertaking other work-related training in the first quarter of the panel increases the probability of moving jobs over the next year by 1.4 percentage points.

The impact of employer-funded training is even larger when we only consider women under 30 in our QLFS panel, as shown in Table 5.8. If a young woman undertakes employer-funded training in the first quarter of the panel, then the probability of moving jobs over the next year is reduced by 3.4 percentage points. For young women, other training has a positive but insignificant impact on the probability of moving jobs. These results are somewhat different from our NCDS female sample. In our NCDS sample, the biggest impact on mobility came from undertaking qualification training courses in the previous quarter. However, for NCDS women, employer-provided training in the woman's 1981 job did have a significant negative effect on the probability of moving jobs in the future.

D.1.5 Overall summary of major results

In our NCDS sample, mobility (ignoring training) increases with qualification level and with employment in the wholesale and retail trade industry, and decreases with employer size. In the LFS, mobility increases with employment in the wholesale and retail trade. The major

TABLE D.1

The effect of training on mobility: summary

Change in probability of moving jobs as a result of training (percentage points)

Type of training	NCDS		LFS		Young LFS	
	Men	Women	Men	Women	Men	Women
Any training	(-1.0)	ns	ns	ns	(-1.5)	ns
Employer-funded training	-2.9	ns	-1.1	-1.6	-3.1	-3.4
Non-employer-funded training	2.5	ns	ns	1.4	ns	ns
Qualification training	ns	3.4	ns	(1.4)	ns	ns
Non-qualification training	(-1.5)	-3.4	ns	ns	ns	(-3.0)
Employer-funded & qualification training	-2.7	ns	-4.0	ns	-1.9	ns
Employer-funded & non-qualification training	-3.2	ns	ns	-1.7	ns	ns

Note: 'ns' signifies not significant at the 10 per cent level. Coefficients in parentheses are not significant at the 5 per cent level. Other coefficients are significant at the 5 per cent level. 'Young LFS' refers to a sample of individuals aged under 30 taken from the LFS.

effects of training on mobility in our NCDS and LFS samples are summarised in Table D.1.

D.2 The Effect of Mobility on Work-Related Training

In looking at the impact of mobility on training, we again begin by using a 'before-and-after' approach which involves estimating models that look at the impact of mobility (variously defined) in an earlier period on the probability of receiving training in the current quarter. We again consider different types of training, and this involves estimating sequential models of training determination. In the first stage, we look at the impact of mobility on the probability of receiving any type of training. In the second stage, we restrict ourselves to the sample of trainees and see whether mobility has a different impact on employer-provided versus other training, qualification versus non-qualification training and completed versus continuing training. We estimate an alternative sequential model where, in the first stage, we look at the impact of mobility on the probability of receiving employer-funded training and, in the second stage, we look at the impact of mobility on undertaking other training versus no training for all individuals who have not received employer-funded training. Reassuringly, the results obtained from the two sequential models are broadly consistent.

For our NCDS panels, we also allow for the possibility that mobility is endogenous in our training equations by employing instrumental variable techniques. In order to carry out instrumental variable estimation, we require at least one suitable instrument for mobility — that is, a variable that determines the probability of moving jobs but not training controlling for mobility. Finding a suitable instrument is very difficult, as most characteristics that determine mobility, such as employer characteristics, region and education, also determine the probability of receiving training. From the 1974 NCDS, we know how many times the child moved between 1958 (when they were born) and 1974 (when they were aged 16). There is a clear positive relationship between the number of times a child moved up until the age of 16 and both the probability of moving jobs and the total number of jobs an individual has held at a particular point in time. It would appear that children who moved a lot during their first 16 years are more likely to have higher job turnover (variously measured). We argue that the number of times a child moved home up until the age of 16, while being an important exogenous determinant of job mobility, does not affect the probability of receiving training controlling for mobility. As such, it can be used as an instrument for mobility. We also use the employment status in 1974 of the person's mother as an instrument for mobility, though this has fairly limited explanatory power in most of our mobility equations. This has important implications when interpreting the results from our QLFS sample, which are based solely on our 'before-and-after' methodology.

For our NCDS sample, we also estimate simultaneous models of training receipt which look at the impact of current and lagged mobility on the probability of receiving training. The results from this work suggest that models that only look at the impact of lagged mobility on current training may be missing an important part of the relationship between training and mobility.

D.2.1 NCDS men

The results that look at the effects of mobility on training for our NCDS male panel are given in Tables 5.11, 5.12, 5.25 and 5.27 of Chapter 5 and Tables B.50 and B.52 of Appendix B.

Tables 5.11 and 5.12 give the results of undertaking the 'before-and-after' approach in which we assume mobility is exogenous (that is, the unobserved determinants of training are uncorrelated with the probability of moving jobs). The results from this model suggest that a person who has moved jobs in the previous year has a lower probability of receiving training in the current quarter (by 0.6 percentage points). This negative impact of a job move appears to be strongest for employer-provided training, reducing the probability of receiving such training by 0.9 percentage points (using either of our sequential models).

The instrumental variable results in Table 5.25 give a very different picture from that of the 'before-and-after' results of Tables 5.11 and 5.12. The results now suggest that mobility in the previous year is positively related to the probability of receiving training, and, in particular, employer-funded training, in the current quarter. There are two likely explanations for this result. The first is that there are unobserved individual characteristics that are positively related to the probability of moving jobs but negatively related to training. If we do not take this into account, we erroneously estimate a negative relationship between moving jobs in the previous year and receiving training in the current quarter. The second possibility is that our instrumental variable results are picking up the effects of induction training when a person first moves jobs, rather than the impact of mobility on training necessary to upgrade skills as part of an ongoing career process. We explore this in more detail in Table 5.27, where we estimate a simultaneous model of training receipt. The results from doing this suggest that job movements in the current quarter are associated with an increase in the probability of being trained, whereas movements in the previous year are associated with a reduction in the probability of being trained. By only considering lagged mobility, we are missing an important part of the story in the relationship between mobility and training.

When we consider the impact of the total number of jobs a person has held over their entire working life (rather than just recent mobility) on the probability of receiving training, we find that the probability of receiving training increases with the number of jobs held, as shown in our instrumental variable model of Table B.50 in Appendix B. From Table B.52, it appears that the number of jobs increases the probability of receiving employer-funded and other training in approximately the same way.

D.2.2 NCDS women

The results that look at the effect of mobility on training for our NCDS female panel are given in Tables 5.13, 5.14, 5.26 and 5.27 of Chapter 5 and Tables B.51 and B.53 of Appendix B. The results from Tables 5.13 and 5.14 suggest that, for women, moving jobs in the past year is associated with an increase in the probability of receiving training in the current quarter. The instrumental variable results, presented in Table 5.26, suggest that the impact of mobility on the probability of receiving training is insignificant (and not significant and positive as suggested by the results in Tables 5.13 and 5.14), though moving jobs in the previous year still significantly increases the probability of a woman receiving employer-funded training (by 0.7 percentage points). When we look at the impact of the number of jobs on the probability of receiving training and employer-funded versus other training, the results are somewhat different. The instrumental variable estimates from this model suggest that the probability of training decreases with the number of jobs the woman has held by around 1 percentage point for every extra job, though this effect is not significant. This overall result is driven by the large and significant negative impact that the number of jobs has on the probability of receiving non-employer-funded training just outweighing the large and positive impact that the number of jobs has on the probability of receiving employer-funded training (Table B.53). Finally, our simultaneous model suggests that contemporaneous job moves and moves in the previous year are both associated with significant increases in the probability of undertaking training.

D.2.3 *QLFS men*

The results that look at the effect of mobility on training for our LFS male panel are given in Tables 5.15, 5.16, 5.17 and 5.18 of Chapter 5. From these tables, we find that moving jobs in the first four quarters of the survey has very little effect on the probability of receiving training in the fifth quarter of the survey. From our young male sample, there is evidence, however, that mobility in the past year reduces the probability of receiving training by between 3.6 and 3.8 percentage points. All these LFS results ignore the possible endogeneity of mobility.

D.2.4 *QLFS women*

The results that look at the effect of mobility on training for our LFS female panel are given in Tables 5.19, 5.20, 5.21 and 5.22 of Chapter 5. As was the case for our NCDS female sample, mobility appears to have a positive effect on the probability of receiving subsequent training, but this is entirely due to the effect of changing jobs on the probability of receiving other training rather than employer-funded training. A similar result is obtained when we only consider women under 30.

TABLE D.2

The effect of mobility on training: summary of 'before-and-after' approach

| Type of training | Change in probability of receiving training as a result of moving jobs (percentage points) | | | | | |
| | NCDS | | LFS | | Young LFS | |
	Men	Women	Men	Women	Men	Women
Any training	-0.6	1.7	ns	2.4	-3.6	(2.3)
Employer-funded training	-0.9	0.5	ns	0.0	ns	-0.8
Non-employer-funded training	0.2	1.2	ns	2.4	ns	3.1
Qualification training	ns	1.4	ns	ns	ns	ns
Non-qualification training	ns	0.3	ns	ns	ns	ns

Note: 'ns' signifies not significant at the 10 per cent level. Coefficients in parentheses are not significant at the 5 per cent level. Other coefficients are significant at the 5 per cent level. 'Young LFS' refers to a sample of individuals aged under 30 taken from the LFS.

D.2.5 Overall summary of major results

In our NCDS sample, the probability of training (ignoring mobility) increases with qualification level, employer size, union membership (weak), full-time employment (especially women), public sector employment, and employment in finance and other services industries. In the LFS, training increases with qualification level, and employment in other services is associated with the highest training incidence. The major effects of mobility on the probability of receiving different types of training in our NCDS and LFS samples are summarised in Tables D.2, D.3 and D.4.

TABLE D.3

**The effect of mobility on training:
summary of instrumental variable approach**

| | Change in probability of receiving training as a result of moving jobs (percentage points): | |
| | | NCDS |
Type of training	*Men*	*Women*
Any training	0.6	ns
Employer-funded training	0.4	0.7
Non-employer-funded training	ns	−0.3
Qualification training	0.5	ns
Non-qualification training	ns	ns

Note: 'ns' signifies not significant at the 10 per cent level. Other coefficients are significant at the 5 per cent level.

TABLE D.4

The effect of mobility on training: summary of simultaneous model

| | Change in probability of receiving training as a result of moving jobs (percentage points): | |
| | | NCDS |
Measure of mobility	*Men*	*Women*
Moved this quarter	0.5	0.8
Moved last year	−0.7	1.7

Note: All coefficients are significant at the 5 per cent level.

BIBLIOGRAPHY

Acemoglu, D. and Pischke, J. (1995), 'Why do firms train? Theory and evidence', Massachusetts Institute of Technology, Department of Economics, mimeo, November.

Becker, G. (1964), *Human Capital*, New York: Columbia University Press.

Ben-Porath, H. (1967), 'The production of human capital over the life-cycle', *Journal of Political Economy*, vol. 75, pp. 352–65.

Blundell, R., Dearden, L. and Meghir, C. (1996), *The Determinants and Effects of Work-Related Training in Britain*, London: Institute for Fiscal Studies.

Booth, A. and Satchell, S. (1994), 'Apprenticeships and job tenure', *Oxford Economic Papers*, vol. 46, pp. 474–95.

Brown, C., Reich, M. and Stern, D. (1993), 'Becoming a high performance work organization: the role of security, employee involvement and training', *The International Journal of Human Resource Management*, vol. 4, pp. 247–75.

Campbell III, C. (1993), 'Do firms pay efficiency wages? Evidence with data at the firm-level', *Journal of Labor Economics*, vol. 11, pp. 442–70.

Dearden, L. (1995), 'Education, training and earnings in Australia and Britain', unpublished Ph.D. thesis, University College London.

Dolton, P., Makepeace, G. and Treble, J. (1992), 'Public and private sector training of young people in Britain', in L. M. Lynch, *Training and the Private Sector*, Chicago: University of Chicago Press.

Elias, P. (1994), 'Job related training, trade union membership, and labour mobility: a longitudinal study', *Oxford Economic Papers*, vol. 46, pp. 563–78.

Government Statistical Service (1994), *Training Statistics 1994*, London: HMSO.

Green, F., Machin, S. and Wilkinson, D. (1996a), 'An analysis of workplace training and skill shortages', Department for Education and Employment, Research Series no. RS7, London: HMSO.

—, — and — (1996b), 'The determinants of workplace training', University of Leeds, School of Business and Economic Studies, Discussion Paper no. E96/01.

Greenhalgh, C. and Mavrotas, G. (1994), 'Workforce training in the Thatcher era: market forces and market failures', in R. McNabb and K. Whitfield (eds), *The Market for Training*, Aldershot: Avebury Press.

— and — (1996), 'Job training, new technology and labour turnover', *British Journal of Industrial Relations*, vol. 34, pp. 131–50.

— and Stewart, M. (1987), 'The effects and determinants of training', *Oxford Bulletin of Economics and Statistics*, vol. 49, pp. 171–89.

Harhoff, D. and Kane, T. (1993), 'Financing apprenticeship training: evidence from Germany', National Bureau of Economic Research, Working Paper no. 4557.

Hashimoto, M. (1981), 'Firm-specific human capital as a shared investment', *American Economic Review*, vol. 71, pp. 475–82.

Katz, E. and Ziderman, A. (1990), 'Investment in general training: the role of information and labour mobility', *Economic Journal*, vol. 100, pp. 1147–58.

Maddala, G. S. (1983), *Limited Dependent and Qualitative Variables in Econometrics*, Econometric Society Monograph no. 3, Cambridge: Cambridge University Press.

Mallar, C. D. (1977), 'The estimation of simultaneous probit models', *Econometrica*, vol. 45, pp. 1717–22.

Royalty, A. B. (1996), 'The effects of job turnover on the training of men and women', *Industrial and Labor Relations Review*, vol. 49, pp. 506–21.

Schmitt, J. (1993), 'The changing structure of male earnings in Britain, 1974–1978', London School of Economics, Centre for Economic Performance, Discussion Paper no. 122.

Stevens, M. (1994), 'A theoretical model of on-the-job training with imperfect competition', *Oxford Economic Papers*, vol. 46, pp. 537–62.

Wadsworth, J. (1989), 'Job tenure and inter-firm mobility', London School of Economics, Centre for Economic Performance, Working Paper no. 1187.

Winkelmann, R. (1994), 'Training, earnings and mobility in Germany', Centre for Economic Policy Research, Human Resources, Discussion Paper no. 982.